My Life in the Time of the Contras

My Life
in the
Time of the Contras

Bruce P. Cameron

University of New Mexico Press

Albuquerque

This memoir is the story of my personal and public life in the '80s.
I have changed the names of the women with whom I was involved,
their family members, and some others.

© 2007 by the University of New Mexico Press
All rights reserved. Published 2007
Printed in the United States of America

12 11 10 09 08 07   1 2 3 4 5 6

LIBRARY OF CONGRESS CATALOGING-IN-PUBLICATION DATA

Cameron, Bruce P., 1943–
My life in the time of the contras / Bruce P. Cameron.
p. cm.
Includes bibliographical references and index.
ISBN 978-0-8263-4251-5 (cloth : alk. paper)
1. Cameron, Bruce P., 1943–
2. Lobbyists—United States—Biography.
3. Iran-Contra Affair, 1985–1990.
4. United States—Foreign relations—Nicaragua.
5. Nicaragua—Foreign relations—United States.
I. Title.
JK1118.C24 2007
973.927092—dc22
[B]
2006100668

DESIGN AND COMPOSITION: *Mina Yamashita*

To the memory of my mother, Jane Ramseyer Cameron;

to my father, James L. Cameron, and my brother, Scott Cameron,

both of whom have given me unstinting support

in my difficult career path;

to my oldest friends:

Mike Belding, Bill Race, Ed Lystra, and Abel Garcia Bonilla;

and finally, to my wonderful and beautiful wife,

Nely Cameron Rivera,

and our children, Nelly Arely, Juan Carlos, and Edgardo Enrique,

and to the memory of Penn Kemble,

who was taken from us too early

■ ■ ■

Contents

Acknowledgments

This is a memoir, not an academic account. The rules that obtain are often emotional as well as narrative. Nonetheless, I want this book to be as factual as possible. So I did consult a number of people along the way. But if there is merit in this book, it is mine, and my colleagues should be held accountable for its errors.

I have found in writing these acknowledgments that I cannot consistently be humorous about my colleagues. So only comments in italics reflect my attempt at humor in expressing my deep gratitude for their assistance.

Stina Santiestevan was the first to take my 500 double-spaced pages, and she claims to have organized them and translated them into English. Eighteen years later Hugo Blasdel took a Word Perfect document and translated it into Microsoft Word, then patiently produced version after version as Lynn and I struggled with the changes that emerged in such disarray. *Finally Lynn Fredriksson, with whom I've shared my vast knowledge of Washington (and advised on how not to confuse leftist rhetoric with reality) re-edited the whole book. She claims to have helped make my words sing. So if you're not hearing music, you know who's to blame.*

Three members of Congress stand out among countless others instrumental to this writing. Former congressman, now Senator Tom Harkin and I traveled together to Central America. Twice. He was never anything but respectful, even to generals whose actions warranted censure; he saved his venom for press conferences and, in a more moderate way, for the House and Senate floors. Tom was one of a very few who invented respect for human rights as an integral part of U.S. foreign policy and then made it flesh by offering one amendment after another until the Harkin amendment became synonymous with human rights. As I moved more and more to the right, Tom defended me. But finally I crossed too many lines. For some couple of years, we did not talk. Still, eventually, because we had been such good friends in the past, we became so again. Tom has also been the major sponsor of research on the illness that you will read has so totally confounded my life.

Dave McCurdy is one of the heroes of this book, and therefore warrants little attention here. But let me say this: Thank you, Dave, for letting me use your office as temporary sanctuary as I made my rounds on the Hill. Thank you, too, for helping me learn to understand the true meaning of a moderate Democrat.

It's harder to express my thanks to Senator John McCain. He was the first Republican to embrace me after I switched sides, and he tried mightily to find me paid work. His office was always open and his aide, Lorne Craner, was especially generous with his time, especially in trying to devise ways to keep the Administration alliance with the moderates alive. John introduced me to two former members who at times were especially helpful on Mozambique: Newt Gingrich and Vin Weber.

There were five other men from different institutions who were instrumental in this book's genesis and fruition. *I was a loyal source to Doyle McManus of the* Los Angeles Times, *and Doyle was my unofficial legal advisor and political psychiatrist. He often took the time to help me work through my current crises de conscience. Finally, he believes (and he would be right) that he kept me from making (in my life and in writing this book) a hundred small errors . . . In retrospect, I've come to believe that he was an agent of International Liberalism hired to weaken the Contras by getting at their lobbyist.*

Howard Yourman was Dave McCurdy's legislative aide. In many ways during the 1980s what I did began and ended with talking to Howard. We could not have achieved half as much without him.

If there is anyone most responsible for this book and its most unhappy ending (in publication), it is Bob Kagan. I was footnoted often in his book. Upon his first reading of my book, he generously called it a minor classic. We know who wrote the major classic, Bob himself. It was Twilight Struggle. *(It's true: buy it and read it.) More than a decade later when I complained that my book was unworthy, he pointed to one lead story on the front page of the* New York Times *trashing one former president's very big book. "If that miserable big book can be published then certainly you should have no qualms publishing your competent little book." That put an end to any thoughts I had of concealment of this book; in fact, if you read this book you will soon see that I have left little concealed.*

Chris Arcos and Dan Fisk were State Department officials who provided this book with one piece of information after another. Chris is the master of the anecdote and the little-known fact. *Dan is the master at piling argument upon argument to prove that the moderates were wrong, and Dave McCurdy and Bruce Cameron did a disservice to their country. Although we can both claim victory, Dan, in the end it was Dave's and my policy that was implemented, so in that sense you lost. But Dan still provided me with rich source material for the years 1987 and 1988. And the depth of my analysis has depended a lot on what he provided.*

Four Central Americans, while not always providing me directly with their cockamamie views on the Nicaraguan mess, did provide me with information and perspective, warped and twisted though they were. Leonel Gomez, born into a family that issued its own coinage to the peons on their plantations, nonetheless chose to make his lot with the poor of El Salvador. He has a truly unique view of the world, more Hegelian than Anglo-Saxon. Francisco Villagran of Guatemala has probably done great disservice to the world by keeping alive in me the belief that I do indeed know more and better and that I should only yield when I am overwhelmingly convinced of my own error. Arturo Cruz Jr., whose dazzling brilliance has often made clear what should have remained murky, has nonetheless been a very good teacher. Chema Argueta, also from Guatemala, has shared with me his crystalline analysis, keeping fact and concepts in easy balance. I don't know exactly what this means, but Chema also assures me my thinking has been greatly improved by my mere exposure to his.

Mentoring is a difficult enterprise. I was lucky since Bill Woodward insists that I am one of the two or three best at what only I do. Professor Sheldon Appleton of Oakland University with his own unique teaching actually prepared me to assemble and present information in a way I would need to arrange as a lobbyist. Ira Arlook channeled my energy explosion released by the assassination of Salvador Allende into areas and kinds of work that created positive results in Congress and with thousands of others ended the war.

I could not have written this book at all without the friendship of four members of the Nicaraguan opposition: Arturo Cruz Sr., Carlos Ulvert, Alfonso Robelo, and Ernesto Palazio. With bonhomie and lots of drink they made certain that I would never understand Nicaragua at all.

Finally to my editor Luther Wilson. He saw in this book what I actually wanted to portray: interesting (and amusing) stories, a sense of what Nicaragua went through in those fateful eleven years, the dynamics of

Congress (especially the small band of men and women who, as moderates, controlled the winning margin), and, finally, the agonizing, sometimes self-indulgent struggle of one man in his efforts to stay both relevant and true to his principle. ■

CHAPTER ONE

THE CONTRAS

1982–1984

It is a spare but cluttered room. Nothing in it fits a larger design. There is the table on which I write, a beautiful cherry wood table built by a friend and his wife more than three decades ago. They are now separated by his death, at his own hands.

When I tire, I lie on what was once their couch or I collapse into my $900 La-Z-Boy that cushions a body in chronic pain. Two brown shelves hold books I no longer look at. The darker shelf was his. Only after five years did I discover that the movers had placed it upside down, by which time the bottom shelf held more than three hundred record albums. Though the records are now gone, obsolete, replaced by compact discs, I don't think I will ever right that shelf. New wooden CD racks I bought myself, to house my collection of 800 discs. CDs and La-Z-Boy are the luxuries of a middle-aged bachelor who has not yet found anyone to tell him what more he needs.

On one side of the couch is a table left by the previous owner of the apartment, on the other is a small chest of drawers remaindered by Salvadoran refugees who once lived in my second bedroom. Atop the chest is a lamp given to me by a Guatemalan diplomat.

The La-Z-Boy, where I now sit through most of my days, at work or at rest, is flanked by two brown tables purchased at garage sales. The long wall above the couch is covered by three beaded aprons of the Ndebele tribe, purchased in South Africa. Each suggests a flavor, like vanilla, and blends nicely with other browns in the room.

On the wall facing the couch are two Guatemalan weavings, one blue, the other enlivened with bright pink, turquoise, and a rich red against a dark brown background. Though the floor begs for quiet and surcease, it is covered with a bright yellow, orange, and brown rug from Mexico.

The cherry wood table upon which I write is cluttered with paper: some for this writing, others for my work as a lobbyist. Other papers have long occupied the space they fill, no one caring to suggest whence they came, what purpose they could possibly serve, or when they might leave.

My room is like my life. Things are there because I want them there, or I have let them come in and find their places. Behaviors and beliefs are like that, too. But, like the things in my room, there by choice, the way I lived was the way I chose to live. I must remember that.

That we cannot know the consequences of our choices is of course the terrible dilemma of living. It is the price of living with other people, the price of never being as smart as we think we are. It makes day-to-day life endurable.

As I begin to write, it is the 4th of July, 1989.

I have always believed in "the movies," and for a long time I also believed in History with a capital H. Since early adolescence, I have been guided by lessons I gleaned from both. Most Americans, consciously or unconsciously, believe that history moves or at least should move forward, with each generation freer and technologically more advanced than the one before. But few have believed in History, believed that History was a purposeful process leading toward the realization of true freedom in society. That was an idea that seized many of my generation in the '60s.

At first, it was an innocent, homegrown American idea. We had been taught in the '50s that the United States was special, that it had a mission in the world to bring what is best—what we are—to the billions beyond our borders. But my generation turned that vision inside out. Where our elders proclaimed a land of the free, we saw a race subjugated in the South by law and exploited in the North by custom and prejudice. Where our elders proclaimed democracy, we saw just two parties controlled by the wealthy and the powerful, who suppressed the real issues and discouraged participation by most people most of the time.

Our first impulse was not the overthrow of the system but a youthful challenge to its hypocrisy and the lies of our parents. By the tens of thousands we went to participate in freedom rides in the South. On campuses and in cities we began to experiment with new political models to make democracy real in the everyday lives of ordinary people, not the shadow-masking domination by the wealthy and the corporations.

The War changed all that. It is amazing to me, if you were born after 1957, you may ask, "Which war?" For those of us born after 1937 but before

1957 (I myself was born in 1943), there is only one war, the Vietnam War, and that war changed our world forever.

We seriously doubted our elders' commitment to democracy abroad when we saw both U.S. parties supporting an aggressive and militaristic foreign policy. And that policy was oblivious to threats to personal freedom and democracy in many governments of the third world supported by our government.

Vietnam turned what was abstract, distant, and troubling into something immediate and tangible, a threat to our own lives or the lives of people we knew. Suddenly, academic questions and debates about current affairs became deeply personal. What kind of government did South Vietnam have? How did it treat its people? What was the function of our aid dollars? What was the role of the CIA? What kind of support did the Viet Cong guerrillas really command from the population? What was the U.S. role in setting up the Diem regime in the 1950s? What was the U.S. role in overthrowing the Diem government in 1963? Why didn't the soldiers of South Vietnam fight? Would the fall of South Vietnam to communism lead to the fall of other governments in the region? If so, did it matter? Could we win? What price would we have to pay to win? What would be the consequences of withdrawal? Were we on the right side?

This is not a book about Vietnam, my generation's response to Vietnam, or other pivotal events of the '60s. But no one of my generation looked at the '80s except through the prism of the '60s. A very small number agreed with Stephen Decatur's famous 1816 toast: "Our Country! In her intercourse with foreign nations may she always be in the right; but our country, right or wrong!" Most came to believe what Carl Schurz said in his address to Congress in 1872: "Our country, right or wrong. When right, to be kept right, when wrong, to be put right." By the millions, my generation marched to protest the war.

Some of my generation did not stop at questioning the American experience in Vietnam but embraced the beliefs and the ideology of the governments and movements the United States was fighting—not only in Vietnam but in countries around the world. What we saw in Vietnam, starkly and vividly, we saw duplicated in country after country in the third world. The United States did not come to support a free people struggling against a totalitarian foe. Rather, the United States helped create the government of South Vietnam and then imposed it on the South

Vietnamese people, who, given the choice, would have voted to unify with communist North Vietnam in 1956. U.S economic aid went to feed a vast network of corruption, and to prop up a government that could not raise sufficient revenues from its own people. U.S. military aid went to outfit an army that shrank from fighting its Viet Cong or North Vietnamese foes, but engaged in routine killings and torture of the civilians it was charged to protect. The CIA lent assistance to these efforts, sometimes actually organizing the killings. The South Vietnamese government, we concluded, was illegitimate.

At that time one could look around the world and find example after example of U.S. moves to overthrow progressive governments and replace them with dictatorships, of U.S. support for quasi-fascist governments. Witness Iran in 1953, Guatemala in 1954, where the CIA took the lead in overthrowing old governments and installing new governments, which greatly expanded the scope of terror from the previous regime's violations. Witness the Indonesian military launching a coup in 1965 that resulted in over half a million deaths, holding 100,000 political prisoners in jail thirteen years later. Witness the Brazilian military, which came to power in 1962 with CIA assistance, whose urban death squads killed hundreds of opponents, and Zaire, whose democratically elected president was assassinated by forces allied with the CIA. The image we had absorbed so well in the '50s—the midnight knock on the door in countries behind the iron curtain—became for many of us the motif of the '60s and '70s in countries allied with the United States.

Coupled with seemingly systemic racism and phony democracy, the U.S. role in Vietnam delegitimized the United States government itself. From there it was an easy step (though few took it) to Marxism and Leninism. Marxism promised a society of freedom and equality which would be the inevitable product of purposeful History. Leninism provided a special role for bourgeois intellectuals who had renounced their class to lead that inevitable march of History. History was moving forward toward true freedom and equality, without America's "bullshit elitism, racism, and sexism," a common cliché of the time, and we were History's agents.

Did I believe that? Yes and no. My estrangement from U.S. foreign policy began in 1968, and I began to flirt with Marxism-Leninism in 1969. I came late to these views compared with many in my age group who were often burnt-out Marxist-Leninists by 1968, certainly by 1973, when my own activism began. My estrangement with the U.S. role in the world and my embrace of this alien philosophy grew stronger as, one after another, third world countries with the trappings of democracy fell to military dictatorships, and the U.S. increased rather than diminished aid to the new dictators.

On September 11, 1973, the government of Salvador Allende was overthrown in a bloody coup in Chile. Allende had led a leftist coalition elected in 1970 and had been carrying out a program of nationalization of some industries and modest redistribution of wealth. To many of us, his government seemed to offer a nonviolent alternative. I believed then and believe now that that coup never would have taken place without U.S. encouragement, though I no longer believe that the United States was directly involved. The anger I experienced at the time was so deep and pervasive that it was almost calming. I knew I could no longer remain passive about my convictions. Already I believed the American system was illegitimate and its foreign policy errors were no accidents, but systemic, inevitable products of a corrupt and murderous capitalism. In short, I came to see the United States as an imperialist power.

After Allende's overthrow, I looked around to see how I could act, with others, to reverse the coup. Finding no organized movement and desperately looking for action, I took off from work to hear Tom Hayden. Tom, together with his wife, Jane Fonda, had founded the Indochina Peace Campaign and had recently discovered Congress. That afternoon he explained that it was no longer enough to oppose the ongoing war in Vietnam by marching in the streets, that it was necessary to oppose it by mobilizing to change votes in Congress.

I grasped the concept instantly. Organizing to pressure Congress was not only a way to get the United States out of Vietnam, but also out of Chile and countless other countries. When I looked around the world in 1973, I saw the United States supporting the Park dictatorship in South Korea, the Marcos military government in the Philippines, the ghoulish Suharto regime in Indonesia, the Shah's Iran, racial dictatorships in South Africa and Rhodesia, Mobutu's brutish Zaire, the military government that killed children in Brazil, the military junta in Uruguay, and finally the new military butchers in Chile. From Saigon and Jakarta, through Tehran to Pretoria and on to Santiago and Montevideo, there were gulags for democrats and leftists whose only crime was peaceful opposition to military rule. And the

Figure 1: The actress and activist Jane Fonda attends a fundraiser for the Coalition for a New Foreign and Military Policy with the author acting as emcee. Seventy-eight pickets, seventy-six Vietnamese, and two Americans were in attendance, and being picketed infuriated the author. One of the American pickets was Penn Kemble, who figures prominently in this narrative. Photo courtesy of Rick Reinhard.

government of each of these countries enjoyed U.S. collaboration and support. The United States had become an imperial power, using political, economic, and military means to dominate the third world. Torture, killing, and disappearance were simply tactics used to discipline third world populations. The only course that made sense to me and to many others was to support revolution. We would be the anti-imperialists providing solidarity to the revolutionaries.

The most tangible contribution I believed we could make was to use the U.S. political system to force an end to government support of and collaboration in military rule. Believing that U.S. support was vital to the survival of repressive regimes, our role in ending it was historically significant. We were serving History. And I adopted a new slogan: "One side right! One side wrong! We're on the side of the Viet Cong!"

But if we did not believe in the system, one might ask how we could think we could manipulate it to change its direction. Our reasoning was simple: There is a ruling class. It has objective interests counter to the needs and interests of the working people in this country and in every country in the world. However, most workers, fooled by a false ideology of democracy, religion, or nationalism did not see this clash of interests. It was our job to reveal it to them and bring them to an objective understanding of their interests—and the need to overthrow the system.

Most anti-imperialists stopped at that point. They refused to use the system except to raise worker consciousness. But Marxist analysis pointed to splits in the ruling class that would sometimes allow the interests of the exploited to find relief through the system. The Vietnamese people were the exploited in that war imposed by U.S. imperialism. From the very beginning, the U.S. ruling class had failed to unite in its support for the war. Significant opposition persisted in both parties, insufficient to stop the war, but sufficient to force the withdrawal of most U.S. troops by January 1973, as it became clear that the United States could not win the war. Yet the war dragged on, as the United States supplied billions of dollars to the South Vietnamese army. In our analysis, the war would have raged on and on, absent a calamitous split in the ruling class that would allow us to act.

That split was occasioned by the series of scandals collectively called Watergate. We saw the events of Watergate not only as attempts by the Nixon White House to weaken its Democratic opponents in an election year, but as part of a larger plan to concentrate so much power in the executive that others of the ruling class with strong representation in the Congress would lose power to advance their own interests. With Watergate revealed, those who would have lost their power in Nixon's machinations organized to impeach him and made common ground with all kinds of challenges to his power. In order to bring Nixon down, members of the ruling class were even willing to work with people like me. In doing so, they risked defeat in Vietnam and Cambodia. In short, Watergate made democracy real for us (albeit briefly), and we believed that the split in the ruling class would allow the voice of the people to affect congressional voting.

What was so wonderful about this kind of analysis was the meaning it gave to our work. We had identified the enemy: U.S. imperialism. We saw its point of strategic vulnerability in Vietnam. The split in the ruling class provided opportunity to use democratic procedures of the system to put an end to its war in Vietnam. It told us our work was important. It gave our work urgency. And it distinguished us from liberals who saw Vietnam as just one more issue.

Most of my anti-imperialist allies were also anti-Soviet, seeing in the Soviet Union a form of state capitalism internally even more murderous than U.S. capitalism. However, we insisted that Soviet foreign policy was mostly progressive, in its support for anti-imperialist struggles against U.S. imperialism in the third world. We even saw communist experiments in Vietnam, China, and elsewhere as positive and progressive.

How did we deceive ourselves into distinguishing between a bogus communism in the Soviet Union and its Eastern European colonies, on the one hand, and what we saw as real democratic communism in China and Vietnam? In the Soviet bloc we could plainly see the corruption, and a vast gulf in living conditions between the leader and the led; in communist China and Vietnam we saw a modest, incorruptible leadership practicing a form of "democratic centralism" which, we argued, allowed real democracy at the base. The apparent real democracy at the base, most notably in the workplace, allowed us to excuse restraints on freedom of press, speech, and assembly (the centralism part of "democratic centralism"). In the American workplace, after all, the corporation or boss was the dictator who laughed at the suggestion of democracy in the shop.

From the vantage point of the '90s, the view I have just described seems inexcusably naive. Communist rule in both Vietnam and China have long been characterized by entrenched corruption and immodest, whimsical rulers who now desperately seek a formula that will enable them to enjoy capitalist growth without getting involved in democracy. What had seemed like democracy at the base in Vietnam and China was really only a means to consolidate support for government policies or (more ominously) to out those who would become targets of future purges.

That was my Marxist-Leninist side. But the main reason I began the work was that I had held a dominant interest in the third world since I was a child. Marxist analysis gave me theoretical justification to pursue my interests through full-time political work, and it gave that work urgency.

I bought into Tom Hayden's analysis of the importance of Congress because my impulses were always constitutional. My analysis could justify, on the level of theory, damage to property on the streets. A mass movement of tens of thousands of anti-war protesting window breakers convinced Wall Street and the Eastern Establishment to oppose further increases in troop levels in Vietnam, and eventually forced President Lyndon Johnson to withdraw from the 1968 Democratic primaries. But on an emotional level, I had always seen the American political system as sufficiently open to allow a genuinely disaffected populace, when organized, to bring about change without recourse to violence. If this were true, then the system was not illegitimate, only its behavior; and its behavior could be corrected.

That belief completely contradicted my Marxism-Leninism. After the war, an aide to Michigan's Don Riegle, then a member of Congress, later a senator, complained that there were always two voices coming out of the Ann Arbor Indochina Peace Campaign. I explained that there had been liberal elements like myself, and communist elements who took over the organization toward the end. The real truth is that the only communications she had seen were ones I wrote or edited, and the dualism was not only the organization's, it was mine as well.

Many in our movement hated America. I never did. I reasoned that the United States was on the wrong side of history, that our freedom had become a sham that benefited only a privileged few. Sometimes I conceded that those few included a majority of Americans. I also insisted that to guarantee our pleasures, our prosperity, even our formal freedoms to Americans, the United States had become an imperial system, extracting resources from the third world and imposing dictatorship on it.

But I was so intoxicated by our continual stream of victories in Congress that I also rejoiced in the American system and the basic decency and goodness of average Americans. A chief reason we were so effective in Michigan was that I took our work off campus and into the Greater Michigan community, articulating our message using the liberal voice. In my advocacy, I never mentioned imperialism, the ruling class, the proletariat, exploitation, or any of the other buzzwords of Marxism. I stressed instead the futility of our efforts in Vietnam and their basic immorality. And I made little attempt to make a positive case for the rule of the North Vietnamese communists.

When the war ended in April 1975, I used my liberal voice to apply for and win a job with the liberal Americans for Democratic Action (ADA). The premier liberal lobby in the '50s, its support had been declining as liberals flocked to single-issue organizations in the '60s and '70s, with the explosion of participatory democracy. But my loyalty was given to like-minded anti-imperialists, carefully placed in other liberal organizations.

In the aftermath of the war, the movement split regarding the next phase of the anti-imperialist struggle. Some argued that the next focus of political struggle should be the multinational corporations and U.S. military budgets that supported them. I sided with those who believed we should use the rhetoric of human rights to end aid to oppressive governments. We argued that reducing or eliminating U.S. aid would persuade these governments to temper or terminate their use of torture, killing, and disappearance. At least, we insisted, it would end U.S. association with barbaric acts. In fact, many of these governments were waging counter-insurgency warfare against third world revolutionaries, people we saw as our comrades.

My boss at ADA, Leon Shull, was an old anticommunist socialist. Old in the sense that he belonged to an earlier generation, the '30s, which had had its own unique experience with communism and communists. He was tolerant of my views. My friends were safely anti-Soviet, looking nearsightedly to China, Vietnam, and Cuba for guidance on matters theoretical. He would listen as I recited the sins of the United States in the third world and denounced U.S. bourgeois freedoms that masked the real dictatorships of the corporations. He understood my outrage at the mistakes we made in the third world, but he refused to believe that they were systemic, or the inevitable product of a corrupt and murderous capitalism. The freedoms, he insisted, were real.

In my work for human rights from 1976 until 1980, I was forced to focus increasingly on the so-called liberated countries in the third world: Vietnam, Cambodia, Angola, Cuba, North Korea, and China. Increasingly I found that no intellectual gymnastics I could perform could make it possible to excuse their governments' repeated violations of basic human rights. But human rights in those countries were not the focus of my work. My work as legislative director of ADA concerned the countries in which U.S. influence was strong and, in my judgment, often applied in the worst ways.

Then, on a night in Chicago a few days after the 1980 election of Ronald Reagan and the first Republican Senate in twenty-six years, I sat down to write some thoughts on human rights and world capitalism (already I had ceased to see it as imperialism but used the term capitalism with little of the emotional freight it had formerly carried).

Freedom of speech, freedom of assembly, and freedom to act politically were not mere icons to mask slavery, they were vital to the functioning of capitalism. Capitalism subverted the very dictatorships I had previously thought imprisoned by it. The dictator of Chile, Augusto Pinochet, was not undone by any revolution or by anything that we would-be revolutionaries accomplished using the powers of Congress. But because he had embraced capitalism, capitalism undid him, because capitalism (Chilean capitalism and the international corporations) demanded freedom of speech, of assembly, of political action.

It took longer than I had thought it would. Pinochet did not leave the presidency until 1990 and he remained Army Chief of Staff well into the '90s. Still, in 1989 he gave the Chilean people a choice: to confirm him as president for another ten years or not. They chose not to. In monies requested by Ronald Reagan, approved by Congress, and spent by the National Democratic Institute, U.S. experts taught the Chilean opposition how to beat Pinochet: how to go door to door, how to work a precinct. "Do it," they were advised, and they did. Pinochet received only 43 percent of the vote.

In 1980 I re-embraced America, though I still believed in History. And the movies. *It's a Wonderful Life* is one of my favorites. Jimmy Stewart, a small town savings-and-loan proprietor, has a lovely wife, three children, dozens of friends, and makes no money. His loan from the bank, owned by monopoly capitalism in the figure of Lionel Barrymore, is called in, and Stewart cannot pay. He decides to commit suicide. But his guardian angel shows him his hometown as it would have been had he never lived.

It is a terrible place. Men work hard, get paid little. They live with their families in overpriced slums and get drunk in Nick's Bar. Their wives leave them, taking the children. His mother, once the embodiment of civility and charity, is a bitter old woman, a friend to no one. And his uncle, his partner, is in a hospital for the insane. His children do not exist, his wife has never married.

He saw that his life had made a difference, that his world was a world he had helped to build, that many people lived better lives because of his efforts. He re-embraced life. He had been a force for good, for making things a little better and—God help me for confessing this bourgeois value—a little more decent.

A friend, John, visited me in May 1979, after his wife had left him. "What do you want out of life?" he asked.

In those days, the left-of-center human rights community was enthralled by Nicaragua. Its ruler, Anastacio Somoza, the third of his clan to rule the country in forty-five years, was fighting for his life. He had almost no support from any major group in his country, and no international support, either. Israel, grateful for the support Somoza's father had given the fledgling country in the 1940s, had ceased to provide him with arms (because of U.S. pressure). But Somoza had his army. And perpetrated a killing frenzy.

"I want to see Somoza fall and Nicaragua free. That would be enough," I answered.

What is sad is that I really meant it when I said it. It bespeaks two things: my narrow horizon of possibilities at the time, for both Nicaragua and myself, and my single-mindedness, which when provoked becomes obsession.

Managua 1982

In late February, I traveled to El Salvador and Nicaragua with my boss at that time, Representative Tom Harkin, a Democrat from Iowa. I was serving as his special assistant on Human Rights. It was our second trip together to those countries; we had been there in 1979, three months before Somoza fell.

In 1979 Managua, Nicaragua's capital, was very tense. Soldiers were everywhere. Every day they made sweeps of poor neighborhoods, and young men were taken away and killed. The enemy, thought Somoza's National Guard, was everyone and everywhere.

A Nicaraguan doctor had met us at the airport and we visited his home. The day before he had traveled by car, a Mercedes with driver, to Masaya, the artistic center of Nicaragua, some thirty miles from the capital. On the way back, his trunk carried rifles and ammunition. In between there were countless checkpoints. He sat in the back ostentatiously reading the *Wall Street Journal*. Who would suspect that a rich doctor with so many privileges would carry guns to the guerrillas? He was never questioned or searched. Young, poor, and male, those were the characteristics of the enemy Somoza recognized.

Somoza had made two mistakes.

In 1972, Managua had suffered a terrible earthquake from which it has never recovered; one to this day searches in vain for downtown Managua. Massive aid to rebuild the country poured in from the international

Figure 2: Senator Tom Harkin and the author at a fundraiser in 1990. Photo courtesy of Kitty Hawk.

community and Somoza should have left that aid alone. Nicaragua had been enjoying more than a decade of economic growth. The opposition Conservative Party was tame. Students held to the left as they did everywhere in the world, but most of them did nothing. Those who went too far disappeared, but they were few.

But Somoza did steal the earthquake relief money for his family and his cronies, while other rich Nicaraguans were denied what they regarded as their due share of the international pie. These turned against him and began to wait for someone else to choose the time to fight.

A small guerrilla force called the Sandinistas, its leaders trained in Fidel Castro's Cuba, roamed the countryside. They posed no real threat, but Somoza killed by the hundreds the peasants who dared support them. These killings, however, did not ignite Nicaragua or the world.

Then, in February 1978, Somoza or someone in his government ordered the assassination of Pedro Joaquin Chamorro, the editor and publisher of Nicaragua's opposition newspaper, *La Prensa*. Chamorro, whose name in

Nicaragua had the patina of George Washington and Nelson Rockefeller combined, had led the nonguerrilla opposition. He symbolized the possibility of change within the system. His assassination was Somoza's second mistake.

The day after twenty bullets shattered Chamorro's body, Alfonso Robelo, who led Nicaraguan businessmen, organized a strike. The strike failed, but it mobilized the disorganized business community against the government. Forty days later, an Indian community within Masaya rose in rebellion when the National Guard (the name of Somoza's army) attacked a crowd leaving a mass commemorating Chamorro. Resistance spread to other cities where youth clashed with Guard.

Overnight the regime lost its legitimacy. It was a time to rebel, and Sandinista training camps in neighboring countries began to attract more and more recruits. The Sandinistas were a small group of Nicaraguan Marxists who had picked up guns in the early '60s. They had grown very little in the next fifteen years. Workers and peasants did not rally to their cause. It was only when the leader of the bourgeois opposition was killed that Nicaraguans, irrespective of class, flocked to the Sandinistas.

Less than seventeen months later Somoza fled, his army disintegrated, and the whole of Nicaragua welcomed the Sandinista leaders and their business allies to Managua. Alfonso Robelo, the young business leader, was in the parade, a member of the five-man junta that would rule the new Nicaragua.

In 1982, Tom Harkin and I were back, sitting in Robelo's living room. His honeymoon with the Sandinistas had been short. He had come into government in a triumphant parade on July 21, 1979, and left eight months later, on April 22, 1980. In June 1979, while Somoza still ruled Managua, the Sandinistas and their business allies had agreed that there would be a thirty-three-member Congress in which the Sandinistas would control only one-third plus one of the representatives. Robelo resigned from the government when the Sandinistas used their monopoly of arms to insist that the Congress be enlarged to forty-four, more than half of whom would be pro-Sandinista. He left to organize an opposition.

But when we visited him in 1982, he seemed relaxed and expansive.

"We are stymied at every turn. We can't have rallies. They won't let us on television. It is their TV, not the people's. They mobbed my house, burned my cars . . ." said Robelo.

Figure 3: Congressman Gerry Studds (D-Mass.), Commandante Carlos Nunez of Sandinista Directorate, our translator Valerie Miller, and Commandante Dos, Dora Maria Tellez. Commandante Dos along with Commandante Zero, Eden Pastora, were leaders of a successful occupation of the National Palace (their Congress) on August 22, 1978, which led to the release of many prisoners including Daniel Ortega, who was later the unelected Sandinista President of Nicaragua. Author photo.

"They?" asked Tom.

"The mobs. Gangs of Sandinista youth. But they don't operate sponta-neously. They're told whom to attack. It is the violent side of the Sandinista effort to deny us democracy. Worse, there are no plans for elections. There is no electoral law, no party law, no registration of voters.

"And on top of that the Sandinistas are internally divided on many issues. But who resolves their difference? Not another Nicaraguan. It is Fidel. Cuba's ambassador sits in on most of the Directorate meetings, resolves differences when he can, calls Fidel on those issues where he is in doubt.

"It's such a shame. We had the whole world supporting us, and they've squandered it. The country's going to hell," he said, finishing with a Latin flourish.

Tom looked at him nervously. Alfonso was too rich, too much at ease in the comfort of his richly decorated home. Tom wanted to believe in the revolution's humanist goals of equality, health care, literacy, opportunity for everyone. Alfonso sounded too much like the Reagan Administration. There was talk of former Guardsmen setting up bases on the Honduran border and others training in camps in Florida. Tegucigalpa, the capital of Honduras, had turned into a center of anti-Sandinista plotting and conspiracy. Alfonso disdained them all. Then he turned his fury, to Tom's surprise, on the U.S. Administration:

"Tell your Secretary of State Alexander Haig to shut up. Every time he breathes the word 'invasion,' they [the Sandinistas] consolidate their hold; it's their excuse for a military buildup.

"Tell him not to act alone. Your government has no influence here. Work with the Mexicans, the Venezuelans, the Spanish. One day we will want to begin negotiations with the Sandinistas and we'll need guarantors to insure that they carry out their commitments. Your government is useless to us.

"And tell Haig this. Everything the Reagan Administration has done since they came to office has been wrong. Their rhetoric is shrill. They cut off aid. Worse, they stopped the shipments of wheat that helped feed the poor. The Soviets had to replace it. And your government is training the Guardsmen in Honduras."

He shook his head in despair, but immediately turned jovial again. We talked of other things, of friends in Washington, the beautiful weather, and his determination to stay in Nicaragua.

What I remember most was how comfortable he was in his role as the beleaguered opposition inside Nicaragua. The Sandinistas, he believed, were inflexible and dogmatic. But he admired them for what they had done for the people with respect to health care and literacy. He also acknowledged that for the first time in history, the Nicaraguan people had a sense of their own identity and a pride in what they had done together in overthrowing Somoza.

He believed that ultimately international pressure would force the Sandinistas to seek accommodation, and then he and his party could take their case to the people in an election. He relished that possibility and he looked forward to traveling from capital to capital—Madrid, Mexico City, Rome, Bonn, Caracas—to organize and focus international pressure.

Within two months, Alfonso had left Nicaragua. He would not return for seven years. A month earlier the *Washington Post* had exposed a $19-million CIA program to organize and train the Contras. To ensure

Figure 4: The author and Alfonso Robelo. Photo courtesy of Rebecca Hammel.

maximum impact of the article, the Contras had blown up two bridges. The Sandinistas took their cue and imposed a state of emergency, with censorship of the press and the banning of all political activity.

Alfonso, following the relentless logic of the moment, wanted out, but under the state of emergency he and other political leaders could not leave without government permission. I had the idea of bringing him north to speak out against the Reagan Administration's support of the Contras. I convinced Tom Harkin, Tom convinced Nicaragua's Foreign Minister, Miguel D'Escoto, and Alfonso and his closest aide were allowed to leave.

His aide came to Washington. He was the doctor who had carried guns in the trunk of his car. Robelo went to Costa Rica to conspire. He was already thinking of war.

Does this sound implausible? Can an honest man sit with you in February, talk contemptuously of those fighting and playing out petty conspiracies in Honduras, and in April begin similar conspiracies in Costa Rica?

When there are no politics, no parties that reach into the neighborhoods, no interest groups to articulate the unorganized wishes of the people, no media to report the politicians' speeches and the demonstrations, there is only conspiracy. The people, their money, their wishes are beyond your reach. You seek instead a general, a rich international backer, if possible guns. You meet in hotel rooms, in the living rooms of the rich people you trust, or in the houses the CIA rents for your use. If you are truly desperate you seek out a member of Congress.

In 1982 Alfonso Robelo gave up the possibility of real politics in Nicaragua for an endless series of hotel rooms and countless visits to congressional offices.

Two years later, in 1984, I was sitting outside the Hart Senate Office Building, telling my best friend and fellow lobbyist an amusing story. I have this friend, I told her, a Central American diplomat, you know him, Julio. He said to me one day:

"Your lobbyist friend from Latin American Advocacy, she's like"—he pauses—"stunning. Don't you think we'd make an outstanding couple?"

He was very correct when he posed his question, standing erect, his suit smartly pressed, every hair in place, even his smile was correct, sufficient to assert the lascivious nature of his request, not sufficient to make it a request of friend to friend. Instead it was male to male.

I was outraged and equally formal. "You are married. And, more to the point, so is she. If you so much as make a move into her life, I will rupture relations with you and those you represent."

I was adamant, and I knew he would withdraw. I was key to his access to many congressional offices and he, consummate Central American conspirator, prized that access over any woman. He never raised the subject again.

The day I retold the story it was September, I think. The air was crisp, sun-filled, and clear. I retold the story matter-of-factly. I thought it would amuse her. She and infidelity were not concepts I entertained simultaneously. She was a wife and mother, my colleague. Honor had required that I repulse the barbarian and I had done so.

But she asked me, in a voice, with a look, neither of which I had ever heard or seen before, "Why did you say that?"

Without thinking, not knowing whether I was responding to her words, or to a change of feeling that in time would cause me to melt, I said, "Perhaps I was saving you for me."

Figure 5: Senator Sam Nunn (retired D-Ga.), the author, and Arturo Cruz Sr. at a PRODEMCA fundraiser. Photo courtesy of Rebecca Hammel.

I want to believe that my response was just left there to hang, to swing back and forth for the two of us to ponder. I want to picture her sitting quizzical but silent. That is certainly not what happened. In those days she talked too much, she always had an answer.

When Robelo left the junta in April 1980, he was quickly replaced by Arturo Cruz. Cruz lasted about seven months, then took the post of Nicaraguan ambassador to Washington, in January 1981. Ten months later he resigned that post and returned to an international banking job he had held for ten years before becoming embroiled in the politics of his country. At that time, he had a private lunch with Tom Harkin and me.

He gave many reasons for resigning but one evoked his passion. An opposition politician by the name of Jorge Salazar had been gunned down the year before by Sandinista police. After his death, seven men were convicted of conspiring with him to overthrow the government.

It was all true, Arturo admitted. But the second man in the conspiracy was a Sandinista planted to entrap the conspirator, then set up the kill.

Salazar was killed in a rain of Sandinista bullets at an abandoned ESSO station in the countryside, in circumstances still clouded.

"How can you trust such people?" demanded Arturo Cruz at our lunch that day. "And nothing has gotten better since then."

Throughout 1982 and 1983, Cruz remained largely aloof from politics, occasionally writing and always available to meet with his country-men when they visited Washington. Of course he engaged at the edges of one or another conspiracy. He acted as an advisor to the most charismatic Sandinista commander, Eden Pastora, when the latter went into exile in Costa Rica in 1981. But his preference was to remain above the fray, to comment on developments in his country.

In February 1984, the Sandinistas finally set a date for elections: November 4, 1984. By that time, the battle lines had been drawn in Congress. The issue was not elections, but the Contras.

When Tom and I returned from Nicaragua in February 1982, Tom testified, but only about El Salvador and the many people we spoke with whose relatives had been victims of the armed forces. Nicaragua had not yet become our concern.

Throughout the year we heard more and more about training camps of former Guardsmen in Honduras, and trainers who came from the Argentine army, which only two years before had finished a massive bloodletting of people suspected of being subversives. The *Washington Post* revealed the $19-million covert program, and there were further reports of U.S. bases being built in Honduras to give logistical support to the Contras.

Contras. Such a strange word. It was not what the men, fighting the Sandinistas from their bases in Honduras, called themselves. It is the shortened form of the Spanish word for counterrevolutionaries, "Contrarevolucionarios." The Sandinistas shortened it, and used it, and it stuck.

The revolution stood for progress, equality, and all other good things. They, the Contras, were against all those things and, worse, for a lot of worse things. Certainly the latter appeared to be true.

The first stories to come out of Honduras were chilling. Contra forces operating inside Nicaragua took no prisoners, and often mutilated the corpses they left behind. The leader of that force, appropriately named Suicide, was executed the next year. But the image of those fighters as chicken thieves and murderers stuck. It was not a good thing to be labeled a "Contra."

A few days before Thanksgiving, I was called by Cindy Buhl of the Coalition for a New Foreign and Military Policy. She was frustrated: "Why will no one offer an amendment to the Defense Appropriations Bill to stop funding the Contras?"

"I don't know," I responded. "Nobody has asked Tom. Let me call him and get back to you."

When I asked Tom Harkin, he responded without a moment's hesitation, "Let's do it!" Harkin's great gift is his own sense of himself and what he believes to be right and to be wrong. If his moral compass tells him that what you propose is right, even when other members think the move is premature, that it will alienate the Democratic congressional leadership, or that it won't do any good anyway—he nevertheless agrees to go ahead.

And Harkin still believed that the Sandinistas were a force that would improve the lives of most Nicaraguans. He believed their alliance with Cuba and the Soviet Union to be the inevitable historical result of decades of wrongful intervention by the United States. Nicaragua was not in his view a threat to the United States. I no longer shared that view. But we were united on the Contras. They were the worst Nicaraguans. They were the discredited former Guardsmen, torturers and murderers, who remained loyal to the rapacious Somoza to the end.

The Nicaraguans I listened to—Alfonso Robelo, Arturo Cruz, and Eden Pastora—would have none of the Guard. They were opponents of the Sandinistas, but they were also vehement in opposition to U.S. aid to the Contras operating out of Honduras. Pastora put it best: "Every family has at least one person who was killed by the Guard."

Association with these men had changed me. In May 1982, I had traveled to Costa Rica to meet with Pastora, the most charismatic military commander in the war against Somoza. In August 1978, together with twenty-five other Sandinistas, he had seized the National Palace of Nicaragua and held over 1,000 people hostage for days. His *nom de guerre* was Commandante Cero (Zero). Following successful negotiations on the part of the Archbishop of Managua, which led to their peaceful exit from Nicaragua, Pastora became an instant hero to Nicaraguans and to people around the world. But when the Nicaraguan revolution became triumphant, on July 19, 1979, the nine commanders, the Sandinista directorate, who ruled the Sandinista Front, immediately began to relegate him to the sidelines.

In the early days Pastora could have challenged them, when the troops he commanded entered Managua. He chose instead to submit himself and his men to the authority of the Sandinista Directorate. He left in 1981 and tried unsuccessfully to gain support for the Guatemalan guerrilla group, Organization of the People in Arms (ORPA), which he hoped would lead a revolution that would not be dominated by Marxist-Leninists. But the commitments to provide arms for ORPA were undone by the Sandinistas. Finally, Pastora returned to exile in Costa Rica and began to plot against them (and took up fishing).

When I met with him, he admitted that he had not believed that the Directorate would align itself with the Soviet Union. He said his greatest fear had been administrative corruption. He noted, however, that one of the first things the nine leaders did was to order uniforms modeled in the Cuban army style. Almost immediately, he found himself struggling against the nine on the issue of aiding the Salvadoran revolution.

"The political and economic conditions aren't right," he insisted. "The repression is bad, but it is not at a level that will lead to a popular insurrection."

He said that Cuban pressure to support the Salvadoran revolution had been very strong. "I told the Cubans not to pressure us on El Salvador. We could lose in El Salvador what we won in Nicaragua."

The Pastora who spoke these words still saw himself as a revolutionary anti-imperialist. He called Reagan policy stupid because it supported the "fascist government in El Salvador." But he always returned to the question of Nicaragua. He had been a "Tercerista."

The Sandinistas had emerged in the early '60s, inspired by the model of the Cuban revolution. In the mid-'70s, one faction broke away, leaving two groups: the Prolonged People's War faction favored raising an army in the countryside, while the Proletarian Tendency concentrated its work in the cities. In 1977, a third group was formed, the Terceristas, the Third Ones, who sought an insurrection allied with the bourgeoisie. Pastora and his principal civilian aide, Carlos Coronel, joined Daniel and Humberto Ortega, the principal authors of this strategy. When Pastora entered Managua before seizing the Palace, he and his soldiers did not stay in the homes of the poor, but in the homes of the rich.

Figures 6a and 6b: Commandante Eden Pastora, the author, and Arturo Cruz Jr. celebrate after ten days of hard work on the hill. The woman in the second picture is Maria Pallais, a member of the wealthy Nicaraguan aristocracy who chose to spy in the West for the Sandinistas. Ours was her first mission. Author photos.

With pride he told me: "For fifteen years, we tried to sell the vision of the Cuban revolution. Then one group separated itself from Cuba and developed a revolutionary strategy that was genuinely Nicaraguan and rooted in the ideas of Sandino. In twenty-one months we accomplished with a nationalist model what they could not accomplish in fifteen years with their Cuban model."[1]

Pastora believed in his vision of Sandinismo, which was revolutionary and anti-imperialist, but Sandino's vision, he insisted, also opposed alliance with any imperial force, including the Soviet Union. Sandino, he asserted, believed in democracy and ideological pluralism.

> The Directorate began betraying the revolution as soon as we took power. They made no laws to guarantee political and ideological pluralism. They made no laws to guarantee a mixed economy. They made no laws to encourage foreign investment. They turned the government into a terror regime, a police regime. And they allied themselves with the Soviet Union. How could things not go wrong for Nicaragua when the 'nine' turned Nicaragua into a battle ground between the East and West. They managed to alienate the backing we once received from the whole world.

But he also denounced the Contras in Honduras, and said he would never take funds from the CIA. What he offered was a damning critique of the Sandinistas, but no program. That came from Robelo. He held a press conference in Managua in April, on the day he left to lay out his proposal for peace in Central America.

The proposal called upon the Central American governments to come up with plans to gradually reduce their armies to simple police forces and to phase out foreign military advisors. It called upon the developed countries to provide substantial economic aid. And finally it stated, "[T]hese negotiations between countries would be incomplete if, in a parallel manner, conversations between governments and opposition forces are not initiated in Nicaragua, El Salvador, and Guatemala in order to search in every nation for democratic and permanent peace and stability."

To a liberal mind, the call for negotiations in Guatemala and El Salvador was not exceptional. We already believed that those governments, guilty of the grossest and most appalling atrocities against their own people, were illegitimate and that negotiations with their armed oppositions were only proper. For many of us, their overthrow was preferable. But to call for the same kind of negotiations in Nicaragua, even excluding the debased Contras, was revolutionary.

For me, all this experience with the Nicaraguans crystallized a new way of thinking. Democratic principles, not revolutionary ones, were the criteria by which to judge third world revolutions, and the Sandinistas had failed the test. But the Contras, rooted in Somoza's National Guard with their Argentine trainers, were not the alternative.

The alternative, I believed, was to be found in Alfonso's peace plan, particularly his call for parallel negotiations in each of the conflicted countries. That summer he formed an alliance with Pastora and an Indian leader, Brooklyn Rivera. They were an exile movement with democratic credentials, untainted by association with Somoza. And they had not gone to war.

When he spoke with me that spring, Pastora had been disingenuous. He was already in discussions with the CIA. Alfonso told me that he was sure some of their funds came from the CIA. "Nominally, the funds appear to come from Venezuelan and Mexican sources. But the payments are too regular and they come on time. It has to be the CIA."

In September, I met Carlos Coronel for the first time. He was accompanied by Arturo Cruz Jr. who had served with the Sandinistas for two years before the revolution and three years after. He had left in August, and by September he was already conspiring with Pastora and Coronel. In all three, the vision of revolution was still a bright and shining star, something not to be opposed, but corrected. Over the next year and a half, both Carlos and Arturo would have extensive contacts with the Cubans, hoping they would intervene to force the Directorate to reverse course.

But when they came to me, they were coming to seek liberal support for two things. They wanted liberals to support the call for negotiations with the opposition. And they wanted the Contra program shut down. They did not hide the fact that they were hedging their bets. They acknowledged that already Pastora's group was assembling arms and training men in Costa Rica. But they insisted that war was not their preferred option.

That fall, prior to the vote on Harkin's amendment, the media and most liberals in Congress were focusing on developments in Honduras and the buildup of Contra forces. I was not. Until Cindy called me, I gave the Contras little thought. My energies were concentrated on building support for a critique of Reagan policy that would endorse the call for negotiations in Nicaragua as well as in El Salvador and Guatemala.

The document, "Central America: A Democratic Alternative," received little notice and had no influence, so far as I know, on later events. But it had one particular line, the line for which I fought hardest, that would guide my actions for the next several years: "Additionally, we believe that an effort to reconcile Nicaraguan opposition groups, including democratic exile groups, with the government of that country through a negotiating process . . . should be strongly encouraged."

On December 8 Tom offered his amendment to terminate all covert assistance to the Contras. The chairman of the House Intelligence Committee, Representative Edward Boland (D-Massachusetts) listened to fifty minutes of liberal speeches bashing the Reagan Administration's creation of the Contras, and then offered a substitute. The substitute prohibited U.S. aid to the Contras only if it were for the "purposes of overthrowing the government of Nicaragua." In other words, if the aid was for the purpose of using the Contras to block military supplies coming from Nicaragua to El Salvador, the official Reagan line at the time, it could continue. It was adopted 411–0.

When I look at that debate today, what I find most notable is that none of the liberal speeches except one expressed a concern for democracy in Nicaragua. And even that one is misleading. The congressman had delivered his own speech outlining his views and then, as a favor to me, inserted in the middle of his speech a statement I had written on the need for democracy and negotiations:

> Peace is the proper objective. Covert destabilization is not the means. The key is negotiations—a dialogue with the intent to terminate hostilities. . . .
>
> Clearly that is what is needed between Honduras and Nicaragua today. Their border skirmishes threaten to launch a regional war. There must also be a larger regional discussion involving these countries and El Salvador to agree on ending all acts of subversion by one country against another.
>
> None of these negotiations, however, will lead to a lasting settlement, in my judgement, unless there are internal negotiations in each of El Salvador, Guatemala and Nicaragua.

In Nicaragua, a (negotiating) process would have to include the Sandinista-led government and both exiled and in-country democratic opposition groups. It is unreasonable to expect the people of Nicaragua at this time to accept the reemergence into politics of forces associated with former President Somoza.

The Sandinista leadership apparently has decided that although the moderates were useful in achieving victory, there is no reason to let them truly compete for power in a democratic manner.

To promote negotiations leading to elections should be the policy of the United States. . . . That is how to achieve peace, not covert operations.

It soon became obvious that the Administration had no intention of limiting the activities of the Contras. In early 1983 the Administration let slip to all the world that they intended to overthrow the Nicaraguan government. The U.S. ambassador in Honduras was heard to say that the Contras would be in Managua by December, and that there was no chance that the Administration would hesitate, as Kennedy had in the invasion of Cuba in 1961. Contra attacks in Nicaragua increased dramatically, many far from the Salvadoran border.

The House of Representatives had been had, and its members knew it. In July, the House passed comprehensive legislation to end all Contra aid. The Senate, however, was silent. And the best the House could wrest from the Senate in conference was to limit Contra aid for the next year to $28 million, $22 million less than the current year's aid. The legislation was a defeat for liberal activists like me. What we could not know was that this limitation on funds would have great repercussions later, in 1984.

My friend Alfonso and his associate Eden Pastora went to war and began to receive CIA training and weapons. In February of 1984, the Sandinistas announced that they would hold elections in November of that year.

Shortly thereafter, Alfonso visited Washington. He knew, even if we didn't, that the war was not going well for the Contras, and he himself was now a Contra, even if being based in Costa Rica made him a bit cleaner. He had never believed that the Contras by themselves could beat the Sandinistas militarily. He believed the main battle had to be political, and now that the Sandinistas had thrown down the gauntlet, setting a date for elections, the democratic opposition had to compete.

Alfonso came to me with a simple proposition: "You and your allies have been giving lip service to democracy in my country while you opposed arming us so that we could fight the Sandinistas and make them hold free elections. If you are serious, then you must do something now to insure that these elections they have promised are free and fair."

By chance later that afternoon, I met House Majority Leader Jim Wright at a reception of the House Foreign Affairs Committee. Although supportive of military aid to the government of El Salvador, Wright opposed aid to the Contras. Still, he was deeply interested in the issue. In 1980, after Alfonso had resigned and before Arturo Cruz had agreed to take office, Wright had traveled to Nicaragua. During his trip, the Sandinistas made various promises, including guarantees of freedom of speech and press and elections. When Wright returned to the United States, it was his leadership and his voice alone that insured that the House would give the Sandinistas $75 million to help rebuild their country. In the years that followed, I took one Nicaraguan after another to visit him, Nicaraguans who had left the country despairing that the Sandinistas would ever honor their democratic commitments.

Wright responded to Alfonso's idea with enthusiasm. He organized a lunch in which Arturo outlined the idea to twenty-six liberals who had steadfastly opposed aid to the Contras. Ten members of this group subsequently sent a letter to Commandante Daniel Ortega, head of the Nicaraguan junta and later Sandinista candidate for president. In it, they made clear in polite but blunt terms that if the Sandinistas wanted to see an end to Contra aid, they had to hold free and fair elections.

The letter was supposed to be secret. But Alfonso had wanted it only as propaganda to discredit the Sandinistas, and he released it in a press conference a week later. Immediately there was a firestorm of criticism from the right wing in Congress, directed at Wright and the others who had signed the letter. How dare these members of Congress usurp the role of the president? The Constitution charges the president, not Congress, with the responsibilities of diplomacy. For ten years, members who signed that letter were criticized in editorials and in letters from their constituents. Wright was seared by the experience and for three years refused to play a major role in the Nicaragua debate.

In early June, Arturo called and asked me to arrange a set of appointments for him with members of Congress. I didn't ask why, I just did it. In our first meeting with Chairman Dante Fascell of the House Foreign Affairs Committee, Arturo revealed what he wanted, and surprised the hell out of me. The House was about to vote on an Administration proposal to give $21 million more to the Contras, and Arturo supported the proposal.

It shook me doubly because Arturo had told me that the night before, he had spent hours on the phone with his sister, whose son, a former U.S. Marine but at that time a Sandinista officer, had just been killed by Contra forces.

The House turned down the Administration request, but top Administration officials had already made new arrangements for funding the Contras. (But that came later, and at the time we hadn't a clue.) We thought that the vote had cinched it, that it meant the end of the Contras. I should have been happy, but I wasn't. Contra aid might die, but the war in Central America would continue. I still believed that the key to the elusive peace was a series of simultaneous negotiations in Nicaragua and in El Salvador between the governments and their opponents.

In July, Arturo surprised me again. A coalition of small moderate and conservative parties, labor unions, and organizations of the private sector wanted to nominate him as their candidate for president. He agreed, but the coalition leadership did not want to register his candidacy until the Sandinistas had met certain conditions.

In the morning before he left Washington for Nicaragua, I met him and his son in the lobby of the Inter-American Development Bank. His son was in a fury. He wanted his father to register his party immediately and begin to campaign. "Don't temporize with those old women," the name he used for the leaders of the Democratic Coalition. "Tell them. They need you. You are the candidate. You must lead them."

It was good advice. The parties were little more than the personal friends of the leaders. Years of dictatorship under first Somoza and then the Sandinistas had given them little opportunity to build a party apparatus.

Arturo campaigned in three towns in Nicaragua. In Chinandega, he faced mobs of Sandinista hooligans who tried to disrupt his rally. Nonetheless 7,000 came to hear him, and youth from the small democratic parties repulsed the Sandinista mobs.

I saw him shortly after he returned. We held a meeting with Jim Wright, and in it Cruz described the events in Chinandega with a passion that revealed that through his voice and his candidacy he had made contact with the people. The power of the people was in him, but it was not strong enough to force the leaders of the Democratic Coalition to register his candidacy.

Instead, the coalition leaders placed conditions on their participation. After all, they had the backing of the Reagan Administration, and it held the Contra card. They were Nicaraguan democrats strutting the world stage with everyone watching.

Shortly after Arturo flew off to Nicaragua, an American colleague by the name of Bob Leiken took the same journey. A liberal working for the equally liberal Carnegie Endowment for Peace, he shared my heresy of believing that, to bring peace to Central America, a historical compromise was necessary in El Salvador and Nicaragua.

He returned animated with more passion than I had ever seen in him. For two weeks he and his brother had traveled all over Nicaragua and what they learned had transformed them. Nicaragua was no socialist paradise. The Sandinista vision was cynical, devoted only to power and personal aggrandizement. It had taken the Cubans ten years to create a new class with special privileges and party stores. The Sandinistas had created the new class in two and a half years. The benefits of the revolution were shallow at best, at worst a sham.

Leiken published his findings in an article in the *New Republic* entitled "Untold Stories." It has been suggested that Bob's transformation was expedient, a device to curry favor with the Reagan Administration. Not true. Bob traveled out of obligation. If you're a specialist you must visit that upon which you proclaim expertise. He didn't want to go. I know this. I took care of his dog. I was the last to see him before he left, and the first to see him when he returned. Bob was angry. He had found that the Sandinista revolutionary claim was a fraud.

We both looked to Cruz's nomination as an opportunity for Nicaragua. It could be the vehicle for the historical compromise we both sought. But Cruz's candidacy did not go well.

After Chinondega, he suspended his campaign for five weeks and began traveling, asking Latin America leaders what he should do next. He had already made things difficult by demanding, as the first point to which the Sandinistas must agree if he participated in the elections, that they negotiate with the Contras. During his travels that demand was dropped, leaving one last chance.

That took place in Rio de Janeiro in late September 1984. For the first time since the elaborate dance had begun between the Sandinistas and the opposition over the elections, the two parties met, Cruz for the opposition and Bayardo Arce for the Sandinistas.

These two were the right two. Arce was one of the nine-member Sandinista Directorate and in charge of the Sandinista party. For the Sandinistas, the elections were important because they could serve to legitimate the government and delegitimate the Contras. For Cruz, this was the last chance to find a way to run, to give Nicaragua the chance to oppose the Sandinistas with ballots instead of bullets. But he felt he had to walk a narrow line: a line between his desire to rally the people through a campaign, on the one hand, and the likelihood that he would be accused of a sellout if he agreed to participate without real concessions, on the other.

The key was to move the election beyond November 4. The Democratic Coalition demanded a postponement until February 24, 1985. On the second day, Arce stunned everyone by agreeing to delay the voting until January 13, providing ample time for Cruz to campaign personally in every province in Nicaragua. Arce's only condition was that the Coalition must arrange for a cease-fire and the withdrawal of Contra troops by October 25. On that day, too, he suggested the Coalition could withdraw its registration if their members did not feel that the Sandinistas had provided the proper conditions for a free and fair election.

Cruz was elated and called Managua to talk to the "old women" of the Democratic Coalition. "Do it," he said. "Register now. We have the guarantees. Our prestige is not at risk. Do it for the country." They refused.

Nonetheless, Cruz and Arce continued their discussions and papers were drawn up to be signed. Then abruptly, without explanation, Arce bolted. The next day Daniel Ortega was quoted in the *Washington Post*, saying that elections would take place as planned on November 4 and that there would be no more talk of delay.

The elections did take place on that day. But at the time, in late September, many of us thought the issue was still open. Arturo had returned to Nicaragua and was lobbying furiously for the Democratic Coalition to agree. And they did. At that time both Cruz and Daniel Ortega, the Sandinistas' presidential candidate, were expected to attend the inauguration of a new president in Panama, and it was hoped that negotiations could be reopened.

Our Congress was then in the final stages of working out its position on aid to the Contras for the next fiscal year. The House had disapproved further funding, while the Senate wanted to continue. Bob Leiken and I both favored ending the funding, but we hoped for sufficient ambiguity so that the Sandinistas would still feel pressure to conduct an open and representative election. At a dinner one night at La Fonda, a restaurant in Washington, I explained how that could be done legislatively.

Taking ideas and putting them into legislative language sounds like a straightforward proposition. But it's like learning a language. You need to take time to learn and then practice. Once in 1978, there was a major campaign on the Hill to loosen restrictions on the sale of certain types of military equipment to the Argentine and Chilean military dictatorships. The campaign had been well financed and well staffed by industry lobbyists. As I sat listening to the debate, I saw how it could be blocked with just the addition of a few words. I was an ADA lobbyist in those days. I went to a friendly congressional office, typed up two versions of the amendment, and ran them over to another member on the floor. He offered one and it was accepted. The campaign faltered, and the Senate rejected loosening of restrictions outright.

I left ADA in 1981 to work for Tom Harkin and returned to ADA in 1984. And I was back at ADA in October when I tried to explain to Bob the three steps required to put our ideas into legislation. First, the legislation must appropriate money for the Contras. Second, it must put a fence around the money so that it could not be spent until Congress specifically released it. Third, that release could take place only after April 28, 1985, and only if both Houses of Congress approved. Alas. Although we worked closely for the next two years, Bob never wholly grasped the language of Congress.

He wrote English, however, very well, and put all our ideas into an op-ed piece for the *Washington Post*: "The fate of a country—even a region—may be in the balance. Our best hope to avoid regional war and a national bloodbath would be to suspend a decision on aid to the Contras until after the Nicaraguan elections."

When there are differences between the House and Senate versions of a bill, selected senators and representatives meet in a conference committee. Appropriations for covert aid are part of the Defense Appropriations Bill. In that year, the Contra issue had prevented agreement on that bill, so it was rolled into a larger Continuing Resolution which contained all the appropriations bills Congress had failed to resolve. The conferees were meeting in marathon sessions on the Senate side of the Capitol.

Bob was not part of the lobby effort. Instead, I initially sought the assistance of two Senate staff assistants who worked for key senators on the Appropriations Committee. We, in turn, were joined by an official of the State Department who was representing Administration views. Neither he nor I should have had any part of this effort. The Administration wanted its covert program without any restrictions and he was specifically enjoined from seeking any compromise. And ADA's position was also clear: we opposed any aid to the Contras or any compromise.

Bob's article was not expected to appear until Wednesday, October 10. Monday arrived, and we were getting nowhere. Finally, one of my Senate allies told me to get copies of the article and "get them here right away." Within two hours we were circulating them.

To the best of my knowledge, no one with whom I spoke subsequently or to whom I gave a copy of Bob's article was moved to take action. But somehow the basic idea filtered upward, probably through my Senate friends. The conferees agreed to the formula. Aid was cut off, but President Reagan was given the opportunity to ask the Congress to unfence the $14 million appropriated for the Contras the following spring.

It had been an amazing experience. Bob and I, two good liberals, had worked closely with two Senate aides and an Administration lobbyist, conservatives who supported the Contras, in order to forge a compromise we all thought would make possible a more inclusive Nicaraguan election and establish a middle ground in our endless wrangling on Nicaragua. I had been accustomed to seeing all Administration officials dealing with Central America as just slightly less than the devil. Instead of the devil, I had found my first conservative friend.

We had won, and it was time to celebrate, with Bob, his friend Leslie Hunter, and Corinne. Conversation was free-form, expansive, and silly. The food was Salvadoran, and triumph was in the air. In retrospect, it does not seem so important. But it is always a kick when your ideas emerge into legislation, and in this case doubly so because there was an element of danger in acting outside the liberal consensus represented by the organizations for which we worked.

Corinne drove us all home. I was first. When I—I'm a big guy—got out of the front seat, Corinne stepped out of the car to say good-bye. Still feeling celebratory, I took hold of her shoulders to better plant a kiss on her cheek, a kiss of gratitude for her intellectual and emotional support in the first days of my emerging heresy. But instead my lips briefly found hers, and her eyes looked up at me with happy smiles.

The next days were spent in the park. Our affair was conducted wherever we could find a remote spot. A quick kiss, a furtive embrace, a touch, holding hands. When she would leave to go home, and I would sing: "We kiss in the shadows . . ." and then I would mumble-hum, for those were the only words I knew.

Some days later we were naked together for the first time, in my apartment. We did not make love, not yet, but she brought me to that point where passion becomes fluid.

In those first days, I felt giddy; this dalliance with a married woman, my colleague and friend, caused me to smile, to find the world sweet. What was I thinking? What was I planning?

The compromise legislation was my last hurrah in 1984. The illness that I had been suffering for seven years, a combination of severe muscular pain and weakness, which at the time I believed to be a complication arising from Crohn's disease, was sapping all hope from me. I was finding it ever harder to go on functioning without relief, and without knowing what was wrong or what to do about it.

Additionally, our other colleague at ADA who worked on our Central America project was totally at odds with what I had been doing on Nicaragua. Like me, Michael was one of those middle-class Americans who grew up in the '50s when America was "perfect," who came to believe in the '60s that his country and the capitalist system were the cause or at least the brake on the solution of most of the ills of the third world. He could not yet see that third world leaders made their own mistakes, producing horrors often quite unconnected with the United States.

I remember feeling beaten. In December I decided to suspend my project at ADA to seek medical advice and treatment. Michael left to join another organization with whom he had been secretly negotiating. Secrecy had been unnecessary, I wished him well.

Nicaragua, too, was going downhill. Ortega did not go to the Panamanian inauguration. There were no further negotiations, and the elections took place as scheduled on November 4. Prior to the elections, both of the remaining opposition parties tried to pull out, citing the failure of the Sandinistas to allow for an honest election. Predictably, Daniel Ortega won with 63 percent of the vote.

Arturo surprised me again by stating that Ortega should be given a chance, that now that he was president maybe he would be the president of all Nicaraguans, not just the Sandinista party. Alfonso shared that view privately; Arturo was very public. He wrote that the Reagan Administration should "give Ortega a period of grace." But the Sandinistas weren't listening to moderate voices anymore. They refused to enter into a dialogue with the opposition unless the opposition condemned U.S. aggression. Worse, *La Prensa* now faced major censorship, and Arturo's friends in the opposition leadership were once again restricted from leaving the country.

For me that year ended on January 3, 1985. Arturo Cruz, in the first press conference of a new American organization called Friends of the Democratic Center in Central America (PRODEMCA), led by hawkish Democrats, publicly endorsed aid to the Contras for the first time. I was shocked. After working with him for so many years, I was surprised that he would make such a decision without discussing it with me.

But I understood. As a candidate, there had been only a brief time to forge a middle ground. With the failure in Rio and the subsequent crackdown after the election, he saw no middle ground left. I would have encouraged him to wait. His decision, as I learned two years later, was reluctant. But when you make a decision like that, when you change a major public position, more often than not there comes a time when you stop seeking outside counsel. Instead you seek solitude, or the company of like-minded people with whom you go over and over the lines you have prepared to explain your decision.

I did not seek him out. I had doctors to see. ■

CHAPTER TWO

THE MAKING OF A LIBERAL APOSTATE

January–June 1985

In the first two months of 1985, I saw every kind of doctor imaginable; some might well be called quacks. I used a shotgun approach. I would see any health care professional, take any (legal) medication. One doctor put me on a diet of fruits, rice, and vegetables, with occasional raw hamburger, and daily injections of vitamins. Self-injections were easy at first, but quickly got harder. My respect for the courage and staying power of diabetics grew beyond measure. By the end of one month, my hand shook when I moved the needle toward my thigh.

Another doctor would take two hours listening to my descriptions of my agony. After numerous tests and x-rays he concluded the pain arose in the muscular system for reasons unknown but it could be treated by exercise. He recommended a quiet yoga or tai chi, but he also gave me permission to run, play tennis, or do anything else I wanted to do. The doctors I had seen for the previous seven years had restricted me to swimming.

Other doctors cautioned that certain foods might cause the symptoms I suffered. After trial and error, I concluded that wheat and dairy products were harmful to me. Mixing and matching prescriptions and medical advice, I began to feel better. In retrospect, my special dietary regimen may not have helped at all. But my belief in it probably did.

Sometime in early 1985, Corinne and I made love for the first time. Vividly I remember her dancing at a Republican-Bush inaugural ball on January 20, 1985. I can still see her dancing joyfully, with her husband, wide smiles on both their faces. I did not dance with her that evening. I didn't dance much at all, still in the early stages of my new therapy. My illness was in full force. I felt three times my normal weight; I felt as if knives were cutting my extremities.

On March 1, Arturo Cruz, Alfonso Robelo, and Adolfo Calero, leader of the Honduras-based Contras, released what came to be called the San Jose Declaration, after the capital of Costa Rica where they held their press conference. In this document, they and many other prominent Nicaraguan exiles laid out a formula for national reconciliation inside Nicaragua without the overthrow of the Sandinistas. The document did call for dissolution of the national assembly that had been elected with the president the previous fall. But it postponed a decision on the role of President Ortega, calling instead for a plebiscite on the reminder of Ortega's term to be held a year after a new assembly election. It called for a cease-fire, and a Church-mediated dialogue between the leaders of the Contras and the government.

For me, it was a bombshell. The despised Contras, now enjoying association with my two friends Arturo and Alfonso, had put forward a proposal that in effect agreed to accept the Sandinistas. As an opening gambit for negotiations, the entire proposal with all was reasonable.

There is a context in which I found this initiative so compelling, partly theoretical. I had been doing some reading. Two books in particular had begun to influence me: Jean François Revel's *Why Democracies Perish* and Bob Leiken's *Soviet Strategy in Latin America*. Both authors saw 1975 as a watershed year in world history, with the Soviet Union as a global power moving for the first time beyond the Eurasian continent in pursuit of its imperial vision. In that year, "the Soviet Union backed armed coups, assassinations, invasions, occupations, and guerrilla movements in Angola, South Yemen, Sudan, Ethiopia, Kampuchea, Laos, Zaire, Afghanistan and elsewhere."[2] In that same year, the Soviet Union airlifted Cuban troops to Angola to fight off the challenges of nominally pro-Western guerrilla forces. Three years later a similar airlift aided the government of Ethiopia, which had just embraced Marxism-Leninism, to fight off rebellion and invasion in its Ogaden province.

I had never doubted the reality of Soviet determination to spread itself and its social system to the rest of the world. On the other hand, I had never believed it had the capability. But in 1985, looking back at the late '70s, I recognized historic change. The Soviet Union, the leader of global Marxism-Leninism, had developed the ability to move its forces or surrogates by air or sea anywhere in the world. Important regional actors, communist Cuba and Vietnam, acted in concert. Important Arab states like Iraq, Syria, and Libya, while not communist, pursued their own brands of totalitarianism, and often acted in concert with the Soviet Union. (I did not grasp the importance of the appointment of Mikhail Gorbachev, that same year, to the post of Secretary-General of the Communist Party of the

Soviet Union. And certainly I could not have imagined that within six and a half years of his appointment both the party and the Soviet Union would cease to exist.)

With the twisted thinking of a revolutionary anti-imperialist, I had always seen the human rights terrors of places like China and Vietnam as mistakes, or as necessary but regrettable steps in the progress of human history. I had seen similar violations in the Soviet Union, however, as systemic, caused by incorrect application of the principles of Marxism-Leninism. In the years 1975 and 1976, I approved of Soviet aid to Vietnam and Angola in their efforts to liberate themselves, while I continued to denounce Soviet actions at home and in Eastern Europe.

Life in those liberated states, however, was anything but free, and the horrors that I had rightly associated with American clients in the early '70s were now routinely perpetrated by Soviet clients in Afghanistan, Vietnam, Angola, Ethiopia, Syria, and Iraq.

From my new human rights perspective, Nicaragua suddenly seemed to be at the end of a long chain of death dealing that began in Moscow and traveled through Havana to Managua. The Marxist-led guerrilla movements in El Salvador and Guatemala also began to take on a different cast. They had risen against tyrannical military governments, and they spoke for a significant segment of their societies, long oppressed and denied. But for me they no longer represented the possibility of genuine liberation.

The governments these movements opposed were military, in alliance with the wealthy few who had kept the majority in poverty and fear. But, like the Somoza government of Nicaragua, from the early '60s they pursued strategies that led to sustained economic growth and the rise of a significant middle class. But alternative political parties, free to compete for power, were thwarted. And, as in Nicaragua, some of the best and most visionary opted for violent revolution because of that. What they didn't know was that in grasping Marxism-Leninism as their vehicle for change, these new revolutionaries had chosen a road that would lead to less freedom than that of the governments they opposed.

I still believed that the solution to the Central American crisis was a negotiated settlement. But whereas in earlier years I had supported diplomacy to achieve this outcome, my new understanding of the Soviet imperial challenge caused me to consider the need for force to compel serious negotiation on the part of the Sandinistas.

Figure 7: Penn Kemble testifying on Central America. Photo courtesy of Rebecca Hammel.

Two months of injections seem to have overcome my continuing pain sufficiently for me to begin work again by the middle of March. Bob Leiken's views and my own (with respect to Nicaragua) were already well known. Penn Kemble was a conservative Democrat I had known for almost a decade, but we had usually been on opposite sides of the issues most dear to us. Penn had many titles and affiliations, but was best described as one of the keepers of the flame of the Henry Jackson wing of the Democratic Party. In a word, he was a hawk. Penn invited Bob Leiken, Bernie Aronson, and me to a meeting to talk about Nicaragua. Bernie's work started with the United Mine Workers and continued as a speechwriter for President Carter. At the time of these events, he was a PR consultant.

In Washington, little groups like this are not unique. Foreign policy, especially when there are great divisions, invites the creation of ad hoc groups trying to make an impact. What was unique about this one was that all four of us were reasonably adept at what we did, and we had access to many members of Congress as well as the media. Most important, Bob, Bernie, and I, all well-known liberals, were prepared to think about the unthinkable: support for the Contras.

Before we could get far in our deliberations, the White House jumped the gun and announced its own plan to "unfence" the $14 million. Reagan cloaked his policy in the rhetoric of negotiations and elections, and San Jose declaration. But the position made no concessions to moderates, and none had been consulted. My key contact in State called me the night before the President made his announcement. He apologized, and we agreed to talk later, since we both knew that the President's position would be defeated.

As I was back on ADA's payroll, and did not like the President's plan, I lobbied vigorously against it in both the House and the Senate. The Senate in the eleventh hour agreed to release the aid, but only nonlethal, in exchange for a letter pledging reforms in human rights and a return to bilateral talks with the Sandinistas.

In the House, there was total chaos. Members easily turned down the President's original request to release the covert assistance without conditions. Then they voted 219–206 in favor of an amendment that would have provided $4 million to promote the Contadora negotiations[3] on security issues (bases, outside military advisors, and cross-border subversion) and another $10 million to assist Nicaraguan refugees. Then, by only two votes (the votes of two Democratic hard-liners who supported aid but would not go against their leadership) the House defeated an amendment to transform the $14 million into food, medicine, and logistical assistance to the Contras.

Then came the shock of the night. On final passage, only 123 members voted for a combined negotiations-refugee assistance package. Almost every Republican opposed the amendment because it did not give direct aid to the Contras. It gave aid only to those fighters who laid down their weapons and went to refugee camps. Liberal Democrats opposed it because they feared that the aid could be misdirected, or that direct aid to the Contras might emerge in a compromise with the Senate. It was also revealed that President Daniel Ortega had just announced that he would go to Moscow.

One of the 123 approached me right after the vote on final passage, got in my face, and said: "Cameron, that is the last time I vote for your pal, Ortega." He told me that others among the 123 felt the same way.

One of these was Representative Dave McCurdy, a Democrat from Oklahoma. The next day I read in the *Washington Post* that he planned to reverse his position on Nicaragua during the next vote because he wanted to support an affirmative policy toward Nicaragua. What he meant was that there had to be some policy to meet the Sandinista threats to their neighbors and their own people. He was infuriated by the refusal of a sufficient number of Democrats to support a policy to meet this threat. His announcement signaled an end of the liberal-moderate alliance that had cut off aid to the Contras just six months before.

That Friday, Alfonso came to visit the four of us, now dubbed the Gang of Four by the Nicaraguan community in political exile.[4] Ten months before, Alfonso had split with Eden Pastora and entered into an alliance with the main Contra faction in Honduras led by Adolfo Calero. At the time I was appalled, and I called him in Costa Rica to ask why. He said many things, but one of them stuck:

I will never again be part of a movement for liberation in my country where I do not directly control those who carry the guns. The Sandinistas had the guns and that gave them the power which they used, ultimately against me. Pastora also had the guns and the power and he used both as he wished. In both cases, our alliance was meaningless.

In his new role, he still had no guns.

In our meeting, Alfonso and I both thought it would be better if another vote could be postponed until the following fall. We thought that it would give negotiations a better chance, and the issue of Sandinista intransigence would become clearer. Bernie Aronson, Bob Leiken, and Penn Kemble disagreed.

The four of us began to visit Congress to test the mood. It was clear that a majority in the House now favored aid and were ready to act. Speaker Tip O'Neill was wary, and postponed consideration of the Foreign Aid Authorization bill in fear that the House would attach direct aid to the Contras.

On May 9, the four of us met with Dave McCurdy for the first time. He had already introduced a bill that would provide aid to the Contras through the Agency for International Development (which disburses most U.S. economic aid), forbidding participation by either the CIA or the Defense Department. Bernie, Bob, and Penn congratulated him and pledged support. I was silent.

Sitting in McCurdy's office afterward by myself, I was deeply troubled. This was no longer some intellectual game to come up with legislation on El Salvador and Nicaragua too complicated for anyone to take seriously. I was involved in what had become an effort to provide aid to the Contras. My liberal soul was in peril. I grabbed a courtesy phone to call the office of Representative Matt McHugh, a Democrat from New York, and I asked for his aide, Gary Bombardier. I requested an appointment the next day.

There is a movie called *Three Days of the Condor*. In one of the last scenes, Max Von Sydow, who plays a hired assassin, is explaining his craft to Robert Redford, a CIA analyst who by force of circumstances had to become an operative. "It is almost peaceful. No need to believe in either side or any side. There is no cause. There is only yourself. The belief in your own precision."

That is the code of many lobbyists. But neither then nor now have I ever been able to operate in that way. It was not a question of the "precision" of applying my craft. To support the Contras raised questions of fundamental values, and my own identity.

The next afternoon, with some unease, I explained to Matt McHugh and Gary Bombardier what I had been doing. To my relief it became quickly apparent that Matt was sympathetic to my intellectual torments. We both believed that through pushing and pulling, the Administration and Congress had arrived at a reasonable, workable policy for El Salvador (though both of us would change our minds within the course of a year). Matt could imagine that happening for Nicaragua as well.

"I am not against the use of pressure, but it must be pressure for the purpose of promoting negotiations," he told me. "It has to be a two-track policy."

"Two-track" is a Washington term used most often in reference to U.S. policy in conflict situations in the third world. One track is military pressure, the second is negotiations. A sophisticated two-track policy can employ sham negotiations to reinforce support for a military solution by revealing the other side's intransigence. However, the Reagan Administration hard-liners were so fearful of negotiated solutions that they opposed negotiations in any form.

They absolutely opposed renewing the bilateral negotiations with the Sandinistas which had collapsed in December 1984. They also opposed giving serious political support to the Contadora negotiations. They did support, at least rhetorically, the San Jose plan of Arturo Cruz which called for a cease-fire and a Church-mediated dialogue between the Sandinistas and the Contras. In a letter sent to the Senate in April, the President had pledged to renew talks with the Sandinistas but only for the purpose of promoting a cease-fire and dialogue.

The hard-liners feared negotiations, not only because they feared the Sandinistas might make a concession but, more important, because they feared that the proponents of negotiations inside the Administration would gain the upper hand and they themselves might be excluded from the policymaking process. Then it would just be a matter of time before an unprincipled peace would be made with the Sandinistas, excluding any chance of the Contras coming to power.

This was the real opposition Matt and I faced that day, but neither of us knew about the endless internal battles inside the Administration at the time. I was energized by the meeting and believed that I had a mandate to try to create the best possible Nicaragua policy.

The following Monday I told Ann Lewis, National Director of ADA, that as a matter of conscience I had to spend time working to achieve a compromise on policy toward Nicaragua. She suggested I take another leave of absence.

The meeting was amicable, but the conclusion was based on a misunderstanding. When I said that I needed time to try to work on a compromise, she understood that compromise to be between ADA policy, which would not allow for aid to the Contras (even as refugees), and congressional liberals. What I meant by seeking a compromise was between the congressional liberal position and the Administration position. ADA's position was irrelevant. And why should it have been otherwise? When I came to ADA, I was a revolutionary anti-imperialist. My Leninist training would certainly not have condoned my being bound to the decision-making of a bourgeois organization, no matter how progressive. Perhaps in 1979 I had moved to a position that was roughly the same as ADA's, but by 1981 I was already somewhat further right. It never would have occurred to me that what was most important was ADA policy. I was an operator. I made things happen. If they were liberal and consistent with ADA policy, that was good, but it was not important. What was important was what was right.

Leaving Ann's office, I felt an enormous sense of relief. I could now think and say what I thought openly. The next step was to find out what that really was. The next day I wrote out the "Cameron Position." Its key elements were six:

1. $28 million in nonlethal economic aid to the Contras for the remainder of the calendar year 1985.
2. No consideration of military aid until 1986.
3. The appointment of a new ambassador for bilateral talks with the government of Nicaragua, chosen with real consultation with the Democrats.
4. Administration of the aid to be carried out by neither the CIA nor the Defense Department (but the CIA could provide intelligence to the Contras on the movements of the Sandinista army).
5. Reform of the military leadership of the Contras, removing those officers guilty of human rights violations and those tied to the deposed Somoza dictatorship.
6. A clear presidential statement that it is not U.S. policy to overthrow the Sandinistas.

The following week, I gave a copy of my paper to Dave McCurdy's assistant, Howard Yourman. On May 23 Dave invited me and the rest of the Gang of Four to review a new legislative alternative before he began discussions with the Republican leadership. It had incorporated three of my points, taking the human rights language word for word. It provided $27 million in economic aid over a nine-month period, and laid out a policy emphasizing negotiations between the United States and Nicaragua, support for Contadora, and negotiations between the Sandinistas and their opposition.

I fought hard for language that would require the U.S. President to return to bilateral negotiations with Nicaragua. I was still looking to expand support in the liberal ranks of the House. But none of us considered making direct negotiations a precondition to the release of any aid. And no other language I could devise seemed appropriate to any of us, including me. I was also the only strong advocate of this. There was, however, a requirement that the Contras—termed "the democratic resistance"—be willing to negotiate as a condition for aid.

Why the one and not the other? There is a reluctance to use legislation to insist that the Administration enter into negotiations with a foreign power it does not want to negotiate with. After all, the conduct of day-to-day foreign policy is the province of the executive.

In any case, I was now committed. The negotiations requirement placed on the Contras and the language on human rights made it possible for me to support economic aid. Had it been military aid, those two conditions would not have been enough. Writing out my position had enabled me to better understand that position, as well as my own emerging perspective. I believed the Administration was moving toward a new policy, and it was getting there not through its own internal devices but the actions of two Central Americans: one Salvadoran, Napoleon Duarte, and one Nicaraguan, Arturo Cruz.

In 1984 the Administration would not even mention the idea of dialogue between the Nicaraguan government and its opposition. To do so would lend legitimacy to calls for dialogue in El Salvador between the guerrillas and the government, a dialogue that the Administration vehemently opposed.

El Salvador's President Napoleon Duarte had made dialogue acceptable overnight by inviting Salvadoran rebels to meet him at La Palma, El Salvador, in October 1984, but he did not get there by himself. Former Senator Paul Tsongas and two Salvadorans, Leonel Gomez and Colonel Roberto Santivanez, had pulled a group of Americans together to change the face of El Salvador. The initial effort was very simple: to reveal the role of the Salvadoran army in the death squads. Santivanez, a former intelligence chief, was willing to talk. I set up interviews for him with the *New York Times* and Walter Cronkite.[5] Paul Tsongas had heard the Colonel's testimony before he went public, and his assurances of Santivanez's authenticity gave both the *Times* and CBS News the confidence to carry the story.

Strangely, this inspired the Chief of Staff of the Salvadoran army, Colonel Blandon, to reach out to the liberal Americans who had come together to support and protect Santivanez. From April to August, Tsongas conducted a series of private negotiations with select members of the Salvadoran army close to Blandon and with key Farabundo Marti Liberacion Nacional (FMLN) leaders. Promises made to Tsongas by high-level Salvadoran military officers led the Salvadoran army to cashier certain officers and send those associated with the worst human rights abuses out of the country.

Subsequently, Tsongas and his staff helped arrange a major prisoner exchange between the two armies. And, more significantly, the shuttle diplomacy of Tsongas and his associates created sufficient support in both militaries for sustained negotiations. By the time Tsongas journeyed to the United Nations in New York to meet President Duarte and convince him to negotiate, Duarte informed Tsongas that he would invite the rebels to La Palma, El Salvador.

The second round of talks produced only deadlock, and subsequent efforts to restart the negotiations failed. Nonetheless, Duarte's party, the Christian Democrats, won an overwhelming mandate in the February 1985 National Assembly elections on the issue of which party could better lead the country to peace.

I had played a major role as paymaster in the early phase of the Tsongas/Colonel Santivanez collaboration. I raised most of the money given to the colonel once he went public, to compensate for his job loss for telling what he knew. (He had been El Salvador's Consul in New Orleans.) I also arranged to pay the expenses of the man who became Tsongas's key advisor, who would shuttle between the Salvadoran army and the guerrillas to arrange prisoner exchange and create an environment suitable for negotiations.

ADA even paid for one of Tsongas's trips to Mexico City to meet with the Salvadoran guerrillas. I wanted to go, but Tsongas vetoed that idea. Left out of the *Times* story were the Colonel's revelations about CIA links with certain Salvadoran officers, notably Colonel Nicolas Carranza, former defense minister and chief of the Treasury Police. The first story had revealed that Carranza had established death squads through former Major Roberto D'Abuisson in late 1979, and that he regularly passed on orders selecting victims for authorized hit men, and delivered funds for safe houses and assassins.

But the *Times* would not print the charge about CIA involvement without corroboration by U.S. officials. In discussing these issues with another reporter, I told him about efforts we had made to get funding for the Colonel. It was news to the *Times* and they printed it. Even though the newspaper eventually printed a second article putting into context our efforts to raise money for the Colonel (we provided less than $50,000, while the CIA often provided Soviet defectors with more than half a million) the first story hurt the Colonel's credibility and cut attendance at a briefing in the Capitol arranged by Tsongas.

Tsongas blamed me, unfairly. Many people knew about our funding efforts. I had talked to dozens before I found the one donor willing to give enough to provide for the Colonel's needs for one year. When I was talking to the *Times* reporter, I was not revealing any secret. But Tsongas was right to exclude me from his trips. He no longer had confidence in me, and he was the elected official whom the Salvadorans took seriously. The rest of us were just supporting actors.

Returning to action in 1985, I remembered all of this, and saw the effort in El Salvador had stalled. The political climate was positive, with the Christian Democrats controlling both the Presidency and the National Assembly in El Salvador, but an effective process for achieving negotiations in Nicaragua was still lacking.

The Sandinistas had refused to sit down with their internal opposition after the elections, even though the demand for talks had come from a united opposition including the Cruz coalition and the other center-right parties, and the Communists and Socialists. The Sandinistas, triumphant, felt no need to make concessions to anyone.

The second Central American to act was Arturo Cruz. Much has been written about the San Jose Declaration, and many commentators believe that the real author was either Colonel Oliver North of the National Security Council or Alan Fiers of the CIA. Indeed, both have claimed authorship.

But the style of the document is unmistakably a blend of Arturo Cruz and his son, Arturo Cruz Jr. It did not call for an overthrow of the Sandinistas, but for a Church-mediated dialogue leading to new elections for the National Assembly. Father and son were also saying that the Honduras-based Contras were a real force in Nicaraguan society that had to be dealt if peace was to be achieved.

It is not that the proposal was perfect, or even stood a chance. What singled it out was that it was reasonable in the Central American context. Through it, the signers, including most of the leaders of the Honduran-based Fuerza Democratica Nicaraguense (FDN), were announcing they would accept something less than the overthrow of the Sandinistas, that they would not require a coalition government. Simple elections would be enough, provided they were honest.

It made sense. If negotiations in Nicaragua began, they would nourish the search for negotiations in El Salvador. I was eager for action. My colleagues had had a chance in El Salvador and had taken it as far as they could. Now it was my turn.

On June 4, Congress returned from its Memorial Day recess. McCurdy appeared before the Rules Committee to seek a rule on the Supplemental Appropriations Bill that would allow him to offer his amendment. The evening before, in a marathon session with the Republican leadership, White House officials, and conservative Democrats, McCurdy had worked out the final language.

When I read the amendment, I found that the human rights language, giving the United States a special responsibility to curb abuses by the Contras, had been removed. In its new form the legislation called on the Administration to try equally hard to end abuses on the part of both the Contras and the Sandinistas. A ridiculous notion, held by too many moderates and conservatives who should know better, the United States is perceived to have equal responsibility to curb human rights abuses in countries and forces we support as well as countries and forces we oppose. In the case of the Contras and the Nicaraguan government, the notion was particularly ludicrous; The U.S. government was trying to overthrow the one and had created, funded and trained the other.

Shortly after reading the new language, I ran into a lobbyist from Common Cause.[6] She asked which side I was lobbying for. There are no secrets in Washington. With great anger and frustration, directed at no one in particular, I replied: "I don't know! I don't know!"

It got worse. From the House lobby, where I had run into the Common Cause staffer, I climbed the stairs to the Rules Committee on the third floor. There I learned that the Democratic Speaker had used his power to prevent McCurdy from offering his amendment. The rule for debating the Supplemental Appropriations Bill would allow the Minority Republican leader Bob Michel to offer the amendment, but he could not designate McCurdy as the author. McCurdy, therefore, lost control over his own language.

The next day I was told that Michel had stripped from the amendment the requirement that the Contras be willing to negotiate with the Sandinistas. That night, the Gang of Four met with McCurdy. He listened to our frustrations, then reported that other members, notably Republicans, were also disturbed that the negotiations requirement had been removed.

Dave put in a call to the White House and asked that efforts be made to restore the language. Colonel Oliver North, Deputy Director of the White House Anti-Terrorism Office said he would try.

But I was pessimistic. In many cases, the language of an amendment can be changed up to the last minute, but not this time. I made calls to everyone I knew who might be able to do something, as well as many who couldn't do a thing. The answer was always the same.

I was miserable. And frightened. Not only had I betrayed my former position and longtime allies, I had betrayed myself. And I could not change this. The Republicans had control of the legislation and they wanted Democratic allies only long enough to gain victory.

I saw just one last hope: a presidential letter laying out U.S.-Nicaragua policy, including negotiations and human rights protections. But I did not know how to get such a letter.

When this kind of thing happened in the past, I would go to the House side of the Capitol and wander around, first to the restaurant, then to the Democratic door of the chamber where lobbyists wait to buttonhole members. When none of that worked, I would go loiter in the offices of members with whom I was working. Most have those nice courtesy phones (with Watts lines) in their reception areas, and you can make dozens of phone calls, depending on the tolerance of the staff.

At four o'clock I arrived at McCurdy's office. As I crossed the threshold someone told me the President's office was on hold waiting for Dave to return. That was my chance. Dave and I had discussed a presidential letter, and he thought it was a possibility. Before he got on the phone I handed him a copy of the President's April 24th letter to the Senate (with key human rights sections underlined) and reviewed what I thought we needed.

The President first thanked Dave for his work, then described his policy as one of promoting negotiations, reconciliation, and support for the democratic center against the extremes of the right and the left. Dave said, "Mr. President, I am glad to hear you say that; that is exactly the kind of policy we need to win the vote next week."

A brief parenthesis (as my Nicaraguan friends like to say): I was not surprised to learn about the President's words. They had been scripted the day before. Twenty-four hours earlier, I was in the same room with Bernie Aronson and Steve Patterson, McCurdy's Administrative Assistant. We knew the call would be coming at some point and we wanted the President to say the right things. So Bernie had drafted some remarks and called Ollie North.

During the previous month, the Gang of Four had begun to meet with North. I should probably remember every detail of our first meeting I had with him, but I do not. It was sometime in May. He mostly told stories. The one I do remember was about the early days of the Contras, when the official mission was the interdiction of arms from Nicaragua through Honduras to El Salvador. He told us the mission was very effective, until the Hondurans inexplicably ordered the Contras to move their bases in Honduras from the areas along the path from Nicaragua to El Salvador to the borders of their frontiers, far from El Salvador. He also spoke about meeting with Holden Roberto, leader of one of the anticommunist guerrilla groups in Angola, when the Congress cut off aid in 1975.

In all likelihood, neither of these stories was true. Ollie told stories to make a point. The stories he told, whether true or not, served the larger truth.

Ollie was also good at listening. We talked a lot about the need for a genuine bipartisan policy, about the necessity of allowing Democrats to participate in the writing of the bill.

Thus a month later we were writing that script.

"And one more thing, Mr. President," said Dave McCurdy. "We need a letter saying exactly what you said, plus one more thing, what you wrote in your letter to the Senate on April 24th." Dave read the President the human rights paragraph acknowledging a special U.S. responsibility to promote human rights among the Contras.

Now I needed to see the letter the President had promised. If a letter really did enunciate a new policy, I would be happy, we could win.

Later that evening I returned to McCurdy's office to discuss an op-ed, drafted by Bernie, which Dave planned to submit to the *Washington Post*. At some point I told Bernie about the President's promise to write a letter, I told him how important that was to me, and I told him about my apprehensions. Bernie suggested I write a draft. He had worked in the Carter White House. He knew Ollie would not have the time to write the letter himself, nor did he find it likely he would assign the task to someone else.

First I wrote that it was not U.S. policy to overthrow the Sandinistas, or to install the former Guardsmen in their place. Then I inserted Senate human rights language. When I got to negotiations between the United States and Nicaragua, I hesitated. Bernie, Bob, and Penn did not feel strongly on this subject. Dave too remained unenthusiastic about direct negotiations. To me this was key. But I was so intent on securing the other language I temporized. The letter would commit the President to consult with the Contras and our allies in the region about the desirability of direct negotiations.

That was the first time in an alliance with the Administration that I compromised my own fundamental principles. It would not be the last.

It has taken me many years to understand why I believe my failure to insist on bilateral negotiations was a compromise of "fundamental principle," and why I had perceived negotiations between the United States and the Sandinistas to be "key." The simplest explanation begins with my identity as a lobbyist. Language promising bilateral negotiations with the Sandinistas would have reached farther to the left. Certainly that would have made me more comfortable.

But "comfort" is not fundamental. The issue of negotiations was at the very core of my alliance with the Administration. What the McCurdy Democrats and the Gang of Four shared with the Administration was the determination to bring to (or force on) Nicaragua "genuine democracy." Where we differed was on how to get there.

My good friend, Bob Kagan, who enters this story at the end of 1985, has written that the McCurdy Democrats "wished to support the war as briefly and as parsimoniously as possible, while probing constantly for any signs of accommodation. Their great hope was that the Sandinistas eventually would see reason. The Reagan Administration was not inclined to probe, however, in part out of fear that the Sandinistas would pretend to negotiate only to kill aid to the Contras, in part out of the conviction that the Sandinistas would never abide by any pledges made. Their great hope was that the Sandinistas would eventually collapse."[7]

What Kagan leaves out is moderates' belief that the Contras could never win an outright military victory. A negotiated settlement, which would lay the foundation for genuine democracy, lead to reductions in the size of the Sandinista army, and ban support for irregular forces such as the Contras and the FMLN was not simply the best alternative, it was the only alternative. We would use a mix of incentives, military, economic, and diplomatic, to force the Sandinistas to make an agreement. We never envisioned their overthrow.

We shared with the Administration the belief that the most important behavioral change to impose on the Sandinistas was the practice of democracy. In 1984, President Reagan's National Bipartisan Commission on Central America, chaired by Henry Kissinger, made this linkage between security and democracy:

> Because of its (the Sandinista government's) secretive nature, the existence of a political order on the Cuban model in Nicaragua would pose major difficulties in negotiating, implementing, and verifying any Sandinista commitment to refrain from supporting insurgency and subversion in other countries. In this sense, the development of an open political system in Nicaragua, with a free press and an active opposition, would provide an important security for the other countries of the region and would be a key element in any negotiated settlement.

This linkage of security issues with a democratic regime in Nicaragua, coupled with the belief that the Contras could not win an outright military victory, were so fundamental to the moderates' vision that we often took them for granted and did not always articulate them well. This carelessness sometimes led us to misunderstand Administration statements, as well as positions to which we and the Administration had mutually agreed.

In that letter, I wrote the following language for the President's signature:

> My Administration is determined to pursue political, not military, solutions in Central America. Our policy for Nicaragua is the same as for El Salvador and all of Central America: to support the democratic center against the extremes of both the right and left, and to secure democracy and lasting peace through national dialogue and regional negotiations. We do not seek the military overthrow of the Sandinista government or to put in its place a government based on supporters of the old Somoza regime. . . .
>
> [W]e also endorse the unified democratic opposition's March 1, 1985 San Jose declaration, which calls for national reconciliation through a church-mediated dialogue. We oppose a sharing of power based on military force rather than the will of the people expressed through free and fair elections. . . . It is . . . the position

of the Nicaraguan opposition leaders, who have agreed that executive authority in Nicaragua should change only through elections.

For the moderates, these words meant that the Administration was abandoning its earlier (and to us impossible) goal of military victory. By foreswearing "military solutions" and agreeing to a change in "executive authority in Nicaragua" through elections only, we believed the Administration was changing course. We believed they should use every opportunity to probe for signs of Sandinista accommodation. Therefore, we were not always clear when we said the Administration should support "negotiations." We did not know whether Contadora was the right forum, or bilateral talks, or a church-mediated dialogue. We supported all of them, and none of them, at the same time. What we knew is that the Contras could not win, but Contra pressure could be effective in forcing the Sandinistas, somehow, sometime, to make concessions in the direction of democracy. It was fundamental, in our eyes, to seek out any and all negotiating forums to pursue this goal.

For the Administration, this was quite different, and clearly inconsistent with the plain meaning of their text. In Administration minds, the key phrase was *a Church-mediated dialogue between the Sandinistas and the Contras.* The Sandinistas rejected this formula when the Contras offered it on March 1, and they rejected it again in October when the U.S. negotiator on Central American issues, Ambassador Harry Shlaudemann, met briefly with Ambassador Carlos Tunneman, the Sandinista envoy to Washington.

For the Administration, that was enough negotiating. It was time to turn to the real task at hand—building up the Contra fighting force enough for them to win. But the Administration would never openly state this position.

To be fair, dealing with us moderates must have been frustrating to the Administration, because we would forget why we favored a specific forum for negotiations, we would forget to link negotiations to the goal we did share, achieving genuine democracy in Nicaragua. But we had every reason to doubt the good faith of the Administration in pursuing a negotiated settlement. Therefore every negotiating forum, however remote from our goal, became important as a sign that the Administration might be changing course.

On Tuesday June 11, the letter was released during a press conference on the White House lawn, with the President, Minority Leader Michel, Dave McCurdy, and two other members. At long last I was prepared to declare, through lobbying, which side I was on.

During the debate on June 12, Dave took fifty copies of the President's letter to the House floor to distribute to moderate Democrats. He would sit for a while, then get up and walk over to one and then another. Always he left a copy of the letter.

I thought the first vote would be close. Representative Edward Boland, a Democrat from Massachusetts and former chair of the House Intelligence Committee, had offered an amendment restating current law prohibiting direct or indirect CIA support for the Contras. This ban would continue until Congress repealed it in another law. Without this amendment, it would lapse on October 1. The effect of this amendment would have been to prevent the CIA from sharing intelligence with the Contras.

The vote was not close. The amendment went down 196–232, and the letter had played a decisive role. *Time Magazine* wrote:

> Reagan's most effective step in changing congressional minds was a declaration that U.S. assistance was not designed to over-throw the pro-Moscow Sandinista regime, but to pressure it into coming to peaceful terms with its domestic opposition. In a letter to Oklahoma Democrat Dave McCurdy, who helped shape the compromise bill, Reagan said, "My Administration is determined to pursue political, not military solutions in Central America."

The vote on final passage of the Michel-McCurdy amendment was 254–174. The liberal-moderate alliance was shattered. A new moderate-Administration alliance took its place.

But from the beginning there were strains in the new coalition. William Broomfield (R-Michigan), ranking member of the House Foreign Affairs Committee and frequent spokesman for the Administration's policies on Central America, gave only grudging support to the amendment:

> I ask all of my colleagues to support on a bipartisan basis an amendment I wish was stronger. I think many do wish that we

were providing military assistance and not just humanitarian.

The amendment introduced by the Republican leader, Mr. Michel, . . . is far from an ideal bill. It does not provide enough aid, it does not provide the right kind of aid, it does not involve the appropriate administrative agency [by which he meant the CIA].

Moderates who were supporting aid to the Contras for the first time, on the other hand, made clear their limited support for this kind of aid only, and only in this package. McCurdy gave his reasons for supporting aid:

The issue is not whether we are for negotiated settlement or military intervention. This amendment provides for a cease fire [and] for negotiations. . . .

The issue is not whether the CIA will be involved in distributing . . . assistance inside Nicaragua. Our amendment specifically prohibits the CIA and the DOD from doing so. . . .

My colleagues, the only real issue today is whether we provide real incentives for both sides and particularly the Sandinistas to negotiate with their people.

J. J. Pickle, Democrat of Texas, was stronger in conditioning his support:

I think it is important that we apply pressure on the Sandinista government. We should continue to make clear our concerns about the policies of the Sandinista government. We must continue to press for freedom of the press and religious freedom in Nicaragua. We must not turn our backs on those in Nicaragua who want more for—and from—their country. . . .

It seems to me that our goal should be a friendly government in Nicaragua which allows basic freedoms for its people, free from external intervention, in strong pursuit of the ideals which spawned the 1979 assumption of power of the present government. . . .

[The Contras] are a fighting force which leaves much to be desired but it is all that we've got. We cannot at this time simply wash our hands of the entire matter and leave them to their own devices.

My anticipated votes on this issue are consistent with my past position on aid to the Contras. I have consistently opposed covert direct or indirect military or paramilitary aid to the Contras, but rather continued support for those seeking changes in the Nicaraguan government.

Representative Bill Richardson, a Democrat from New Mexico, is a man of my generation who worked for many years as an assistant to Senator Hubert Humphrey before returning to New Mexico to run for Congress. He was liberal, strongly pro-human rights and anti-interventionist. In the first hearing on international human rights held by Humphrey and organized by Richardson, he had invited me to testify. He spoke eloquently about why a liberal could support this package.

It is not a perfect amendment, but it does give some good points: it says that we support the Contadora process; it says we will push for bilateral negotiations with the Sandinistas; it condemns Contra atrocities; it says that we will work toward a cease-fire. It says no to the CIA in disbursing the aid and I am completely for that, because the American people don't want military assistance nor do they want the CIA involved. . . .

I am voting this way because I think the President of the United States for the first time is saying that he is for negotiations and meaning it. He met with us yesterday, and he said in a letter and verbally that he is not for overthrowing the Sandinista government . . . that he supports the Contadora process, that he wants us to give him a chance.

For nine or ten months, this Congress has voted no on aid to the Contras. That hasn't worked. There is still bloodshed. I think we should try a new approach, and I frankly don't know that the Michel amendment is the right thing to do. But we must at least try. I am willing to give the President of the United States a chance and the benefit of the doubt. I hope and pray that he does not let us down.

Two days later, on a Friday, I went to see Ann Lewis, my boss at ADA. Since taking leave, I had told her nothing about my activities. But her brother, Barney Frank, a congressman from Massachusetts, had been told by anti-Contra lobbyists that they had seen me buttonholing members, urging them to support the President's package.

In fact, I had lobbied no one. Except for McCurdy, I spoke with only two members during the vote. One had always supported the Contras and was intrigued with my position. The other, a longtime friend, was so liberal that, if he could get away with it, he would vote against aid to the Pentagon. He voted against Contra aid.

Ann asked me to resign, and recounted false stories of my vigorous lobbying for the Contras. I denied them, but it was denial based on distinction without difference. I thought about it over the weekend and submitted my resignation on my forty-second birthday, June 19, 1985. For nine and a half years I had been associated with ADA, the organization that for me had come to symbolize pure liberalism. After what I had done, my resignation was inevitable. But I hate change nevertheless and this did not feel good.

After the vote on July 12, Dave, Bernie, Bob, and I were joined at dinner by Ollie North and his secretary, Fawn Hall. Celebratory dinners are silly and fun; little of consequence is said. Ollie suggested before Fawn arrived that she was single and available, and that both Bob and I were good-looking men. Bernie took Dave aside to tell him that I would probably be fired, and to ask if he might be able to help me. (I started work in Dave's office ten days later.)

Over the July 4th weekend, I wrote a long paper about my work on Nicaragua and an explanation of why I had changed my position. I concluded:

I asked in the beginning of this narrative if I had changed my mind. I had. I agree with the President's letter:

"We do not seek the military overthrow of the Sandinista government or to put in its place a government based on supporters of the old Somoza regime.

"Just as we support President Duarte in his efforts to achieve reconciliation in El Salvador, we also endorse the Unified Democratic Opposition's March 1, 1985, San Jose Declaration which calls for national reconciliation through a church-mediated dialogue. We oppose a sharing of power based on military force rather than the will of the people expressed through free and fair elections. That is the position of President Duarte. It is also the position of the Nicaraguan opposition leaders, who have agreed that executive authority in Nicaragua should change only through elections."

I think this is still a good statement, and it was a good guide for policy on Nicaragua. Though it was what I wrote and what the President signed, it was never really a good representation of Administration policy.

I had written into a major presidential communication what I had believed for three years. Successful negotiations in El Salvador depended on successful negotiations in Nicaragua. Whereas before I had formerly believed that negotiations should result in coalition government, I had come to believe that negotiations should result in elections. And the goal should be how to make elections free and fair so that opposition parties in each country would feel free to participate. It would take strong guarantees to convince either the Contras or the FMLN guerrillas to lay down their arms and trust their fate to elections. But it was the only way I could see to finally end the seemingly endless cycle of violence in Central America, where the victor always suppresses the loser and the loser always picks up a gun. I believed I had witnessed the Administration move in this direction, and I saw the President's signature on my letter as vindication of that belief.

But I was also wary, so I wrote the criteria for an evaluation of Administration policy over the following nine months:

> Members of Congress and opinion makers like myself are . . . making a lot of risky bets: 1) that the President's letter is believable; 2) that the main Contra force, the FDN, can be reformed and will settle for less than overthrow of the Sandinistas; 3) that the Salvadoran government will negotiate in good faith; and 4) that either the Sandinistas or the Salvadoran guerrillas are prepared to accept a historic compromise through negotiations.
>
> . . . whether Cruz and Robelo, who have both acknowledged the FDN's human rights abuses in the past and who want a political solution for their country, will be able to share real authority with Calero and the FDN military leadership is still in doubt. . . .

This offered good criteria for assessing progress in my alliance with the Administration. Unfortunately, politics is not very generous. It is rare when you can sit down and review performance in such a straightforward fashion. More often you are simply responding to the day's or week's events. What you know clearly is what side you are on, not how well that side is performing, measured against a clear set of criteria.

On the same day I resigned from ADA, a squad of Salvadoran guerrillas killed two dozen people, including seven Marines, in the Zona Rosa of San Salvador. I learned from a Salvadoran source that the Sandinistas had early knowledge of the planned assassinations and had approved.

One concession I had wrung from my Administration allies was to allow a Salvadoran leader, a democrat of conviction but allied with the guerrillas, to visit the United States. If there were to be successful negotiations in El Salvador, his participation was crucial. And he needed to consult with key American actors. But after the Zona Rosa murders, as spokesman for the alliance of leftist political parties and the guerrilla organizations, he had defended the killings. His ban from the United States would no longer be lifted.

Positions hardened. On one side were the Sandinistas, the Salvadoran guerrillas, the Guatemalan guerrillas, and the Cubans backed by the Soviets. On the other were the Guatemalan government, the Salvadoran government, the Honduran government, the Contras, and the United States. Despite calls for peace in the amendment we helped write, there was now only talk of war and an escalation of violence.

I observed it all with relative equanimity. No, the immediate events following the vote did not augur well for peace. But what else could the Contras do? I told myself that the $27 million in nonlethal economic assistance would not allow the Contras to go on the offensive in the war; and the offensive would bring peace.

I could not have been more wrong.

While we were speculating about who would run the new aid program, Ollie was actually looking for a way to expand the war.

When congressionally approved aid ran out in May of 1984, Bud McFarlane, the National Security Advisor, was able to find a replacement: Saudi Arabia. Ollie was the go-between. He received a bank account number in the Cayman Islands from Adolfo Calero, and passed it on to the Saudi ambassador in Washington. The Contras hardly missed a payment.

The money began flowing in July 1984 at the rate of $1 million a month, just a little less than the CIA had been providing.[8]

Oddly enough, the Gang of Four never speculated about who might be providing money to the Contras during the year of the official cutoff. Newspapers suggested rich Americans or third world countries, but to the best of my memory, no one guessed that it was Saudi Arabia. (More often people guessed it was Israel.)

When the official U.S. money ran out, the CIA agents remained, and ran the war until October when the Boland amendment was signed into law by the President. Then their leaving created a big problem.

Adolfo Calero had been a good businessman in Nicaragua. He had directed the Coca-Cola franchise before becoming a Contra leader. For the most part, he had used the Saudi money ($32.5 million) well, buying arms and ammunition for his troops. But he did not know how to run a war. There was no structure for delivery of the arms. The CIA had taken care of that, and now the CIA was gone. No Nicaraguans knew what to do. In part, this was because the most talented former Guardsmen had quit or been purged in the endless infighting that characterized the Contra movement.

On July 1, Ollie flew down to Miami to meet Calero, Enrique Bermudez, the FDN military chief, and retired General Richard Secord, in a conference room in the Miami International Airport Hotel inside the terminal. Ollie was blunt. He cited numerous reports of Contra officials "lining their pockets" and of recent purchases of faulty equipment. He said the whole project could go down the tubes unless the CIA came back, and soon.[9]

In the end, the participants agreed that they would have to create a viable resupply operation and build up a new southern front. Contra operations based out of Costa Rica had fallen on hard times after the Administration withdrew its support of Pastora, and Calero only grudgingly agreed to share a small amount of the Saudi money with that southern-based group, known by its initials FARN, led by "El Negro" Chamorro. Like Pastora, a former ally of the Sandinistas, Chamorro had tried to operate out of Honduras, but was banished by Honduran strongman General Gustavo Alvarez. He then tried to work with Pastora, but was kicked out by him in January 1983. He had a tiny force in Nicaragua and now the Administration felt it needed him as the foundation of the new southern front.

What Ollie did not tell Calero at the meeting was that he had decided that General Richard Secord would run the new resupply operation for both the north and the south. He was no longer going to trust Nicaraguans to do the job. Albert Hakim, an Iranian-born business partner of Secord, shortly thereafter set up an account, Lake Resources, in Switzerland. After that, Lake, not Calero's bank account, received the monies that were raised.[10]

I knew nothing of Ollie's trips or these decisions, but I had been to Miami a few days before Ollie's meeting. When I had visited Nicaragua in 1980, '81, and '82, the congressional delegations had been organized by John McAward of the Unitarian Universalist Service Committee, a very liberal organization. Obviously, I was no longer a candidate for their trips, but they now thought I could help them establish a better working relationship with the Contras. It was the first time I had ever been to Miami. Our meeting with the Contra leadership took place in the conference room of an electronic components warehouse owned by a Nicaraguan exile sympathetic to the cause. The trust I had in John and his staff was adopted by Adolfo, Alfonso, and Arturo, the new leaders of the Contras.

In the evening, John arranged a meeting with Edgar Chamorro, formerly allied with Adolfo in the FDN leadership. I am sure Chamorro passed on stories over dinner that should have made me wary. But even looking back on what was to take place over the next year, I remember none of them. In 1982 he thought he could fix the Contras, but found he could not. I had not tried yet. Why should I have listened to him recounting his failures?

The next morning we flew back to Washington just in time for me to meet with liberal House staffers on the question: Whither U.S. policy toward Nicaragua?

My body ached for Corinne. I don't believe that ever before or since have I wanted a woman so badly. It was lust at a level that I had never experienced at eighteen when men are supposed to be at the height of their sexual powers. I had called her before I left Miami. She was there and she was game.

Our lovemaking that day formed embraces so tight, a meshing of bodies so complete, that we were both incredulous.

Corinne, in those days, in that summer, was my only release. It was not love, not grand passion, only grand sex. She was a witch. With her my body reached a level of sexual passion and release that I had not found with other women since my late twenties.

Meanwhile, my heart prowled elsewhere. I had had an ongoing relationship that now was fading, and I was madly smitten with one of the doctors

I had encountered in my search for better health. And I told Corinne every-thing. I asked her why she put up with me. I explained over and over that I could never love her. I told her about an article I had read, an article about married women having affairs outside the home they wished to preserve. Hearth and husband were not quite enough.

Corinne talks a lot, but I don't remember a word in reply, perhaps because there was none. It was a strange time. She was at LTA, I was at Dave McCurdy's office. There was work to do, as I will soon describe, but I was at loose ends. I was running almost every morning, more often than not trying to counteract the effects of too much drink the evening before. And, let loose by the white-haired, wise old doctor, I had returned to the squash and racquetball courts, playing two or three times a week.

It was a lonely time, without the ADA office, cut off from so many former liberal colleagues. And, having taken this great risk and won, I felt that there should be a woman in my life whom I loved. And yet I didn't look at Corinne, not for one second. The emotional center in my life that summer was Ollie North. ■

CHAPTER THREE

THE SUMMER OF OLLIE NORTH

July–December 1985

My responsibilities at Dave's office were simple: to follow legislation adopted by the House through final passage. His staff was extraordinarily friendly even though I was the only one not from Oklahoma. In fact, Oklahomans were quite new to me, and I delighted in the lilt of their speech. Other than Dave himself and his administrative assistant, the staff really did not grasp the significance of Nicaragua. Still, they were very open and they radiated great love for their home state. Over the years, I grew very fond of them. Until his very last day in office, I always felt at home in Dave's office. I always experienced a decency, friendliness, and curiosity there.

In those days, I looked to Ollie to make sense out of all that had happened. I met with him only four times that summer; three of those meetings are listed in his appointment book, an Iran-Contra document. The other time I tagged along with Alfonso Robelo. But we talked often by telephone. Our meetings took place at night. They had no form and, for me, no real purpose, except to draw closer to power with which I had become aligned.

During one meeting, he told me that two commandantes from the Frente Sandinista Liberacion Nacional (FSLN) had tried to reach him. This was supposed to provide proof that the renewal of Contra aid was working, that the Sandinistas were looking to negotiate. And indeed this was the formula I believed in. I now think he told me this story to reinforce that belief.

Ollie also told me about a trip to El Salvador in 1983 with Vice President George H. W. Bush. He described a meeting with top colonels in the Salvadoran army to whom he supposedly read the riot act on human rights. The vice president's security people insisted that the colonels be asked to remove the revolvers that they wore on their hips, but Ollie objected. Such a request would have demonstrated a lack of respect, and the meeting was already problematic; if this happened, it would be doomed. He told me the argument was settled when the vice president arrived, asked what the problem was, and immediately agreed with Ollie. Thereafter, a receptive group of Salvadoran officers received the vice president's message and began to clean up its act.

In retrospect, I don't believe the first story; I do believe the second. But in neither do I buy Ollie's spin. As a result of the vice president's trip, two officers were sent out of the country because of their involvement in human rights violations. Our effort in 1984, led by Senator Tsongas, had resulted in the exile of five officers. But neither effort led to prosecution, and that remained the case. Salvadoran officers killed or ordered killings with total impunity. With one exception. In October 1991, two officers were convicted in the killing of six Jesuit priests, their housekeeper, and her daughter.

Despite the gravity of our topics of conversation, what remained important to me was not the stories. It was simply being there sipping coffee with Ollie. Our meetings and calls were my proof that the alliance made sense.

In an earlier meeting with the Gang of Four before the vote, Ollie had told us about a little-known part of the Foreign Aid Authorization Bill, the Pell Amendment. This bill did incorporate aid for the Contras, but it was not the legislative vehicle for the $27 million. That was the Supplemental Appropriations Bill.

Inexplicably, since Contra aid was a popular topic in the Senate, that body adopted the Pell language in the authorization bill that barred the United States from giving aid or military equipment to any country that provided aid to the Contras. If enacted into law, it would have had a chilling effect on any government that might want to aid the Contras, especially militarily.

At the time I knew nothing of the Saudi Arabian contribution of $32.5 million to the Contras. I realized the aid was coming from somewhere, but assumed it came from private donors in the United States. I also knew that Ollie had some control over it.

But I would not discuss that aspect of his work with him. In my view, any material support he directed to the Contras was against the law, though I never articulated this. I was ambivalent about the Pell Amendment. I saw the necessity for some military aid, but did not want to see enough to increase the Contras's military capabilities in the field. When in May Ollie asked for my help in getting it repealed, I was silent.

After my dismissal from ADA, the situation looked different. I rationalized, "in for a dime, in for a dollar." But my real reason was that I was on

Ollie's side now. It was my responsibility to change this law.

The most logical member to approach was Representative Dante Fascell, chairman of the House Foreign Affairs Committee, who would lead House conferees in their meeting with the Senate. He supported Contra aid, had worked closely with Dave, was the Democrat who accompanied Dave to the Rose Garden when the President released his letter to the press. I had an appointment with him on the day of the conference, but he had to cancel. I took the issue to his aides, but sensed they could do nothing. I argued that it was ridiculous to approve economic aid to the Contras on the one hand, and on the other adopt a law that would make our allies unable to provide the military aid we could not by law provide.

Fascell's aides did not listen, and when I finally encountered Fascell himself in the Capitol, he couldn't focus, his mind filled with several dozen items he would have to confront in just a few hours.

On the evening of the conference, Representative Henry Hyde, a Republican from Illinois, saw me lingering outside the Senate Foreign Relations Committee in the Capitol where the conference was to take place. Henry was one of the brightest of the hawkish conservative Republicans. He knew me from the days when I was working for Harkin, and associated me with liberal efforts to cut aid to allied governments with human rights problems.

He approached me and quipped: "What little country are you beating up on today?" I pointed to my new identification, a congressional badge, hanging from a chain around my neck, bearing Dave McCurdy's name. I told him about the Pell Amendment and the illogic of adopting it just after renewing aid, and I urged him to lead an effort to delete it.

He stunned me with his response. "I will, and I will call it the Bruce Cameron amendment."

"For Christ's sake, you can't do that!" I replied in horror. "I'm in enough trouble already for someone who is supposed to be a liberal Democrat."

I also approached Ed Fox, chief lobbyist for the State Department. He, too, was astonished and did a double take to look at my badge. I gave him the same short memo I gave Henry.

Both were stunned at my new position. But they did not take my information to the rest of the pro-Contra conference committee members. Was that surprising? It seemed so to me at the time, but in retrospect, it was understandable. Neither Ed nor Henry, despite their leadership positions, had been involved in the formulation of the compromise on Contra aid. That had been done out of channels, with people like Dave and the Gang of Four who worked directly with Ollie. Trying to bring Henry Hyde and Ed Fox in at the eleventh hour did not work.

Finally, in despair, I called Jonathan Miller, Deputy Director of the Office of Public Diplomacy on Central America in the State Department. I explained the situation. He called back, and Ollie joined him on the phone. I explained again. Ten minutes later every Administration lobbyist available had their copies of the conference working document open to the section on the Pell Amendment.

Still, it was too late. The elected officials who needed to be briefed on the amendment's importance were the Republican senators who supported the Contras. They were not briefed. I did have one opportunity to talk to Senator Richard Lugar, chairman of the Senate Foreign Relations Committee, when we were standing at adjacent urinals. But I just couldn't. A good lobbyist takes whatever opportunities he is given to make his case, but when he asked me what I was doing in the Capitol so late at night (it was close to 11), I just told him I was following the conference. He replied, "I was afraid of that." I didn't know what he meant, but it seemed clear he was as tired as Fascell, and silence was best.

When the issue was finally raised, Henry gave a spirited speech against the amendment. But no Republican senator picked up on it. Fascell just said, "My guys," referring to six or seven liberal members sitting to his right, "will accept no change." It was over in minutes. Henry looked at me and shrugged.

How our democracy works can defy understanding. I had another amendment in the same bill, so I kept following its progress. This was an amendment that would prohibit all military aid to the government of Guatemala until (1) there were free and fair elections, (2) a new president had taken office, (3) he had requested such aid in writing, and (4) President Reagan had certified that there had been a reduction in government-sponsored killings and disappearances. Lugar had been fully briefed on this issue. For twenty-five minutes he fought to create a loophole that would allow for $100,000 to be made available for military training to Guatemalan army officers, even in the absence of a certification. He or his staff probably would have been fully briefed by Department of Defense lobbyists who did not want their program interrupted, even for four months.

The difference between the two amendments was this: aid to Guatemala was subject to regular processes. Nicaragua, on the other hand, had become an issue handled out of channels. Dave McCurdy had assumed leadership of the new Administration-moderate alliance and had chosen the Gang of Four as his key advisors, which linked him with Ollie.

Ollie found a way, overnight, to make a new precedent in the annals of Congress. The next morning, the conferees were informed by White House lobbyists that the bill that included the Pell Amendment would be vetoed. Fascell refused to reopen the conference, so in a startling move Claiborne Pell from Rhode Island, ranking Democrat on the Senate Foreign Relations Committee, agreed to a "technical modification" which was incorporated into the bill as it was reported by the conferees to both House and Senate for final passage.

In its new form, the Pell Amendment prohibited using aid as leverage to seek support from other governments, while it specifically allowed officials to explain the goals of U.S. policy in Central America and allowed other governments to provide military material from their own reserves to the Contras.

Shortly after that, Ollie told me that, privately, he would have to raise $1.5 million per month in military aid to supplement the $3 million per month in economic aid authorized by Congress. I remember hearing this with unease mixed with pride in the lobbyist's craft. Raising this money would now be legal. My timely information on the conference had allowed Ollie to mobilize forces in the White House to generate a veto threat.

But I didn't think very hard about who or what Ollie might be soliciting. I vaguely imagined the money coming from El Salvador, maybe Honduras or Venezuela. While associated with Pastora, Alfonso Robelo had received funds from Venezuelan sources. Like others, I also suspected Israel. But I didn't ask Ollie. In my wildest dreams I could not have imagined that Ollie was trying to create a new organization to run the war.

On August 8 of that year, the modified Pell Amendment became law. That same month an aide to Secord held discussions with the Contras in Honduras. They came to a mutual decision that the resupply operation could not be set up there, because the Honduran army was nervous about its high profile and pressing hard for more U.S. assistance (from which the officers expected their cut). Honduran army officers were notoriously corrupt.

Instead, Secord approached General Bustillo, Chief of the Salvadoran Air Force, to seek permission to operate out of Ilopango Air Base near San Salvador. My hunch about El Salvador was right; I was just wrong about the type of support being sought.[11]

The plan, however, did not become operational immediately. Even as late as February 1986, seven months after it was conceived, the Enterprise, as General Secord named it, had only one plane, a C-7 cargo. Because supplies were so limited, many FDN troops had quit Nicaragua and fled to Honduras and Costa Rica. In desperation, Ollie had one of the planes carrying some of the $27 million in nonlethal aid make its legal delivery to an FDN base in Honduras, then directed it to pick up an illegal cargo of weapons and drop them to troops inside Nicaragua. The act so clearly breached the boundary of the law that the State Department, in charge of administering the $27 million, refused to pay for the drop in Nicaragua.[12]

By March the new system was finally in place. A full team of men was put in place at Ilopango, and each of the key players was linked to the others by a special communication device, provided to Colonel North by the super-secret National Security Agency. They had hoped to start earlier, they had hoped to quickly capitalize on the new funding and escalate the war. But by the time the Enterprise it was needed simply to rescue the Contras.

Each resupply operation was slightly different, but this was the common pattern: an L-100, the nonpassenger version of the Boeing 707, would carry nonlethal supplies to the FDN, and the operator, Southern Air Transport, would be paid by the State Department. The plane would then pick up stock from the FDN's Saudi-funded purchases of lethal weapons and fly them to Ilopango, a flight paid for by the Enterprise. Then, under the guidance of Ollie and certain Defense and CIA officials, all acting illegally, an Enterprise plane would make air-drops into Nicaragua.[13]

Of all this I knew almost nothing. Retired General John Singlaub, president of the World Anti-Communist League (WACL), was believed by many in the press to be Ollie's key agent with the Contras, buying them weapons and supplying them with training and tactical advice. In one of our late-night conversations, I asked Ollie about him, pointing out WACL's unsavory reputation, with rumored links to various Latin American death squads and neo-Nazis.

"Singlaub serves a useful function," Ollie replied. "He diverts attention from someone else whose function is vital." He was referring to retired

General Secord, of course, but at the time I did not know of him and didn't ask. The significance of the remark was lost on me until December 1986, when Secord's role was exposed, sixteen months after my conversation with Ollie.

There was talk in late August. Already there had been reports in the *New York Times*, the *Washington Post*, and other major newspapers about Ollie's involvement in providing military advice and facilitating resupply of the Contras. I should have linked those reports with what Ollie had said. But I didn't.

I was reaching the end of my brief tenure in McCurdy's office. I was thinking about how I could get funding to continue my work with Arturo and Alfonso, and to carry on my other human rights work as well. I met with a representative of a conservative foundation that appreciated what I had done for the Contra cause, but nothing ever came of it. They wanted to find Ronald Reagan clones seeking to bomb Nicaragua back to the Stone Age.

I was about to go on vacation. The other successful legislation on which I had worked that year was the amendment on Guatemala. Even though it continued the prohibition on military aid or sales to Guatemala (a prohibition that had been in effect, with one minor interruption, for five years), it was well received by the Guatemalan Foreign Minister Fernando Andrade. He saw it as his personal project to return Guatemala to democracy. He thought the amendment would help him convince the Guatemalan army to allow free and fair elections, to stay neutral, even to allow Vinicio Cerezo of the Christian Democrats to assume office if he won. (Earlier the army had twice tried to assassinate Cerezo.) Andrade's closest aide had even assisted me and other congressional staffers in writing the amendment. The grateful foreign minister therefore offered me a free trip to Guatemala, along with a free hotel room, providing me with the opportunity to learn Spanish.

GUATEMALA: SUMMER 1985

For human rights activists, the '60s, '70s and '80s in Guatemala were synonymous with hell. By 1981 everyone was frightened, everyone knew someone who had been disappeared by the death squads.

Say you are a teacher and you just gave an exam. Holding your briefcase full of examination papers, you walk to the corner where you daily catch a bus home. On this particular day a van screeches to a halt in front of you, four men jump out, grab you, and throw you into the van. You are taken to a "safe house." The police do not investigate, because your abductors are the police. They torture you in clever, ingenious, excruciating ways. Eventually they kill you, and dump your mutilated body on a pile of garbage at the edge of town.

Or you are an Indian living in a village when the army appears, rounds up you and your fellow villagers, hacks everyone to death with machetes, and burns your village to the ground.

I saw twelve bodies in a small village outside Chajul in northern Quiche. I had been given the use of a helicopter for a day by the then military ruler Efriam Rios Montt. My army escorts claimed the killers were guerrillas disguised as Guatemalan troops. At the time, I spoke no Spanish and simply stood by, listening to my escorts while Ray Bonner of the *New York Times* interviewed villagers to try to find out what had happened. He learned nothing. The bodies had been laid out under a thatched roof detached from a cement building. There were large cuts on all the bodies, six to eighteen inches long, but there was no longer any blood. They had been dead for seven hours.

There was nothing human about what happened there. That was Guatemala.

But Guatemala is also magical. It is rightly called the land of eternal spring. In the highlands, where the tourists go, where I went that day, where the army had gone before me, the temperature ranges between 60° and 80°F. The clouds are always beautiful, always new, always changing. We were in those mountains, filled with life, filled with death.

Despite it all, I had traveled to Guatemala to find life, and I did. I stayed in the wonderful Hotel Antigua. Each day I studied Spanish for six hours, then hung out with friends I met in school.

Washington reality intruded a week after I arrived. A friend called to tell me about a cashiered Honduran Major Ricardo Zuniga who had disappeared in Honduras. His life, too, had been overtaken by an obsession with things Nicaraguan.[14]

Zuniga had been Pastora's case officer for Honduran intelligence, and had flown Pastora to a meeting with Honduran strongman Gustavo Alvarez in 1982. Eden Pastora and Alvarez hated each other at first sight, and Pastora was not permitted to set up a base in Honduras. After that Ricardo was made the man in charge for the Honduran Chief of Staff, dealing with the Americans on military aid. At his last post, before Zuniga was

Figure 8: These were seven of the corpses. Author photo.

kicked out of the army, he served as deputy commander of the Honduran military base in a primarily Indian area on the border with Nicaragua.

Zuniga had been a fierce advocate of taking the fight to the Sandinistas, but an even fiercer opponent of the way the Americans and General Alvarez had carried this out, relying as they did on the Guardsmen, giving insufficient support to the Indian fighters whose grievances were clear, who could have rallied the vast majority of the Indian population against the Sandinistas.

In June 1984 Zuniga had come to Washington to attend a conference, and to visit his wife and children in Alexandria. Privately he told me an odd story.

While he was deputy commander of the Honduran base in the eastern provinces, his principal duty was to assist in the training and supply of the Indian force MISURA. This force originally had been trained by the Argentines and operated, on paper, in coordination with the FDN. Another force of Indian fighters, MISURASATA, was led by Brooklyn Rivera, allied with Eden Pastora, who opposed the FDN.

According to Ricardo, this distinction did not exist inside Nicaragua, and Indian forces for the most part fought as one. Ricardo told me that in 1984 the combined force had launched an offensive against the Sandinistas and driven them from all their Atlantic Coast garrisons except their bases in two major towns, Bluefields and Puerto Cabezas. The Indians had then gathered forces to move on these towns, and requested additional weapons and ammunition to do so.

But instead of seizing the opportunity to show the strength of opposition to Sandinista rule in Nicaragua, according to Ricardo, the CIA refused their support, and ordered the Hondurans to cancel planned shipments. Within days, the offensive fizzled.

A month later, the Honduran officer corps overthrew General Alvarez and forced him from the country. He was an early supporter of the Contras and close friend of their military leader, former National Guardsman, Commander Enrique Bermudez. After the coup Ricardo returned to Tegucigalpa. What he found there alarmed him.

During his visit to Washington, I arranged a variety of meetings at which Ricardo could tell his story. The FDN had become a separate government inside the Honduran capital, with its own counterintelligence force. Ricardo had uncovered the fact that this unit, led by Colonel Ricardo "Chino" Lau, had carried out death squad killings under contract from General Alvarez in cooperation with Battalion 316, the death squad of the Honduran army. Additionally, Contra counterintelligence units had harassed and surveiled Honduran army officers known to be opponents of the Contra policy. These officers became unnerved by the motorcycles that followed them and the occasional slashing of tires.

But what alarmed Zuniga most was what he learned of a CIA plot to pressure the Honduran high command into removing him and four others from the army, and to transfer sixteen others to staff positions outside the chain of command. His informant had told him the twenty-one officers were deemed by the CIA to be hostile to the agency's preferred Nicaragua policy.

Days after he returned to Honduras, he was placed under barracks detention, accused of making unauthorized statements to the House Intelligence Committee. Unfortunately, that was true; I had arranged the meeting. In late July, together with a colleague from the House Foreign Affairs Committee, I flew down to Tegucigalpa to meet with the head of the Honduran Intelligence, Colonel Grijalva. As I learned later, the whole time we were in Tegucigalpa, we were under constant surveillance. Our calls were monitored, and we were photographed wherever we went during our twenty-two-hour stay.

But our meeting with the Colonel, Ricardo later told me, was successful. As soon as we left, his situation eased, and his superiors began to talk to him about possible posting as a military attaché overseas, probably in Taiwan. Then, abruptly, he was cashiered at the end of August 1984. He later discovered that decision came not from the military because of his activities in Washington (we had satisfied them that his activities were benign) but from the President of Honduras. Ricardo's father had been the President's opponent in 1981, and the President was apparently getting back at the father by sacking the son.

I last saw Ricardo in January 1985, five months after his expulsion. He was, as always, ebullient and confident of the future. He had plans to run for the Honduran Congress later that year, and he was considering a variety of business ventures.

According to the official story of his assassination, one of these ventures misfired; Ricardo and his sister had loaned a Cuban, a naturalized Honduran, $40,000. The Cuban did not want to pay Ricardo back, and hired two Nicaraguans to help kill him. The three men clubbed Ricardo, shot him, put a metal file through his heart, then threw him over a cliff and buried him. Their motivation may sound ludicrous, but in Central America it is not. I was once told of a man in El Salvador who would not spend two nights in the same location for fear that his debtors would kill him. It is a rare killing in that region that is ever brought to justice. Killing a man to whom you owe money is, to many, a sound business decision with little risk.

I had known Ricardo for a total of only twenty-four hours—six in 1982, seven in 1983, nine in 1984, and two in 1985. But they were the intense hours of conspirators, men who saw each in the other, as kindred souls, always ready to drop everything to begin a new plot. He was known as Mr. Human Rights within the Honduran Officer Corps. Oddly, he even had a good relationship with General Alvarez, who liked to tease Ricardo about his tender feelings about the rights of his nation's enemies.

I loved him.

At first I felt nothing when I heard of his disappearance, or even a week later when I learned of his death. I was too deep in the morass of my own confusion. Ricardo had been sacked, and possibly killed, because of his struggle to stop abuses, because of his government's involvement with the Contras. Now I had become a key supporter of that policy.

In our last meeting in January, Ricardo had concluded that it was time to stop, to shut down the Contra policy. This was a profound change. Even when he had told us what the FDN and CIA were doing the previous year, he still supported military resistance to the Sandinistas. Only much later I learned that in April 1985 he had been involved in another attempted coup with like-minded officers who might have made a serious challenge to the presence of the Contras in Honduras, but it failed.

While I was still waiting to learn what had happened to Ricardo, Ed Long, the man who replaced me in Senator Tom Harkin's office, came to Guatemala. His visit was a welcome distraction from my own internal chaos and my sorrow over Ricardo. Together we heard the worst horror stories about the Guatemalan army, and we heard the Guatemalan army explanations: "We have been fighting communist subversion for thirty-one years. They are ruthless. We fight back accordingly."

Our guide to Guatemala's victims was a young woman named Jean Marie Simon, a free-lance journalist and part-time consultant to Americas Watch, the most active of U.S.-based human rights organizations.

Ed's trip came in the midst of three days of lively rioting over bus prices. The riots were centered in Zone One, where the National Palace and other major institutions were located, and Zone Twelve, the location of the country's largest university, San Carlos. (When we returned to the States another Senate staffer, Charlie Flickner, was to quip that the Guatemalan chapter in our autobiographies could be called "Death Taxi to San Carlos.")

We had been witness to rioters grouping and regrouping, to challenge and then fall away from advancing police in Zone One. We were somewhat nervous, and nervous people sometimes see things that aren't there. At one point Ed believed that we were caught in a street at either end of which were advancing troops. He grabbed my arm and yanked me down an alley to escape. But there were, in fact, no troops at one end and the troops at the other were not advancing.

During our taxi trip, it was my turn. We were taking side streets, avoiding the main avenue where students and other youth were massing and setting tires ablaze. But we chose the wrong side street, and we stopped when we encountered rioters advancing in our direction. As we were debating what to do, an advance party approached and threatened us with a Molotov cocktail. In the next instant he drew his arm back and threw it forward. I "saw" the homemade bomb leave his hand, fly toward us, break apart on the taxi's hood, and burst into flame. Except that it didn't happen. My brain immediately corrected the image, and I saw the bomb fall just short of our car. Even the correction was a lie. In reality, he had only threatened; the bomb never left his hand. The taxi driver gunned the car in reverse and we were out of there. Even today, years later, the image of that scruffy student letting loose the Molotov cocktail is still vivid. Vivid, but wrong.

On my last day, I saw Jean Marie's best friend in Guatemala, the Deputy Chief of Mission of the French Embassy. Although Jean Marie was superb in revealing and exposing the brutal nature of the Guatemalan army, and this friend had been her entry into the offices of many army officers willing to talk, his goals in Guatemala were different from hers. He appraised me immediately as one who shared his revulsion at the horror that was Guatemala, but also as one who recognized other realities.

"Your country's relationship with Central America is similar to ours with Africa," he began, referring to the French neocolonial role in a dozen African republics. "You have a special responsibility here and you have not exercised it. You have the worst of both worlds: you criticize the army here, as you should, for their grisly behavior, but you don't offer them anything if they were to change. They are crazy; they live the anticommunist myths of the 1950s, but they have changed. They have ended their alliance with the old oligarchy and do see the need for social reform."

"What do you mean, the worst of both worlds? I don't understand," I replied, gazing at one of the local beauties swimming in the hotel pool.

He smiled back, appreciating my appreciation of local color, but shielding his smile from Jean Marie. "Your government is nuts. You criticize the army, but there is no cost. So they don't take you seriously. On the other hand, you don't offer them anything in exchange for fighting the guerillas. It is no wonder they are anti-American."

I proceeded to explain our legislation and what the military government must do for the army to be eligible for military aid or arms sales again. He liked the concept, but was dubious about a policy developed by Congress instead of the Administration. He was right. We always faced the same problem: writing elegant Central America policy in Congress, leaving it to the Reagan Administration to carry out.

The truth of that wisdom was upon me when I returned to Washington from Guatemala. Arturo Cruz called and announced that he would be at my home in an hour. I pleaded the flu, acquired on the last day in Guatemala. It was mean. I had a headache like I didn't know was possible. But he insisted it couldn't wait.

WITH ARTURO

Arturo's message was simple, he was going to resign. He had visited Tegucigalpa, the capital of Honduras, in August. The FDN had civilian headquarters in Tegu and base camps near the border with Nicaragua. On the same day of the House vote in June, the three As—Adolfo, Alfonso, and Arturo—had created a new organization, Unidad Nicaraguense Opositora (the Unified Nicaraguan Opposition or UNO), to conduct the battle against the Sandinistas.

But when he got to Tegucigalpa, he found that the FDN was totally opposed to the UNO becoming a reality in Honduras. The declaration of the three new leaders was not posted in a single FDN office or camp. Arturo was not treated as a new leader, but a nuisance, someone FDN leaders hoped would just go away. And that was what he wanted to do: go away, resign.

That would have been a break for both of us, sparing us another eighteen months pursuing an agenda of negotiations and Contra reform in vain. But when he announced his desire to resign, I felt only failure—my own. I had taken a year's lease on an office, but I wouldn't sign the lease until Arturo said he would share it with me. If together we were to begin a new life as "Contra" and "Contra supporter," I thought I might have a chance. Arturo was not smarter than other Nicaraguans, he had not sacrificed more, but he did have a reputation as the Nicaraguan who most symbolized decency and integrity. One could accuse Robelo of opportunism and Calero of a wide variety of sins, including corruption, the protection of murderers, and megalomania. The worst that could be said of Arturo was that he was indecisive. How could I go wrong with this man? I pleaded with him to stay, to give us a chance to fix it, "us" meaning Bob Leiken and myself. Bob had his own long meeting with Arturo four nights later. For the moment, Arturo stayed.

Let me stop and look at this more closely. The weight of conservative Democratic organizations had been brought down on Arturo to get him to join the Contras. Millions of dollars had been spent by the Administration and Ollie North's conservative network in their efforts to restore aid to the Contras. They had won. Arturo Cruz became their new symbol, and I, a defrocked, unemployed liberal lobbyist, covertly aided by a wealthy Central American, provided an office for Arturo. It was ludicrous.

I had been gone for four months when I moved my meager belongings from ADA into my new office which I shared with PRODEMCA. What I leased was a room barely large enough for two desks so that when my new assistant Eric Singer was there and Arturo showed, Eric had to do without.

My muscle pain returned with a vengeance. My back, neck, shoulders, legs, and forehead were all in terrible spasms. This time nothing worked—not diet, or exercise. Nothing. I even tried an ashram in Western Massachusetts. Then, as mysteriously as the pain had appeared, it eased one night three weeks later.

Even before the pain eased, the new conspiracy began. Arturo and I met at my apartment, joined by Bob Leiken and Arturo Cruz Jr. After meeting for three hours with the radio on (Ollie had told Bob the radio would interfere with certain kinds of audio surveillance), we identified six major priorities to guide us for the next sixteen months.

- We agreed that Adolfo must be made to choose. He needed UNO as cover, to get aid from Congress. On the other hand, he wanted to remain head of FDN, to block UNO decisions he might not like. He had to choose; he could be the leader of the FDN or a member of UNO, but not both.
- With Pastora's demise, and the fragile state of UNO-related forces there, the FDN had begun operations in southern Nicaragua. This made it difficult for FARN, associated with Cruz and Robelo, to expand its operations. During our last meeting in August, Robelo had given Ollie a copy of Fernando "El Negro" Chamorro's plans for expansion. The FDN had to leave the South. (This was of course a ludicrous position. FDN fighters there included the Jorge Salazar Battalion, the most successful Contra unit, close to the people in the area and totally free of National Guard domination.)

• We all knew that Adolfo had secret resources. We had no idea that he had already received (in 1985) more than $35 million from the Saudis and American conservatives, we simply knew that he had money and we, the liberal Contras, had none. That pool of money would have to be controlled by the UNO directorate, not one man or one party (the FDN).

• There was a group outside UNO called the Southern Opposition Bloc (BOS), led by Eden Pastora and Alfredo Cesar, a Nicaraguan engineer who had replaced Arturo Sr. at the Central Bank when Arturo joined the junta replacing Robelo. We decided Arturo should insist on negotiation with BOS, hopefully leading to integration.

• There were competing Indian organizations. Nicaragua is roughly divided into two parts—the Pacific Coast, densely populated and mainly Spanish speaking, and the Atlantic Coast, sparsely populated, mostly Indian, speaking local languages, English, or Spanish. There are two major armed groups competing for recognition and resources, MISURA and MISURASATA. We had no clear idea of what ought to be done, but we would demand that it be fixed anyway.

• Last, the Contras had long been seen, by members of Congress and informed Americans, as chicken thieves and killers. There is no doubt that in their early years (in 1982–83), they had killed large numbers of innocent civilians. We would insist on a human rights monitoring group within UNO, operating on all fronts—the North, the South, and the Atlantic.

How did these great conspirators plan to implement their goals? Via the press. In retrospect, the reason for this was simple. Bob Leiken and Arturo Jr. were writers, expert at fashioning sentences to convey messages that change the world. Arturo Sr. also believed in the power of words. Indeed, words had often been the substitute weapon of choice for real politik in Nicaragua. Why try to organize a barrio when you could write a poem? I knew better, but I . . . in those days I didn't try to argue.

Our reporters of choice were James LeMoyne of the *New York Times* and Dennis Vollman of the *Christian Science Monitor*. These were easy calls to make. We knew them, they liked us, and they might follow our lead.

James, for example, did a good job of showing how two families, the Caleros and the Sanchezes, controlled the FDN. Adolfo was in charge of Washington for the Contras and his brother Mario Calero was in charge of procurement in the United States. Aristides Sanchez ran Contra operations inside Honduras, and his brother, Enrique Sanchez, was in charge of procurement in Honduras. That was the true face of the FDN leadership.

Dennis Vollman wrote a piece quoting me and congressional allies extensively. I was called a "congressional source," in this case the second so named:

Because Cruz is widely respected in Congress, the FDN needed his help to get the money. But "once Cruz helped the FDN get the money and didn't have that card to play any more, Calero and the others started ignoring him," says a congressional source.

"Calero's people are trying to systematically undermine Cruz," says another congressional source close to Cruz. "He has no control over the troops or any way of knowing how the military money is going to be spent. Neither Cruz nor Robelo have anything to say about the way the FDN operates, either politically or militarily. Cruz and Calero constantly clash over human rights. Calero basically doesn't give a hoot about human rights but looks at it as just a public relations issue to keep Congress happy." . . .

Cruz's biggest problem, says one key congressional aide, is that "he has no place to go." It has been Reagan Administration policy all along "to leave politically-moderate Nicaraguans, who are neither pro-Sandinista nor right wing, with no alternative but to join the armed FDN opposition," the aide continues.

The aide agrees with Nicaraguan exile analysts who say that not only had the United States consistently opposed any opposition attempt to strike a deal with the Sandinistas, but had also consistently supported only the most right-wing elements within the exile movement.

This has left Cruz and other moderates like him, according to these analysts, in the position of having to choose between cooperating with the pro-Somocistas they abhor and being cut off from all the money, arms, and ability to influence events. The former option is a problem also because, according to most politically-moderate Nicaraguans, no organization dominated by the pro-Somocista FDN will never be able to command the support of a majority of Nicaraguans.

In response to this article, Calero exploded at the next meeting of the UNO directorate. The CIA's Alan Fiers was a fourth person in that meeting with the Triple A and, while attempting to appear impartial, he sided with Calero. A reshuffling of responsibilities among the Triple A took place, but it gave Alfonso and Arturo no more control of how funds were spent or how the war was fought.

Corinne asked to stay after the others had left. She informed me that she had had enough of our affairs. It was too confusing, it was crowding her marriage. "I cannot carry on anymore." For a long time I missed the double meaning of her message. Yes, the affair crowded her marriage, but her marriage also crowded our affair.

During that confusing period of my life, with no job, no emotional or political points of reference, Corinne's decision meant little to me. I ended two other affairs as well. I loved none of those women and they did not love me.

But I admonished Corinne. "Okay, but let's not say 'never,' let's review our options two months from now, on December 4." She nodded and we were all business again.

Bob Leiken wrote a piece for the *New York Times* calling the FDN leadership a "shadowy group of former Somoza allies" living in Miami. That was on a Sunday. Elliott Abrams, a neoconservative activist and the new Assistant Secretary for Latin America, received two calls that day complaining about Bob. One was from the egregious Jean Kirkpatrick who, after four years as Reagan's UN ambassador, had become a columnist for the *Los Angeles Times* and defender of every kooky idea to emerge on the far right. She was also close to Adolfo. The other call came from another friend of Adolfo, CIA Director William Casey. They complained such an article could not come from a friend of the resistance. If Bob wrote the article, he was no friend.

Those three articles alone constituted progress in our six-point agenda until December. At that point, unintentionally, I turned to public relations myself. In late October I was invited to a party in honor of Elliott Abrams, only recently appointed assistant secretary of state. The party, at Ambassador Otto Reich's home, was pleasant. I introduced myself to Alan Fiers, who suggested we get together later. Earlier that day I had met with Alfonso and he had given me twenty-five Joya de Nicaraguas, cigars brought from Managua. As was my custom, I gave one to Ollie.

On the following Tuesday, Shirley Christian of the *New York Times* called me. There is a section of the *Times* called "Washington Talk," and she felt she had a cute item for that. In May, President Reagan had imposed a trade embargo on Nicaragua to prove to doubting Democrats that all avenues of nonmilitary pressure had been exhausted, that only military pressure could force the Sandinistas to bargain, on regional security and democracy.

Shirley wanted to write a little piece suggesting that Ollie, by receiving my cigar, had broken the trade embargo. She asked, "By the way, what are you doing?" I told her not much, having been fired by ADA and unable to secure conservative funding for a new office. She said she thought that was news, and on November 19, a story about me, titled "Shift Hurts Human Rights Lobbyist," appeared in the *Times*. The story was straight reporting, accurately reflecting my views and recent experiences:

> The tall slightly stooped figure of Bruce P. Cameron is a familiar one in the halls and hearing rooms of Congress where he has lobbied for ten years on human rights and related foreign policy matters.
>
> To anyone who asks what he has accomplished, he can provide a three-page list of legislation placing conditions or restrictions on foreign military aid to countries that violate human rights. His role in drafting or pushing bills for passage is widely acknowledged among human rights activists and in Congress.
>
> Last June, however, Mr. Cameron played a key behind-the-scenes role in creating the compromise legislation that provided $27 million in nonmilitary aid to Nicaraguan rebels fighting the Sandinista government. As a result, he says, he has been ostracized by most of the human rights organizations and individuals who finance human rights lobbying.
>
> Most human rights groups oppose aid to the rebels, with their reasons ranging from opposition to the overthrow of another government to concern over human rights accusations made against the rebels. Mr. Cameron's supporters, on the other hand, assert

that many human rights groups have as their first priority support for the Sandinistas and other leftist causes in Central America.

She went on to report my forced resignation from ADA and my dismissal from two other foreign policy organizations on the left, the Human Rights PAC and the Foreign Policy Education Fund. She then briefly chronicled my history in the anti-war movement, my evolving views, and my encounters with Nicaraguans who changed my attitude.

Subsequently, the *Miami Herald* and the *Washington Post* also printed articles, equally sympathetic. They also reported on Bob Leiken and John McAward, who had been fired from his job at the Unitarian Universalist Service Committee. There were in fact many reasons for John's firing, but one was crucial: he thought critically about the Sandinistas and recognized some progress in El Salvador. The *Post* reported on January 5:

> Coincidentally, it was the liberals' success in forcing reforms in El Salvador that opened the first rift in their ranks. When death squad murders declined and moderate Jose Napoleon Duarte was elected President, most congressional Democrats switched to supporting increased aid for El Salvador. But leftist-oriented human rights activists continued to protest the aid, charging that Duarte's regime had not reformed enough to deserve U.S. help.
>
> "El Salvador was really where the break in the consensus came," said Bruce Cameron, a human rights activist who supported the Duarte regime and later lost his job over the Contra issue.
>
> The second watershed issue was the behavior of Nicaragua's Sandinista government, which came to be viewed by increasing numbers of liberals as unnecessarily repressive, even in the face of U.S.-sponsored Contra war. Sandinista youth physically attacked opposition activists during the 1984 presidential election campaign, and some Sandinista leaders dismissed the vote as a meaningless formality. After the election, the regime cracked down on dissidents and moved increasingly close to the Soviet Union. . . .
>
> The result has been a three-way split. In one camp are the activists who oppose aid to the Contras under any circumstances as immoral. "The Contras and human rights are incompatible,

period," said Ann Lewis, national director of the liberal Americans for Democratic Action.

In addition are those few, including Cameron and Leiken, who have "defected" to the Administration's side in supporting aid to the Contras even though they insist that their goal is to bring about negotiations toward a compromise between the Sandinistas and the rebels. They also criticize the Administration for failing to negotiate.

And, in the middle are an unknown number of Democrats who say they oppose aid to the Contras today but might be swayed if they could be convinced that Cameron and Leiken are right.

"There is a group that believes some aid to the Contras could be justifiable under some circumstances as a way of giving support to a political effort," said Representative Matthew F. McHugh (D-N.Y.). "The key is negotiations. . . ."

Viewed another way, the conflict is between activists who talk in terms of moral absolutes and politicians who more often criticize the administration's policy because it doesn't "work," and who are looking, without much evident success, for an alternative policy that would clearly work better.

"None of the liberals outside Congress have asked me what I think," Cameron said. "But Members of Congress have."

Until last spring, Cameron was chief human rights lobbyist for the ADA, universally acknowledged as one of the liberals' most effective congressional engineers.

Doyle McManus put his finger on the key issue for Democrats flirting with the Administration: "Does it work?"

Through these articles I was announcing what side I was on, noting I had little choice, and explaining that I was still uncertain if Administration policy would work, because only a policy emphasizing compromise and negotiations could be successful.

The Nation, America's oldest left-wing journal of political opinion, wrote a critical article entitled "A Defection within the Family."

The defection of one person may seem to be a minor matter, but it has touched off accusations of apostasy and counter accusations of neo-Stalinism. . . . Cameron's defection significantly reduces the liberal-left's ability to thwart Reagan's Central American policy in Congress. The crack in its unity has encouraged congressional liberals to be seduced by the myth they can make over Nicaragua, and Guatemala, in their image.

There is little agreement on the reasons for Cameron's heresy. The simplest explanation making the rounds is that he succumbed to the lure of power. Proponents of this view say that Cameron, known for his overbearing style, enjoys plotting and intrigue, and that the Reagan Administration led him to believe he could manipulate its Central America policy.

Doyle believed my shift was due to events in Central America that caused me to rethink my position, to believe that we could collaborate with the Administration in creating a policy to foster democracy and human rights. Max Holland wrote that it was the lure of power and a taste for plotting and intrigue that had caused me to change.

These are different sets of reasons, but they are not mutually exclusive, and I actually believe both to be true. In the years since that time I have examined my motivations over and over, and I have come to conclude there were in fact many explanations.

- As a liberal lobbyist during a conservative administration, I was tired of opposition. The best we could ever do was to block the Administration. We never made or implemented policy.
- I was outraged by the fact that the liberal-left funding community was so stingy in supporting my efforts, despite the fact that I was "one of its rare effective lobbyists," as Max wrote.
- Tsongas had kept me on the fringes of the Salvador plotting. With the Contras, I could be in the middle of everything.
- Ann Lewis, under pressure from left-wingers on the ADA Board, was pushing me to form an advisory committee to supervise my work. I had raised my own money; now I was supposed to assemble a group of people (who were not donors, not knowledgeable about Congress, even less knowledgeable about Central America) to tell me how to do my work. A good many members of the ADA Board wanted the United States to cease aid to the

Salvadoran government and provide it to the Salvadoran guerrillas. When I told the Board in December 1984 about ADA's role in promoting peace talks in El Salvador, and forcing the exile of killers from the Salvadoran officer corps, one of my major critics insisted we should be promoting land reform. What he actually meant by land reform, I would never know; most likely he didn't even know at the time.

In truth, I didn't want to answer to anyone except my own conscience—and my previous boss at ADA, Leon Shull, who had retired on December 31, 1984. I didn't like Ann Lewis at the time, but I do now and we always respected each other. I could not abide many, if not most, of the Board. In a very real sense I was antidemocratic. I had been effective on the Hill on human rights issues because Leon had spared me from dealing with the ADA Board. Ann would not spare me.

- I enjoyed the intrigue and plotting, I really did. Max was absolutely right on that. I relished those late night meetings in Ollie's office.
- I believed in what I was doing.

Oddly enough, that last reason was the largest part of the truth. The others were real, and influenced my willingness to break with the liberal left, my closest colleagues and friends for a decade. But ultimately my choices were made in the realm of ideas, not in psychology, or personal tastes and preferences.

At the beginning of my work on Central America, it was easy and natural to base my policy choices on the liberal principles of the human rights community and its legislative agenda. But the more I came to work with people from the region, the less principle seemed the appropriate guide for policy that would affect those people's lives. What changed were the questions I asked about the political environment of U.S. Central America policy. Different questions produce different answers and different policy. In the early '80s, I had been asking the questions that would be dominant in liberal and left circles for a decade:

- Was it right for the United States to organize, train, and supply a paramilitary group to fight the government of Nicaragua, a legitimate government that had come to power through a popular insurrection against an unpopular dictator?

- Was it right for the United States to support the army of El Salvador, an army that displayed a consistent pattern of gross violations of human rights?

These were questions with the same easy answer: "No." Therefore correct liberal strategy was to find sponsors of legislation and organize support to cut off aid to the Contras and support for the Salvadoran army.

Beginning in 1982, the questions I asked changed. Finally, the only question that mattered was: "What will stop the war?" For El Salvador, a strong case could be made that cutting off aid would stop the war, as the Salvadoran army collapsed and a new government, led perhaps by the guerrillas, took over. Alternatively, one could argue that ending the flow of aid would cause the army-backed government to seek a reasonable peace settlement with the guerrillas, thus ending the war.

If you believed these scenarios, if they were your guide to ending the war, then you had to ask another question: "Would the Administration or Congress ever terminate aid to the Salvadoran military?" Since successive votes from 1980 to 1984, the obvious answer was no, they would never cut off aid to the Salvadoran military. If you were guided by the principle of denying aid to human rights violators, your strategy need not change. But if you were guided by the question of how to end the war, you were forced to rethink your strategy.

Similarly for Nicaragua, the question of how to end the war required more than strategy shaped by the liberal principle of seeking to terminate the flow of aid to the Contras. The situation, however, was entirely different. Congress did cut off aid to the Contras in 1984. Why, then, did I work for its resumption when it was argued that if the ban was retained it would only be a matter of time before the Contras collapsed?

I simply did not believe the argument.

The Contras in 1982 had represented no more than the desire—of former Guardsmen, some extremely right-wing landowners and businessmen, and some peasants outraged at their treatment by the Sandinistas—to get revenge. By 1985, a significant portion of the progressive Nicaraguan bourgeoisie, symbolized by Alfonso and Arturo, had embraced the Contras. In

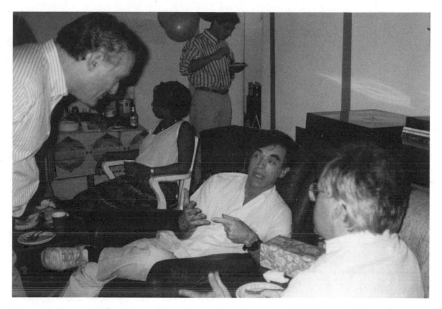

Figure 9: Ernesto Palazio, representative of the Contras in Washington, Bob Leiken, and Bernard Aronson in discussion at fiftieth birthday party of the author in his apartment. Author photo.

addition, a substantial group of moderate Democrats in the House were no longer willing to support a policy that refused to challenge the Sandinistas' export of revolution, military buildup, and increasingly totalitarian rule.

After their victory in the polls in 1984 and the cutoff of aid to the Contras, the Sandinistas could have chosen reconciliation and dialogue with their internal opposition, they could have taken steps to end their military buildup. But instead they refused dialogue, and intensified their acquisition of arms and buildup of military bases. At that point Arturo joined the Contras and began searching for a different policy. Merely cutting off aid to the Contras was no longer a viable alternative to Administration policy. It would not end the war, because an aid cutoff minus policy to challenge Sandinista misrule would no longer command a majority of the U.S. House of Representatives. The search for a new policy was on.

Some have argued that, in the debate leading to the resumption of Contra aid in 1985, Bob, Bernie, Penn, and I were responsible for moderates abandoning their liberal partners. This is a gross exaggeration. Nor is it true that we had any role in the San Jose Declaration. We urged neither Arturo nor Alfonso to join the Contra leadership. The moderates who changed their votes that year were, with two exceptions, people we never met and never lobbied until 1986. The two exceptions are Dave McCurdy and Bill Richardson, and each had changed his own mind on the night of the April 23rd vote, weeks before we spoke to them. What we did do together (through Bernie's and Bob's writings, through the President's letter) was define an alternative that gave the vote policy meaning, an alternative against which to measure and judge Administration policy in the 1986 debate. Our policy of searching for negotiated settlement was also fundamental to the thinking of Arturo and Alfonso, and reinforced their emerging alliance with the moderates, and alliance which I did help broker.

Was I correct in shifting the question from one of liberal principle to the messy practical question of how to end the war? I will not give away the ending to the Nicaragua story just yet. But in the case of El Salvador, the war ended in February 1992. Military aid was never cut off, although it was halved in 1990 in response to the 1988 killings of six Jesuit priests, their housekeeper, and her child. Military aid will continue there indefinitely. Other ways, other strategies to end the war had to be found.

With regard to my views on Nicaragua in 1985, Shirley Christian recorded them accurately: "He favors combining pressure on the Sandinista government with appeals to negotiate, and he has concluded that military action by the rebels, often referred to as Contras, constitutes that leverage." But Max was also correct when he wrote:

> The controversy dramatizes the dilemma of the liberal-left in opposing U.S. policy. Should it accept the logic of imperialism, reducing the struggle over U.S. policy to a quibble over how best to save the world from Marxism-Leninism? Or should it take a cool, tough and candid approach . . . to national security, one that forswears the overthrow of another government unless that government represents a clear threat to the United States.

Max was one of the moral purists Doyle talked about. What Max didn't acknowledge is that he and his fellow purists were out of the debate entirely. The debate was between those of us who were quibbling over how best to respond to the challenge of Marxism-Leninism in the third world. Not to respond was not an option.

But when the *Times* and the *Nation* articles appeared in November, I wasn't still "quibbling." I had given up the six points to change the Contras and reduced my goals to two:

• Starting a Human Rights Commission within the Contra camp, employing competent staff, and
• obtaining funds so Arturo Sr. would be free to carry out his political responsibilities without worrying about taking care of his family.

The reason for the primacy of my first goal was simple: working for human rights is what I do. If I accomplished nothing else, I could live with myself if the Contras were to set up an effective human rights organization.

I thought my second goal was absolutely vital if we were to start pressing for our primary objectives. Arturo had the stature to press for these reforms. He could not do so if he had to spend his time worrying about money.

I also tried to use my apparent new leverage with the Administration to push other issues. I wrote Ollie a memo about Major Ricardo Zuniga and urged him to force an investigation of possible CIA mischief in Honduras. Major Ricardo's last fight was to stop a CIA plot to force the expulsion of five Honduran officers, including himself, and the removal of sixteen others from the chain of command. It was his testimony to Congress about this plot, and the CIA's reporting back to the Honduran high command, that led to Ricardo's imprisonment. Ollie did nothing.

I gave Alan Fiers a thick file on Colonel Roberto Santivanez, revelations about death squads in El Salvador. I hoped it would lead the U.S. government to take his testimony. But, to this day, no one from our government has ever asked him what he knew or what he still knows. I introduced Santivanez to Arturo Sr., who offered to try to employ him as security chief for the Contra politicians in Costa Rica. (There had already been two attempts on Alfonso's life.) But the CIA and Calero blocked Santivanez's appointment.

Ollie did send me as an observer to the Guatemalan elections in early November, and the runoff elections in early December, and I had a great time. We flew on an Air Force jet used by the White House, lolled in enormous seats, were served great food. I got the opportunity to meet senators and congressmen, and to become acquainted with them on a trip, when they were not overwhelmed by hundreds who want their attention every day in Washington.

My favorite moment came during the first trip, in November. We were broken up into small groups and sent to various locales around the country. When we returned we assembled at the Camino Real Hotel to write a press statement drafted by Bill Parry, assistant to Senator Richard Lugar, chairman of the Senate Foreign Relations Committee.

Our drafting committee went back and forth on the text until only one issue remained: whether we should state that fair elections *would lead* or *might lead* to a new Guatemala that respects human rights and democracy. Two neoconservative Democrats, Bill Doherty of the AFL-CIO and John Silber, president of Boston University, argued that the success of the elections proved the problems of Guatemala had been solved. Senator John McCain, a conservative Republican from Arizona, wasn't buying it. He insisted that the document must state our observations in the conditional, with "may" or "could." McCain, a foreign policy hard-liner, was imprisoned by the North Vietnamese for over five years. While that brutal experience might have twisted his whole vision, made him see the world in black and white, he still chooses gray most of the time.

But McCain was also volatile. He stood up from the table, saying: "Okay, gentlemen, it is your document. You have your way, but I will not sign it or endorse it."

I had gotten to know John a little bit on the plane and at a reception the night before at the ambassador's residence. He seemed to like me, because he liked risk takers and because I supported the Contras.

When he began to rise from his chair, I placed my right hand on his left shoulder and gently pushed down. He stayed. Then I said that the election held that day was too important for us not to recognize it as a positive step and to do so unanimously. I also suggested that the senator's way was more prudent in case antidemocratic elements were to prevent the new president from taking office or overthrow him in a coup. Senator Lugar watched all of this, watched Doherty and Silber back off, then watched me take the final copy and bolt three flights of stairs to make sure it would be ready in time for the press conference. Since that time I have been able to see the senators when I've needed to do so, and I consider John McCain a special friend.

Figure 10: The author describes in a press conference in the Camino Real Hotel in Guatemala what actions the new government of President Vinicio Cerezo must take and what improvements in human rights must be made before military aid is released. Author photo.

Bill Doherty invited me to a conference in Costa Rica that started three days later. There I was able to see the new office of Arturo Cruz Sr. I saw that Arturo, through his son, had assembled good staff that looked to him for leadership and, finding none, presumed to fight among themselves. I arranged a breakfast meeting with Arturo Sr. and Alfredo Cesar of BOS, but it led to nothing.

In December Ollie informed me, after my repeated requests and memos, that he had secured funding for Arturo Sr. from a "foreign source." The source of the funds was not in fact foreign, but Spitz Channell, a fundraiser for conservative causes and president of the National Endowment for the Preservation of Liberty, and Rich Miller, president of International Business Communications (IBC), though I would not learn this until 1987. Ollie also told me I was no longer part of the deal, that the foreign principals would meet Arturo directly to work out the arrangement. Arturo consequently received $7,000 per month from January until November 1986, when the Iran-Contra scandal broke.

In early December, the Gang of Four had dinner with Elliott Abrams, his principal deputy on Central America, Bill Walker, and his personal assistant, Bob Kagan. Elliott's purpose was to discuss the upcoming request of the Administration for $100 million in military and economic aid to the Contras. Elliott had been on the job for only three months, but he had been well briefed on who the Sandinistas were and what they had done. He spent some time describing in detail the contents of a truck that had been blown up in Honduras, transiting from Nicaragua to its destination in El Salvador. He knew the contents, and the backgrounds of the people who had been driving it. He knew a lot about the Sandinistas. But Abrams knew little about the Contras, and was totally ignorant of the infighting between Adolfo, on the one hand, and Arturo and Alfonso, on the other. He knew nothing about FDN resistance to UNO leadership. And he offered no ideas for either the Administration or the Contras with respect to a new diplomatic initiative.

The four of us were disappointed, but we gave them all the benefit of the doubt. They were, after all, new to their offices. Still, Elliott, toward the end of the evening, made one remark that was especially chilling. "Anyone who believes that this President will leave office with the Sandinistas still in power does not know Ronald Reagan." I took it as a threat that the Administration would use the Contras as the vehicle to bring down the Sandinistas, or there would be a U.S. invasion. Abrams was giving us a choice—to work with him to make Contra policy work, or to be responsible for the United States again sending young Americans to die in another war in another distant underdeveloped country.

Politically, the year 1985 didn't end for me until January 6, 1986. I was invited to a meeting of the new Human Rights Commission of the Contras. Calero was there, and I thought he wanted to show a new willingness to commit himself and the FDN to UNO. Also present were Ambassador Robert Duemling, the head of the Nicaraguan Humanitarian Aid Organization, the new State Department unit formed to administer the $27 million, his deputy Chris Arcos, and four Nicaraguans who were to staff the new commission.

One of the Nicaraguans was Alvaro Baldizon, a former investigator for the Ministry of Interior in the Nicaraguan government, who had defected and reported on more than 2,000 assassinations carried out by the Sandinistas. He knew about the killings because he was an investigator entrusted to carry out delicate missions, including those in areas where targeted individuals had been assassinated by Nicaraguan government agents. Finally, he had had enough of the killing, and he walked out of the country into Honduras. I believed he would be a powerful symbol of the Contras's commitment to human rights. But his work, I insisted, would have to be in Honduras, not in Costa Rica where they were planning to set up shop.

But Baldizon never saw Honduras again. After he left the Contra Human Rights Commission Office, he died of a heart attack at age thirty.

I left that meeting dissatisfied, but without knowing exactly why. Nothing untoward had happened. In fact, nothing at all had happened. The three Nicaraguan men who were to be in charge of the office seemed to be without purpose. The only man with a purpose was Adolfo, but his purpose was unclear.

Later that afternoon, in my office, I met with Roberto Ferrey, the man who had been named director of the Contras's human rights office. He was a Christian Democrat who, after leaving Nicaragua, had exposed some of the better-known Sandinista human rights abuses. Yet he appeared to be a political hack, seeking office for personal gain, looking for the highest bidder; he was a man without vision. He did go to Honduras, but under his tutelage the office achieved nothing—no crimes were seriously investigated, no reports were made, no one was punished. The following year, his entire office staff resigned to protest his nonfeasance in office and misappropriation of funds. Two years later, he became a director of the Contra movement, when his sister chose not to seek reelection for the Christian Democrat seat in the seven-member body. She, too, had been suspected of misappropriation of funds; her mischief being more recent, her brother was chosen to take her place. Conservative friends told me he appeared even more thuggish than Adolfo. They are both big men, with pockmarked faces and what the Mafia call "bellies of distinction."[15]

I willed myself to feel good about that meeting and about Roberto, but years later I accused Robelo of misjudgment, saying, "It was your idea to appoint him." He responded: "You told me you liked him." He was right and that day I had. But even on that day I had serious misgivings.

Adolfo Calero joined Roberto and me in my office. He distinguished me from Leiken, explaining I was more practical. What he meant was that I was potentially easier to manipulate. He was wrong, but I said nothing.

Often in difficult and challenging situations, I remain silent. Whether with women or Contras, silence often works best.

Still later, Adolfo and I were joined by Penn. Penn knew I was broke and genuinely wanted to help. He bluntly told Calero of my sacrifices for the cause and my importance in the upcoming battle for military aid. Calero indicated that he could help. Again I was silent. I just stood there, my mouth frozen into a smile. Adolfo observed the pause, then turned to other things.

December 4, the date scheduled for review of our two-month abstinence, came and went without discussion. On that day, I was in fact in Guatemala to observe the runoff election.

But we were not immune to the magic of Christmas.

True, the magic appeared only in her office, in full dress; there was only the chance of something later, no promises. It was 1984 all over again, the fleeting touches, the quick embraces, the smiles, the closing of the office door, the long passionate kiss.

So 1985 came to an end. I was without a job, and without a thought of how to change the situation. But I had gained some notoriety. My parents held a cocktail party at Christmas with me and my articles as the featured attractions. ■

CHAPTER FOUR

TURBULENCE

January–June 1986

When I first wrote about 1986, I began: "I sometimes think that my entire life will be devoted to explaining what I did from January 27 until June 26, 1986. Everything before or afterwards will be regarded as of little consequence." I wrote this in July 1987, at a time when to have thought otherwise would have been to ignore hard reality. In fact, this was only true for a time.

By 1993 only rarely did anyone ask about my days with the Contras. Everyone was long since exhausted with the issue of Nicaragua. My closest friends, like the drunks and the homeless I encountered on the walk from my apartment on 17th Street to the YMCA seven blocks south, always seemed to develop pressing engagements elsewhere when I started to tell them my stories.

In January 1986, the events that would ultimately lead to the scandal were already five months underway. General Secord's Enterprise was getting underway in El Salvador, and had already purchased one plane. Private funders, whom I was about to meet, had already transferred $1 million to Secord's Swiss bank account. Taiwan had given $2 million. Nonetheless, the Contras were fleeing Nicaragua to Honduras and Costa Rica to seek food and medicine; no delivery system for the Contras inside the country had yet been devised. The President was about to ask Congress for $100 million, but Ollie would not wait for Congress to respond to the immediate crisis.[16]

On January 22, North met with Secord and Manucher Ghorbanifar. The latter had made himself a go-between for the United States and elements within the Iranian government. Ollie was nervous about the whole operation. Already two shipments of arms had been sent to the Iranians, to secure the release of American hostages held by pro-Iranian Shiites in Lebanon, to gain a political opening. The first shipments had been largely organized by the Israelis. This time the United States was to organize the sale without intermediary, and Ollie was in charge.

He saw the Iranian government—a government of Islamic clerics—as natural anticommunists, and he was committed to freeing American hostages. But Ollie was also NSC coordinator of the administration's counterterrorist efforts, and the Iranian government was categorized as a terrorist government. He was therefore deeply troubled.

In the middle of the meeting, Ghorbanifar suggested Ollie accompany him to the bathroom where the Iranian suggested a new twist: the profits from the sale could go to the Contras. It was perfect, a quick injection of cash to the Enterprise, money for new weapons, and, most important, time for the Administration to build support in Congress for the right kind of Contra aid bill.[17]

A week later Ollie chaired a meeting in the White House with General Secord and other key Administration officials to prepare for the next arms shipment to Iran. It was decided that 1,000 TOW missiles would be sold to General Secord by the Defense Department for $3.7 million. The Iranians would be charged $10 million and the remaining profit would be stashed in the Lake Resources account in Geneva, to be used to resupply the Contras.[18]

I knew nothing about this. In fact, I had been unemployed for five months. During that time I would tell a macabre Guatemalan joke. In Spanish the acronym for AIDS is SIDA. I would say that I suffered from SIDA, "sin impuesto despues de agosto," meaning "without income since August."

Doubts about my alliance with the Administration had been steadily increasing since the June bill. In October, Public Broadcasting's Marty Smith was filming Contra bases in Honduras. At one point, in a meeting with Colonel Enrique Bermudez, military chief of the FDN, soldiers complained about a recent agreement with UNO leadership. Bermudez told Marty to stop filming, but failed to tell him to stop recording. The Colonel was subsequently recorded telling his men he had signed dozens of agreements and complied with none. Marty also filmed an interview with an FDN defector in my office, who described his efforts to investigate and prosecute human rights abuses committed by FDN officers and soldiers, and his inability to convince FDN leadership to do anything about them.

One day Bob Leiken and I poured out our frustrations to Penn. Penn, looking for a way to solve our problems, wrote a paper titled "From a Proxy Force to a National Liberation Movement." It called for the rebuilding of the Contra movement through recruitment of more educated officers; the development of political skills, literacy, and medical care for the population it was trying to win over; and a real strategy for negotiations so the Contras could attract the support of liberal and social democratic Latin Americans and Europeans. The paper made particular note of the new Contadora initiative, which stressed the need for democratization throughout Central America, as well as security issues (army size, the removal of foreign bases and advisors, cross-border subversion). The democracy plank seemed like a breakthrough, a bridge linking Administration goals and the Latin Americans who wanted to see the Contra movement dismantled.

Earlier that month I had traveled to New York to attend a board meeting of PRODEMCA. Bill Doherty of the American Institute for Free Labor Development in Latin America, who was the AFL-CIO point man on Central America policy, had spoken very positively about the new Contadora initiative, a real change in his position. The year before he had urged Arturo to support the Contras, arguing there was no other option. Penn had asked me to attend this meeting in case it was decided I should work for PRODEMCA. I was polite, cooperative, explained the nuances of Congress in detail.

The problem was they were almost right, but not quite. The rhetoric (of human rights, negotiations, Contra reform, democracy) was right, but I didn't trust that they meant it.

This is why:

In 1981, Salvadoran death squads assassinated the Director of Land Reform Rodolfo Viera. They had also hoped to kill my friend Leonel Gomez, but he arrived late to where they expected him to be. Instead they killed two employees of Bill Doherty, Mike Hammer and Mark Pearlman. In 1983 I had succeeded in convincing the House Foreign Operations Subcommittee to withhold one-third of all military aid to El Salvador unless the Salvadoran government made every attempt to bring the authors of the killings to justice; the officers who gave the order and the men who pulled the triggers were all well known.

I tried hard to get the support of both AFL-CIO leadership, represented by Bill Doherty, and those unions who opposed the AFL-CIO leadership position on Central America, liberal labor unions like the UAW, Amalgamated Clothing Workers, and Communications Workers. Conservative unionists supported the government of El Salvador and leaned toward the Contras, liberals supported the government of Nicaragua and leaned toward the rebel-controlled labor unions in El Salvador. I thought this issue could unite them; both claimed to support human rights and labor rights. But neither supported my effort and it was defeated.

In February 1989 my friend Leonel Gomez returned to El Salvador for the first time in eight years. Before he left El Salvador in 1981 and later in the United States as well, he had publicly criticized both the American Institute for Free Labor Development (AIFLD) and Bill Doherty. Leonel and Doherty held their first meeting in many years in El Salvador. Bill told Leonel he shouldn't criticize the Salvadoran army; criticism endangered the greater good. And then Doherty said the following, which served to separate neoconservative from neoliberal:

"Don't you think I know that General Vides Casanova was on hand to congratulate the killers of Pearlman and Hammer when they returned? He said: 'Job well done.' Don't you think I know that?"

What was left unsaid was this: I want to denounce the army, but I hold back, because I do not want to hurt our side.

People like Leonel and me, in our minds, don't take sides. But we do hold vaguely articulated principles about which we are utterly rigid. One of those principles is that you denounce corruption, killings, and torture wherever they occur. You may have to wait a long time to find the right person, the right medium, the right circumstances to tell your story, but eventually you do tell it. Always. But I do not trust neoconservatives to tell the truth about what side they are on.

Truth-telling of this sort need not be difficult or dangerous; you can be the anonymous source for a story so you won't be held accountable. But you are accountable to yourself. In our case, I was also accountable to the American people, Leonel to the Salvadoran people. You do not give up your side. But you do have to risk it at times, in order to ensure it behaves justly.

There had been only two Salvadoran defense ministers since the October 1979 "reformist" coup, and both were alleged to be involved in the Viera killing. The first, General Garcia, presided over the October 1980 meeting of the high command where the Viera and Gomez killings were ordered. The second, General Vides Casanova, congratulated the killers of Viera, Pearlman, and Hammer. Leonel and I tried to get the story out, with limited success. The AFL-CIO in 1983 could have pressured the House to adopt the amendment to cut 30 percent of military aid to El Salvador pending a successful prosecution of the murder of the three labor leaders. Its passage would have risked the stability of the high command and maybe even the government, but it would have established the principle that the army will pay if it covers up for officers who kill civilians.

Back in Washington after the New York meeting, I began a new dalliance. But we were never more than affectionate friends. Not because she wasn't attractive. She was. Very. But she was also a close friend of Adolfo Calero, and I was wary.

I found that I could not work for PRODEMCA. They were allies, close allies, but our difference regarding denunciation was everything. If I was to work with them, I would have to give them my loyalty, and that I could not do. Still, I wanted the respect and credibility that only a paying job can bring.

On January 27 Penn introduced me to Rich Miller. It was an easy, pleasant meeting, and Rich was strictly professional. He needed a service that I could provide: to lobby Democrats to support military aid to the Contras.

I said yes, but I would not do this unconditionally. The Administration had to offer something in terms of negotiations or I would not support the aid package and, more to the point, neither would a majority of members of Congress who had switched from anti Contra to pro-Contra the previous spring. Rich readily accepted my condition, but warned me: "Don't tell Spitz."

"Spitz" was Carl Russell Channell, the president of a slew of right-wing organizations. Both Spitz and Rich would plead guilty in the spring of 1987 to felony use of a tax-exempt educational charitable organization to raise money to purchase arms for the Contras. Rich and Spitz were in fact the guts of Ollie's conservative fundraising network. They were also the "foreign source" which provided a monthly stipend to Arturo and, we later learned, supported Alfonso's political projects. Spitz raised the funds from wealthy benefactors, six of whom gave a total of over $8 million in one year. Rich transferred some to an offshore bank in the Cayman Islands, and later to Geneva, organized tours for Nicaraguans speaking about the horrors of Sandinista rule, and contracted ads to support the President's $100 million aid program. They were spending so much money that my proposal (to spend $40,000 for a lobbyist for three months) must have seemed trifling. Penn had already met Spitz, but thought I should, too, before accepting their money. His exact words were: "You have to see these people."

We had dinner at the Maison Blanche, one of Washington's finest restaurants, two blocks from the White House. Accompanying Spitz was his executive director, Dan Conrad. Both men were gay; while Dan was giddy, Spitz was belligerently reserved.

Conversation was free floating, unfocused, nasty. I was careful not to say too much. I stuck to the public record of my activities, giving no hint of my substantial doubts about the Administration's current policies and behavior. And they gave no hint of what else they might be doing. How could I refuse Penn's money and accept theirs? It was easy. I had no qualms about withholding my loyalty and operating behind *their* backs. So I suppose it was only fair that they withheld their own secrets.

Dan initiated the discussion this way: "Soooooo (which he drew out until it snapped), what other qualifications do you have, besides having been fired?" I remember little else that was said, certainly not my answer, except that Dan did ask if he could come watch me work. I said yes, but I never let him do it. I didn't think he would understand my low-key lobbying style, loitering in the House lobby, saying only a few words to certain members, and never about the Contras. I have done this often. It's a way of reminding them I'm still around and might someday ask for something, In the meantime, "How're you doing, Congressman?" I remember nothing else of the dinner, except that I was totally drained when I returned home.

Did I think very hard about taking the money? Honestly, no. I wanted to be back in the game. Rich, Spitz, and Dan knew nothing of the Hill. For them the issue was relatively simple: the Sandinistas were communists challenging U.S. interests and our way of life in Central America. "Let's get 'em." Spitz once quipped about efforts to reform the Contras: "Do you care about the person who takes out your garbage?" If I could rip them off and still do good, that would be just fine.

Do I overstate my callous approach to Rich and Spitz? Perhaps. But I always felt, throughout our seven month association, that neither worked at understanding either Central America or, for that matter, the United States. I myself worked overtime to understand movement conservatives.

Spitz actually had a rather interesting and complex worldview, despite his insistence on calling the Contras "freedom fighters." It was a Spenglerian view. Societies must inevitably decay. The moral forces that make them

Figure 11: Oliver North and the author entering the Spitz Channell fundraiser in the Hay-Adams Hotel. Photo courtesy of Rebecca Hammel.

great ultimately lose their strength, and other (not necessarily evil) forces in pursuit of their own selfish goals sap the dynamic energy of a country, and it declines. His role, as he saw it, was to act against the inevitable decline. To me, someone who has been Marxist then liberal all his adult political life, believing in either human progress or History, this was an extraordinary view. It was entirely consistent that the character of the Contras would be irrelevant to Spitz's calculations.

Some days later (the same day the *Challenger* went down), I received the first of what would be four installments of $10,000. It felt like a ridiculous amount of money. Liberals never paid like that. With it, I could pay the rent, hire a full-time assistant, and still pay myself $6,000 a month. Thus began what would be five months of intense effort.

Those 151 days were days of Nicaragua. We commanded the front pages of newspapers all over the United States. Everything I did in those days was energizing, important. I had not created the issue nor had the people I worked with; President Reagan and the nine commandantes of Nicaragua had made it. The rest of us came to, fell into, or seized the roles we played.

Figure 12: Fawn Hall and the author at a reception at the Hay-Adams Hotel. Photo courtesy of Rebecca Hammel.

It is hard to recall now, since Nicaragua has long been banished to the back pages. Those who play the game now perform anonymously. They are not even sources; no one calls. But in 1986, what I was doing (though not attached to my name) was chronicled in the nation's major newspapers every week.

The last days of January and the early part of February were a swirl of activities that after much reflection and research I still cannot quite order and untangle.

But I do remember two events, both strange with the strangeness of that time. I think the fundraiser was the first. Spitz Channell had invited his top funders to Washington, to meet privately with the President, a fact I learned only later. I met Spitz and Ollie later at a dinner at the Hay-Adams Hotel, the one closest to the White House.

Elliott Abrams was there, as was Ollie's secretary, Fawn Hall. Penn had also come. But in this group only Ollie was at home. This was the right, this was the far right. Elliott sat next to a man who believed that William

Paley, the founder and president of CBS, was a Jewish Bolshevik agent sent to the United States by Lenin to do us in. That, he said, explains why CBS coverage of Nicaragua was the worst of the three networks. I sat next to an ambassador from Costa Rica who was careful to say nothing.

Ollie was clearly the star. We had a short drink and then went into the dining room. I did not notice that we were photographed, but that comes later. Ollie's speech was short in duration, short on facts, but inspired. He roused his audience that night, as he had probably done earlier when he met with them privately to solicit funds for the Contras.

Fawn and I left early. I had a racquetball appointment with Arturo Cruz Jr. Fawn and he had become involved the previous fall, and much of their courtship had been conducted in my living room watching the Washington Redskins play football on Sunday afternoons. Fawn decided to watch us play racquetball.

The next day, or perhaps the day after, I arranged for Arturo and Alfonso to meet with Dave McCurdy and other moderate Democrats. There were fifteen of them in all, mostly from the South or Southwest. It was a rough meeting. The congressmen had lots of questions, Cruz and Robelo few answers.

A southwestern Democrat with long experience in foreign affairs began, "I know the Sandinistas are bad. But is there an alternative? Who runs the Contras?"

A Texan followed, "I worry about Colonel Bermudez. Would the Contras simply take power if they could and be just as autocratic as Somoza? What would be the difference?"

Cruz, squirming nervously in his chair, tried to answer. "We've begun the reform process. We're going down to Honduras to show the new face of UNO, to begin to establish civilian control over the army."

Dave McCurdy objected. "UNO has not developed and delivered a coherent political message. I asked Cardinal Obando y Bravo about UNO. He said they're strong anti-Marxists and pro-capitalist. I waited, but he said no more. He didn't say anything about democracy."

A Missouri congressman broke in. "I have a different concern. The Sandinistas are Marxist-Leninists, and you say they're terrorists. But there's no precedent of Marxist-Leninists ever yielding to pressure. They will go down fighting. Do you have a strategy to counter that?"

Robelo responded: "I don't know. We will have those discussions in our upcoming visit. In our discussions last fall, I believe we began to make progress with Adolfo Calero."

A member from Florida intervened. "We'll help on that. We can make it a condition of military aid that the Guardia officers leave and that there must be real respect for human rights."

When we left, Alfonso turned to me and said, "Those are bright guys. They ask the questions we ask." Both he and Arturo had sidestepped direct answers about their military strategy and their problems with Adolfo and the FDN leadership.

Shortly after this, the Gang of Four met with RIG, the Restricted Interagency Group on Nicaragua, consisting of Ollie, Elliott, and the CIA's Alan Fiers. It was a measure of how significant our work had become that the meeting took place at all. None of the four of us had jobs in government, we were all Democrats, and we had all publicly criticized Administration policy. Even Penn had finally lost his virginity when the Associated Press did a story on the paper he had written.

We met to discuss how to implement Penn's recommendations. The three of them were lavish in their praise of his recommendations as the perfect description of what needed to be done. But they offered no ideas about what they might do to increase middle-class recruitment within the Contras, or to make UNO rather than the FDN the focal organization in the fight for democracy in Nicaragua, and there was no talk of how they would respond to the Contadora initiative, a key recommendation.

Penn had described the need for a group of Americans in labor, politics, and education to establish an ongoing relationship with the Contra movement, and teach them the skills they needed to successfully compete in the late twentieth century. But Ollie said, "Penn, we don't need to create a new group. It already exists: PRODEMCA." He said this, fully articulating each syllable of PRODEMCA. It was typical Ollie, exuberant yet condescending. The meeting was meaningless.

In retrospect, the RIG's silence on Contadora seems even more bizarre. The day before, thirty-one Democrats, including all those who had attended the meeting in McCurdy's office with Arturo and Alfonso, signed a letter calling on the President to "unequivocally" back the Contadora initiative, and delay his request for military aid until after a meeting of the Central American presidents scheduled for March in Guatemala.

The idea for the letter had come from Alfredo Cesar of the Southern Opposition Bloc, the group of Contras outside UNO who were receiving no U.S. aid. He had given the concept to Brent Budowsky who worked for Congressman Jim Slattery, a Democrat from Missouri. In 1984 Brent had worked for Representative Bill Alexander, chief deputy whip and a Democrat from Arkansas. Brent specialized in centrist Democrats who supported a negotiated solution with guarantees for democratization inside Nicaragua, but would never support aid to the Contras as leverage.

I arranged for Brent to meet with Ollie and Bill Walker of the State Department. Brent was positive about his meetings and convinced he was making progress. But within two weeks, the initiative was dead. Brent could never tell me why or who was responsible. I quipped at the time, "There is a gnome in the White House driving us over the cliff." Later I was told it was not a gnome but the President. Reagan personally, without staff, made the decision to reject a delay that would have given diplomacy a chance.

Is this story true? I think it's doubtful. At no time in recent years was the Administration more united than it was in early 1986, and the point of that unity was aid to the Contras with no concessions for negotiations. But we wanted to believe Administration failure to support negotiations was due to the President's failure to get good advice, or to get good advice in a timely fashion. In a sense we had to believe this, because our legislation was predicated on the Administration in some way carrying out the diplomatic effort.

We wanted to give the Contadora foreign ministers time to work out an agreement before the vote on Contra aid. In effect, what we were asking the Administration to do was suspend its request for $100 million in response to the moderates' demand, so the Contadora countries could use the threat of Contra aid as leverage to force Sandinista concessions. Key in our minds was the symbolism of the Administration doing it for us, the moderates. It would demonstrate that if a treaty were signed, we would be able to shut down the Contra program—since the Administration had been our accomplice in this effort. The Administration rejected the delay, of course, and it was not (as Ollie told Brent) because the President personally made the decision. It was because delay would violate what they all believed in.

One night some days later, I was at home. It was a Wednesday. Corinne had contrived to be out that evening, and had asked to see me. It was a strange evening. I was still under the spell of my new dalliance. Corinne, on the other hand, was no longer cautious and wanted to renew our affair. She had come to feel that she could no longer talk to her husband. She could talk to me. I, on the other hand, wanted to be with my new lady and said so to Corrine.

I must have been crazy.

Corinne meekly accepted my idiotic pronouncements about the superior political skills of "Joan" and then, miraculously, she took me to bed anyway. That night we made love in ways we had never tried before. It was that night that the formula of dominance I had fantasized about for years became flesh. To describe our lovemaking might enlarge an understanding of me and Corinne. But I decline.

As winter and spring passed, our lovemaking became regular—not often, but ever more intense. I ceased to see anyone else. This was an offering to her, an acknowledgment of her singular importance—but I was not in love with her. I would look at her walking with me in the streets and see her as a strange presence. I could not understand her role in my life. Only my body understood. In my mind and my heart, I kept her at arm's length.

This I remember, and the reason seems obvious now, though at the time it seemed curious; I would not let her close to my work. Almost immediately upon receiving my first pay from Spitz, I entered into a conspiracy with the liberal Contras against Administration policy. On the issue of Contra reform I began to work with moderate Democrats to oppose the Administration aid package because of a lack of committment to negotiotions. I was paid by people who belonged to the far right, who supported Administration policy unconditionally. I doubted everything the Administration was doing and had just joined two separate conspiracies to thwart it. I brought all the intensity I had to these tasks every day.

Only once did Corinne try to insert herself into the tactics of our work. Penn had written an ad that invoked democracy, human rights, and negotiations—but its bottom line was support for military aid to the Contras, albeit under specified circumstances. The ad was designed to solicit the signatures of well-known Democrats, and its purpose was to show that Democrats could support arms for the Contras to fight and kill Sandinistas. Without telling us, an aide to Penn put both Corinne's and my signatures on the draft advertisement.

The day after Corinne saw it, she charged into the office in a fury of doubt and confusion. "Supporting economic aid to the Contras was one thing, but, Bruce, this is military aid! Guns! Are you sure about this?" LTA is against it and it could cost me my job even if you got the money for my position. I got up and closed the door to the office.

"I didn't give it a moment's thought. Penn and Spitz are who we work with now. They want it. They believe in the magic of words. I don't. Only deeds will change votes, not words."

"But you're saying," she remonstrated, "that you're for military aid. Is that a position we want to take? Where will it lead? What will it accomplish?"

Over and over she attacked the principle of providing military aid to the Contras from every possible angle, on every possible basis.

Finally, I temporized, "I don't think I have any choice. I have to sign this. But I don't mean it, and it doesn't bother me to fudge. It does bother you, and you shouldn't sign it. I'll have your name removed and I will defend your decision."

It was a good exercise. And it stiffened my resolve, for a time, to avoid compromise in both my dealings in Congress and in pursuit of Contra reform. ■

CHAPTER FIVE

CONTRA REFORM

January–June 1986

C ontra reform. It was a phrase that entered my life and consumed me and others for more than five months. It was used again in 1987 with some frequency, but its real life was limited to those months in 1986. We hadn't used the phrase in 1985, although we were trying to implement the idea. I did not mention it in my proposal to Rich Miller. Yet two weeks later, we had a Contra reform cabal, and by April members of Congress were talking about it and everyone knew what was meant.

A memo I wrote in late February, titled "Aid the Resistance; No Aid to the Contras," may illuminate this:

> Since November 1981, the United States has been aiding the coun-ter-revolutionaries who are seeking to replace the Sandinista gov-ernment in Nicaragua. It is a policy that has failed, a policy that cannot succeed, a policy that should be rejected.
>
> But the United States should aid all the Nicaraguans, includ-ing the Contras, who seek change in Nicaragua, who will work together to establish democracy in Nicaragua.
>
> Is that a contradiction? No support to those we have been sup-porting, but support to a force that does not exist?
>
> Such a force does exist, albeit in embryonic form. It is UNO, the United Nicaraguan Opposition. UNO is mainly three men: Adolfo Calero, Alfonso Robelo, and Arturo Cruz. The latter two served in the Sandinista junta. They are democrats. If they led political parties in elections in Nicaragua, they would receive from 30 to 40 percent of the vote.
>
> Adolfo Calero leads the Nicaraguan Democratic Force (FDN), with upwards of 18,000 soldiers. But what is it? The 18,000 sol-diers are principally peasants who fight the Sandinistas because the Sandinistas, driven by their Marxist-Leninist ideology, would

not leave the peasants alone. The FDN leadership is no more than the former management of the Coca-Cola franchise in Managua (Adolfo), his relatives and friends, many of whom were not very distinguished supporters and officials of the deposed Somoza government.

Tens of thousands of educated Nicaraguans live in exile in Central America and the United States. Some would like to join the forces attempting to establish democracy in Nicaragua. But they will not under present circumstances.

They see a small clique running the FDN, a clique that cannot even establish a minimally effective logistics network, a clique that is afraid of its own soldiers and therefore does not even try to lead them. Public relations? No matter what mistakes the Sandinistas make, the leadership of the FDN is always able to look worse. The FDN civilian leaders see resistance efforts on the part of any other group not as an asset but as a threat. That is the chief though by no means the only reason for the lack of a southern front.

The FDN is a peasant jacquerie, organized in the pattern of Nicaraguan armies 80 years ago. A disaffected family, in this case two families—the Caleros and the Sanchezes—raise the flag of rebellion, hire some officers who raise a peasant army, who then do battle with an army organized along similar lines.

The ratio of men to officers in the U.S. army is twelve to one. Amongst the Salvadoran guerrillas, it is seven to one. With the Contras it is 200 to one.

The Sandinistas, bad as they may be, are not pre-modern, and peasant revolts are almost always defeated. A peasant jacquerie led by an expropriated Coca-Cola salesman will certainly lose, scorned by the rest of the free world.

If UNO can change the smell of the FDN by creating a new face at the top for the Contras, then perhaps new life can be breathed into the whole movement by the recruitment of hundreds of middle-class youth in San Jose, Costa Rica, or Miami, young people who want to be part of a genuinely "democratic resistance" but are blocked by this Coca-Cola cabal.

Congress must tell the Administration that it will support the Nicaraguan resistance, but that it will not support the Contras.

Bob Leiken, in testimony before the Senate Foreign Relations Committee on March 4, made many of the same points, adding further information:

> The United States has, by and large, chosen to support one of the groups—the FDN, which is now part of the umbrella organization UNO. The FDN was created by Argentine military and security agents and by the CIA. Strong ties of loyalty, or fealty, have developed between CIA officials, acting as imperial patrons, and their colonial adjutants in the FDN. The FDN High Command, with one exception, was drawn entirely from the National Guard, and many were senior officers in it. Most of these men are intensely loyal to Commander-in-Chief Enrique Bermudez, are called "Enrique's Group," and have the allegiance of some of the field commanders. However, Bermudez, together with Adolfo Calero . . . and Aristides Sanchez, forms part of a cabal that is closely linked to a shadowy network of expropriated landowners, bankers and industrialists and former associates of Somoza. These exiles influence the FDN leadership through family ties or as former or current employees. FDN procurement is handled mainly by Mr. Calero and his brother and brother-in-law (Sanchez).

But it was a newcomer who coined the term *Contra reform*. In the early part of February, Arturo Cruz Jr. arranged a meeting for me with his friend Carlos Ulvert. Carlos was the political representative of FARN, the small fighting force based in Costa Rica and led by El Negro Chamorro. In the days before UNO and the $27 million, it was Carlos's job to go, on behalf of FARN, to Adolfo and humbly request some of the Saudi millions. Carlos did not know where the money came from, and learned not to like Adolfo very much.

Before leaving Costa Rica to come to the United States, Carlos had been given a copy of Penn's and my paper on changing the face of the Contras. It ignited a fire in him. At least two Americans with access to power had understood the basic problems of the movement. He outlined three major changes that must be made if the Contras were to be made viable.

- The monopoly of power held by FDN civilians in Honduras had to be broken. Calero had to be dismissed and the FDN as a private army had to be abolished and integrated into a new national army.
- A UNO administrative structure had to be created to include a secretary general and secretaries for international relations, politics, and military affairs.
- A major recruitment drive was needed to bring young educated Nicaraguans into the ranks of the Contra army.

Carlos viewed these reforms as necessary for building a truly national effort that would attract international support. Within a week of Carlos's visit, Arturo Sr. arrived for a visit. In December he had moved from the Washington suburb of Bethesda to Miami's Key Biscayne. His return completed the core Contra reform conspirators: the two Arturos, Carlos, and myself. We worked in my apartment on my KayPro or at Arturo Jr.'s on his Apple. The gist of our first 1986 reform proposal resembled the 1985 language and Carlos's demands:

- All military units, FDN, FARN, and KISAN (an Indian group based in Honduras) would become military arms of UNO, not military arms of any particular political group.
- All incoming funds were to flow into the UNO treasury to be allocated and disbursed according to policies established by the UNO directorate.

A third point, a new one, was the requirement of a UNO administrative structure. In the previous year, the UNO directorate had appointed a coordinator and a permanent advisory council. The coordinator was already under the sway of Calero.

On February 18, Alfonso returned to Washington. At a meeting in late December Alfonso had offended Arturo, in a way he could not and Arturo would not explain. Since Arturo the son and Carlos were Cruz people, they both felt uncomfortable approaching Alfonso. I was dispatched to enlist him in the conspiracy.

We met at the Ramada Inn on New Hampshire Avenue in the large dining room with tables surrounding a sumptuous breakfast buffet. Robelo greeted me: "Don Bruce. How are you?" "Don Alfonso," I replied, "I am well." Don is a term of respect used by many Central Americans for older men or men of power or wealth. "Don Alfonso" made sense. "Don Bruce" did not, but was our joke in those times. Always, after a long absence, we greeted each other in this way. But the levity soon ceased and he turned grim, beginning a long speech:

> I have to tell you that I have never felt more uneasy in all my years in the resistance. We were in the camps in Honduras, Arturo and I. UNO has no reality with the soldiers, none. It is all FDN.
>
> And they are a defeated army. Five thousand have fled into Honduras in just the last month. In the camps, there are weapons and ammunition, even enough food. But the FDN has no logistical effort worth the name; it cannot re-supply the troops in Nicaragua.
>
> But this bothers me most: The Contadora governments have really begun a serious effort. I, a Latin American, will not feel right until the diplomatic alternative is fully explored and exhausted. We should delay the military aid. I must know that the Sandinistas are a leopard that cannot change its spots.

When he had finished, I felt an enormous sense of relief. He had married the policy of reform to support for negotiations. It was a day on which I was proud to be associated with this effort and these men. I explained the reform efforts and told Robelo that he must come to a meeting at Arturo Jr.'s apartment to present his ideas on reform.

For the next few days, this group wrote and rewrote the proposal. Little was new in our final product, but we fought each other over every word, and finally even I was not immune. Each of us possessed a sensitivity that had to be revealed, tortured, healed.

On Friday, February 21, the Administration gave advance copies of its proposed legislation to select members and staff in Congress. It provided $70 million in military aid and $30 million in economic aid and made not even minimal concessions to reform or negotiations.

The next day I went with Carlos and the Triple A—Adolfo Calero, Alfonso Robelo, and Arturo Cruz Sr.—to a meeting with Assistant

Secretary of State Elliott Abrams, his staff, and Adolfo. It was an odd meeting. Elliott and his people were reserved, but assured the Contra leaders the Administration was determined and would win in Congress. Each offered his home telephone number to the Contra leaders, but they said nothing about the Administration proposal. It was Cruz and Robelo who took the lead. Cruz began:

> Since the formation of UNO, there has been an excessive emphasis on the military struggle. We—Alfonso and I—have no control over the military. For that reason we must be the catalyst in three areas: one, we must open a diplomatic front, a real diplomatic proposal; two, we must unite the opposition; and three, we must take all those steps that lead to our goal of reconciliation inside Nicaragua, including reconciliation with the Sandinistas.
>
> If I am to go to the Hill and talk to Congress, I must be honest and tell the truth. I will not tell them that we control the military. I will not tell them that we have a diplomatic strategy when we have none.

Adolfo looked straight ahead at the wall, not glancing at anyone or showing any emotion during Arturo's oration.

Alfonso then picked up the theme. "I am uncomfortable, too. The FDN says it was better off before the creation of UNO and the passage of the humanitarian aid bill.

"We need a diplomatic initiative. I am willing to ask Congress to support the President's bill, but only if the Administration and Congress will delay the provision of military aid until May 25. We must give Contadora a chance."

But Adolfo at this point reached the limit of his patience. "You have control of the military through me. And you are forgetting your first responsibility. You promised the commanders in your visit to Honduras that you would get aid for them. That is your solemn commitment before all others."

Robelo objected. "Colonel Bermudez didn't once mention Arturo or me—two of the leaders of UNO—in a speech to graduating officers or in the meeting with the commanders. They don't recognize our leadership. Why should we help them?"

Elliott tried to cool tempers by asking Arturo and Alfonso what concrete things could be done to give reality to UNO.

Adolfo intervened before they could answer: "Our troops are desperate and you are talking of unimportant things. We have not had one cent of private aid since the humanitarian aid program began." That was his big lie of the day, but he said it with such force and apparent conviction that even I believed him.

I thought Arturo and Alfonso at that moment would press their reform agenda, but they both fell silent. What was agreed was that UNO would begin a diplomatic initiative and it would be announced to the press within a week.

That Monday night the conspiracy met again in Alfonso's room at the Marriott. The decision was firm. Alfonso and Arturo would not lobby Congress until most of the reforms were in place. Carlos optimistically agreed. Elliott had told him that afternoon: "We just got rid of Baby Doc (the young dictator of Haiti), we're about to get rid of Marcos (the president of the Philippines who fled the country three weeks later), and in two years we'll be rid of Pinochet (the military dictator of Chile). Certainly, we can have Contra reform."

I was dubious, but I gave a copy of our latest reform proposals to Bob Kagan, Elliott's personal assistant and key aide on Contra reform. Bob is one of my good friends, I trust him enough to share my innermost secrets. That trust comes from experiences we shared in the winter and spring of 1986.

Bob was someone I liked immediately, and I steered Carlos in his direction. He probably spent hundreds of hours with us, "the liberal Contras," during that time. And he would create the one big opportunity we had to achieve serious reform. But we failed to use it, as I will describe. Still, Bob Kagan will make only a few cameo appearances in this memoir, for a simple reason: he came to believe in the reform issue, and in his eyes our efforts were successful. In mine we merely failed, over and over again.

While Bob was able to deliver Elliott to the reform side, he could not convince Alan Fiers or Ollie. They argued that reform would accelerate once aid was passed in the House. We didn't believe them.

I met with Alan that Wednesday. He was concerned about the fact that he was seen as a total supporter of Calero. Then he said that reform must be gradual, because Adolfo was at the breaking point and could walk away from it all. (This is a classic conservative dilemma: you perceive wrong but you don't call attention to it for fear that the whole structure you see as the better alternative will fall if the wrong is revealed.) He took credit for various positive movements in the direction of reform and ended by referring to Robelo and McCurdy, "Don't they realize that Calero represents from 40 to 50 percent of the Nicaraguan people?"

The day before this meeting, Arturo was to have one last meeting with the McCurdy Group, a group of moderate House Democrats, who tried to concert their efforts on foreign and defense policy issues. I believed it was his chance to gain a constituency for reform that could work with him. I wrote him a short memo suggesting what I thought he should say. In it I summarized the reform agenda—integration of separate armies into UNO, creation of a powerful executive secretary, reform of the Permanent Advisory Council, the end of FDN representation in Washington—and the proposed diplomatic initiative. I concluded the memo:

> I (Arturo) wish I could tell you that I am sanguine about the reforms. But I cannot. I cannot tell you that there will be a diplomatic initiative. But I do know that until there is reform we can neither create nor be credible with a new diplomatic initiative or reach out to other resistance forces in seeking the unity of the Nicaraguan opposition.

Arturo chose to ignore the memo. Instead, he described increased cooperation in the UNO directorate and said that he expected more progress. Dave McCurdy didn't believe it, saying, "We believe in you and Alfonso, but we don't trust the FDN and we don't trust the Administration."

Arturo and Carlos startled me in their response. They defended both Calero and the FDN; and worse, from my view, they defended the Administration.

That proved fatal in the initial round on Contra reform one week later. We met at night in Alfonso's room in the Marriott. Arturo, Carlos, and Alfonso had gone to Central America and returned. My mood was lousy and my resolve was weak.

The Friday before, I had been asked to give a talk before a group of congressional aides. I began by noting that President Reagan had just achieved two diplomatic successes—the removal of both Baby Doc and Ferdinand

Marcos—to the applause of our country, and he was about to be defeated by the House in his request for $100 million for the Contras. At the end of my talk a young woman from Senator Biden's office asked me, "What is your position?" I replied with confidence, "The President will lose." "Fine," she answered, "but what is your opinion on the merits of the proposal in its present form?" "In its present form," I responded, "it will lose." Finally, she all but screamed, "Do you have any opinion beyond prediction? What is it?"

Very carefully and deliberatively, I finally answered her question. "In its present form, without guarantees for Contra reform and negotiations, the bill should be defeated." Arturo, Alfonso, and Carlos did not go that far, but resolved not to lobby for Contra aid until Contra reform was underway.

In Alfonso's hotel room, the phone rang. The caller asked for me, which was a surprise. Who knew I was there? It was Elliott Abrams. During our conversation, I said almost nothing. Occasionally, the others could hear a "but . . ." Nothing more. After I put the phone down, I turned to the others and reported. He had ordered me to order them to return to lobbying. He promised that reform would be taken care of after we had won the vote.

This was an opportunity to exhibit moral courage. I could have urged them to refuse Abrams's command. Instead, I let Elliott beat up on me without saying a word. And when I reported to the people gathered in Alfonso's room, they submitted.

We were correct: without reform and without a diplomatic plan, there would be endless killing without purpose. We all believed in these ideas, and their power. But material forces dominated this case, and the dominant material force was money. Each of us—Alfonso, Arturo, Carlos, and myself—was paid by Spitz. Arturo and Alfonso had thought they were paid by a foreign source, and Carlos had thought his money came directly from Rich Miller. But all of us had been bought and paid for and the bill was being called in.

Carlos had bought a book about the life of Ernest Bevan. In it there was a wonderful remark that we both liked, but we never assimilated its message: "Always remember, Francis. The first thing you have to decide before you walk into any negotiation is what you'll do if the other chap says 'No.'"

We had designed our reforms. We had presented them. And Elliott had said no. A possibility we had perhaps surprisingly never discussed.

It is not easy to quit. It often seems better to stay, to use your voice, to promote change. I think that was why I stayed, why I allowed Elliott to issue orders. But there also comes a time (usually well before we are willing to acknowledge it) when the right course of action is to leave, and to shout to the heavens why you left. I rationalized it wasn't that time yet. So, we resumed lobbying.

Shortly before the vote on March 20, the first phase of Contra reform came to an end. There was agreement among UNO and Elliott and his staff to create, within the Contras, a new position of secretary general charged with implementing the Directorate's policies. The logical choice was Carlos Ulvert, reform's staunchest proponent. But for reasons I still do not understand, Alfonso's first choice was a man named Leonardo Samariba, a former Nicaraguan businessman who had spent a year in jail for conspiracy to overthrow the government. After his release, he had moved to Florida and opened a copy store. His position on reform was unknown. Arturo acquiesced in this appointment and Adolfo approved it.

On the morning before the vote, I met with Samariba for breakfast at the Washington Square Hotel. I tried to make reform issues and their congressional implications real to him. I thought if he understood, he would work harder to make the reform take root. He saw his role differently.

I would not talk again privately with Samariba for another year. In those twelve months he saw his role as one of balancing Adolfo's status quo, on the one hand, with Arturo and Alfonso's impulse for change, on the other. In practice, he sided with Calero and the FDN on most issues.

Arturo Jr. had begged me to intervene with Alfonso, to tell him point blank there would be no reform unless someone who believed in it and had worked for it led the implementation process as secretary general. He was right, but I couldn't do it.

I knew that if Alfonso said no, I was unprepared to do anything differently.

Then Alan Fiers (nom de CIA voyage, "Cliff Grubbs") went too far. There was a scheduled meeting of Arturo, Alfonso, and Adolfo with Alan in Fort Lauderdale. Arturo Cruz, habitually punctual for these meetings, arrived early. When he walked in, he saw the man he knew as "Cliff."

Alan began: "Arturo, I know you are concerned about the slow pace of reform, but I promise you it will come. But you have to be careful, you can't push them too hard. Without the FDN, there is no resistance to the

Sandinistas. They are the core, the crucial, indispensable element. Give us time. They'll change."

Arturo snapped. He had never felt right about the enterprise. Now, when he was just thinking about urging a new reform effort, he was told to be cautious and wait. He walked out.

I was in Representative Alberto Bustamante's (D-Texas) office when Bob Leiken reached me to tell me the news. I told Alberto and his staff what was happening and the reasons for Arturo's action, and described the likely failure of reform efforts. I also asked Alberto to keep this in confidence. He agreed, and did not reveal his knowledge until the next day, at a White House session. He asked the briefer to speculate on what would happen to the next vote (scheduled for the 15th of April) if Arturo Cruz resigned before it took place. (In fairness, it was not a secret he had to keep.) The briefer had no answer.

When I finally reached Arturo, he was adamant. This time he would not be dissuaded, this time he would leave. His resignation provoked a grave crisis. Cruz and his people, Robelo and representatives of his political party, and Calero and the FDN all feverishly began drawing up position papers.

Cruz's paper was the most direct, accusing the FDN of preventing Robelo and himself from involvement in military matters and monopolizing the political arena. Privately, Robelo was calling for Arturo to be designated coordinator of UNO. Both of them called for an end to the FDN and its absorption into UNO; they also called for majority rule.

Those documents were drafted over the weekend of the 12th and 13th. On the 11th, I had impulsively called Ollie for the first time since the March 20 vote, when I had run into him after the President's package was defeated, and he had exploded at me, charging that the defeat was my fault and McCurdy's. He said the President would never again send a proposal for Contra aid to the Hill.

Three weeks had passed, and I felt, just maybe, he might have some helpful ideas on what to do. Instead he launched into a vicious attack on Arturo.

"I read the transcript with Alan. Cruz had no justification for such an outburst. Alan said nothing out of line. Cruz's tormented ego is endangering the whole project."

Ollie continued, "God, I can't stand him. I promise you this. One day, maybe not this year, maybe not for many years, but one day I will meet him.

That man living in the luxury condominium in Miami with his Mercedes Benz. And I will tell him what I think of him and what he has done to those poor boys fighting for their lives in Nicaragua."

He then told me that he was being pulled off the Contra account, that he was only staying at the NSC staff out of concern for the American hostages in Lebanon.

When I got off the phone, I found he had won me over again. I was angry not at Arturo but at the liberals who were trying to drive Ollie from office.

I called Alfonso and asked him if he thought Ollie should leave. He replied that while Ollie was a "Caleroista," he was nonetheless dedicated and energetic in support of the cause. We needed him.

When I returned sometime later from a meeting with two liberal friends, whom I had savaged throughout dinner without their having a clue as to why, I had a message from Alfonso. When I finally reached him the next morning, he informed me that Rich Miller had called to arrange a private meeting with Ollie the next day.

In that meeting, Ollie savaged Dave McCurdy, and to a lesser extent me as McCurdy's agent, as well as other members of Congress. He also tried to drive a wedge between Alfonso and Arturo. But Alfonso would not budge. When he left the meeting, he immediately reported to me.

We now had a much better sense of our enemies and our potential friends. Carlos Ulvert and I prepared a letter, to be signed by Arturo and Alfonso, to our friends in Congress, most notably the minority leader, Bob Michel. It would state that there had been no real reform. Depending on the outcome of these meetings, we might have considered going to the press.

The Nicaraguans were staying again at One Washington Square, and we gathered there before going to the Hill. Bob Kagan showed up, and we told him what we were planning to do. He told us we must not deliver the letter, as it would surely go public and jeopardize the vote. Once again we buckled under slight Administration pressure.

A few hours later, the Gang of Four met with Elliott Abrams and Bob Kagan. I had thought of complaining about Bob's intervention, but before I could speak, Elliott did: You guys are too involved operationally. That should not be. You have become meddlers.

Penn basically agreed with that sentiment. He was wary of how involved Bob and I were in the daily plots and activities of the reform-minded

Contras. But that day he vehemently defended us, telling Elliott that without our intervention, the present Contra leadership would have fallen apart some time ago. He had witnessed more than once our interventions to keep UNO alive.

Elliott did not respond directly to Penn's riposte. He simply informed us of the decision he had just made: he would give the FDN directorate an ultimatum later that afternoon. They would agree to negotiate in good faith with Arturo and Alfonso or lose half of the remaining humanitarian aid. If after thirty days they had not negotiated in good faith, they would face another cutoff. The idea had come from Kagan.

This was a victory for reform, but two of our numbers were still dismayed. Leiken was afraid that the decision would create a firestorm among the FDN civilian leadership and, worse, among some FDN field commanders loyal to Calero. And Robelo feared that Calero would go to CIA Director William Casey, and Jean Kirkpatrick, who would cause Elliott's decision to be rescinded and Elliott himself to lose his job.

Meetings were subsequently scheduled for Miami in the first week of May. In the interim, aides to Cruz, Robelo, and Calero were to meet to write a document that would guide the Triple A when they met in person.

In those staff meetings, Cruz's assistants felt powerless to insist upon their position. They saw their man as someone who could quit, leaving them with no position. The FDN representatives easily outmaneuvered them. In the document the aides prepared, all immediately conceded the principal reform demand, and gave the FDN the right to retain control of its army: "The organizations which are part of UNO maintain their own identity and structure within the pluralist unity."

Instead of fighting this, Cruz sulked. When I arrived on May 7 to try to ease communication between Arturo and Alfonso, and help them show some backbone, the concession had already been made. It was no longer on the agenda. And I didn't object.

I didn't completely realize what had happened until a year later. Instead, the principal issue that dominated the session of UNO directorate meetings at the end of May was majority rule. Even the staff document recommended the adoption of majority rule for the UNO directorate, except in the matter of general UNO strategy and military appointments. The minority could appeal to the Permanent Advisory Council, which would be made up of five Nicaraguans who would make the final decision. But Robelo suddenly decided that the minority should be able to appeal in all cases, effectively eliminating the one reform of consequence.

Cruz was really furious; he wouldn't even talk to Robelo. He felt enormously betrayed. Leiken called me at the hotel, insisting that I confront Robelo. This time I did and, though it pained him, he backed off. I didn't argue with him, I agreed that his argument had logic. I just insisted over and over that he concede and support Arturo.

I then called Alan Fiers and told him there was agreement on our side and he had only to bring around Adolfo. He did so, telling a State Department colleague that, "Bruce was the hero of Miami." UNO was still intact, "reformed" in time for the third and final vote on Contra aid, scheduled for June 26. The only real change was in voting procedures. Adolfo agreed to majority rule except in UNO strategy, expansion of UNO, and military appointments. If there were disagreements, the decision would be turned over to the Permanent Advisory Council for final decision. The five would not know that they were the court of appeals until an impasse arose. It was a traditional Latin legalism to mask irreconcilable differences, cute but meaningless, and it was never invoked.

We claimed victory anyway, and I think to some extent we actually believed we had won. Dennis Volman, a reporter for the *Christian Science Monitor* who had served two years with the State Department in Managua, was a friend of most of us, but he was dubious about the whole Contra enterprise and had often used his articles to express opposition. In this case, however, he bought our line, that the moderates had gained strength and authority and would use it:

> Sources close to UNO say they expect UNO will turn toward using diplomatic means to resolve the six-year-old Nicaraguan civil war. There will also be more emphasis on establishing bridges to politically moderate European and Latin American countries. Underlying this is a greater willingness on the part of leaders like Cruz to explore avenues that will increase the power of the opposition within Nicaragua and then pressure the Sandinistas into some form of power-sharing with that opposition.

And Volman correctly described the policy of Calero:

Calero and other FDN leaders have worked mainly toward over-throwing the Sandinistas—an overthrow that would probably necessitate a U.S. invasion.

I had briefed Dennis on the long meetings, their outcome, and, most important, our hopes for the future. I think I believed that, even with the FDN still intact, reforms were meaningful, because Cruz, Robelo, and Ulvert could undertake, as Dennis wrote, "a new diplomatic strategy." And that would have been true had the legislation turned out differently. ■

CHAPTER SIX

LEGISLATING THE CONTRAS

January–June 1986

In a memo to Rich Miller dated January 24, 1986, I wrote, "Our hope is to maintain the large majority in the House supporting aid to the resistance that was forged last spring." The key issue I stressed was negotiations.

But what I was trying to do as a lobbyist in the winter of 1986 was impossible. My organization, the Center for Democracy in the Americas, consisted of a board including Penn Kemble, David Ifshin, a Washington lawyer and Democratic activist, and myself. Both Penn and David were neoconservatives, but Penn trusted me to play a role (a role he would not have chosen for himself as a lobbyist, but a role he found necessary). David trusted Penn.

We were funded by Spitz Channell, on the far right. In late 1986 Spitz would raise money to uphold Reagan's veto of a bill requiring limited economic sanctions against South Africa. From whom did he solicit funds? "People," he said, "who were concerned about preserving the white race." He once told Penn and me that Jews had destroyed the criminal justice system in New York City. It was easy to withhold loyalty from Spitz.

First among my self-described constituency were Arturo and Alfonso and the people of Nicaragua they represented. Second were the moderate Democrats led at that time by Representative Dave McCurdy. After that came my longtime liberal associates on the Hill, mainly Senate staff. The latter would, if they could, shut down the Contras unconditionally and attempt, through bilateral and regional negotiations with the Sandinistas, a limited democratic opening in Nicaragua, along with Sandinista agreement to reduce its army and forswear support of guerrilla forces in neighboring countries. My agreement with them was on the importance of negotiations. We obviously parted ways on the Contras.

On February 21, the Administration released its proposal for aid to the Contras. It was written without reference to the concerns of Democrats, or Cruz and Robelo, not to mention the moderates.

Administration stupidity, however, apparently had no limits. They decided (who *they* were, I don't know) on a simple up or down vote. In effect they were asserting they could fashion a bill ignoring the concerns of over 50 percent of all House members and shove it down their throats.

In fact, every Administration tends to believe that once it reaches internal consensus, long and contentious discussion should stop, and everyone should just climb on board. Systems in which the executive branch emerges from the elected parliament have the advantage of a majority ruling party support before embarking on controversial foreign policy. In the United States, the separateness of the executive branch encourages key policymakers to believe that wisdom resides in the executive and Congress is merely a necessary evil.

The speaker of the house at that time was Representative Thomas "Tip" O'Neill, a Boston Democrat. The speaker was very sensitive to reports from the religious community concerning serious Contra human rights abuses. He remembered the U.S. occupation of Nicaragua in the '20s, and the subsequent assassination of General Sandino, who had resisted the occupation, an assassination ordered by General Anastacio Somoza, installed in office by occupation forces.

O'Neill opposed any aid to the Contras, and he knew the mood of the House, which (in the winter of 1986) the Administration did not. To rule out any possible amendments, he used rules that had been laid down the summer before during passage of the humanitarian aid package.

Both sides, the liberals and the Administration, were in agreement that the moderates should be forced to choose sides, and that they should not be given the opportunity to write their concerns into legislation.

Dave McCurdy's key aide on the Contra issue was Howard Yourman. Howard had spent years in the office of Speaker Carl Albert and was a very adept legislative tactician and a professional. He worked for a moderate Democrat and he did his best. His best in this case required him to ignore both the Administration and the Democratic leadership. We started writing our own Contra aid bill.

Our concerns were as always: reform, negotiations, and measures to improve the program and drive the Administration crazy. It was only fair; they were already driving us and most sane Americans crazy. Patrick Buchanan, White House Communications Director and standard bearer for the lunatic right, wrote in an opinion piece carried in the March 5 *Washington Post*: "With the vote on Contra aid, the Democratic party will reveal whether it stands with Ronald Reagan and the resistance—or Daniel Ortega and the Communists."

Then Secretary of State George Schultz put it this way—he stated that the alternative to support for Administration Contra policy is "a vision of two, three, many Nicaraguas—a hemisphere of burning churches, suppressed newspapers and crushed opposition."

Reagan himself said Nicaragua had become "a command post for international terror," describing the Nicaraguan government as an "outlaw regime" which gave sanctuary to agents of all America's enemies: Castro, Libya's Quaddafi, the Ayatollah, the PLO, the Red Brigades of Italy, not to mention the Soviet Union and its Warsaw Pact allies.

But what did rhetoric like this really mean? Senator Arlen Specter, a Republican from Pennsylvania, asked Schultz in testimony before the Appropriations Committee whether the Administration was "seeing a military victory for the Contras." Schultz responded that the goal was a "rearrangement of the way of governing Nicaragua" through "a church-mediated policy of national reconciliation," and Contra forces who would "make it plain that the communists cannot win a military victory."

Specter responded: "I don't understand your answer and I don't understand the Administration's policy."

One thing we were sure of: the Administration policy could not be fixed with a letter. Dave McCurdy told the *Washington Post*: "It's got to be a lot more than a letter. I've been the recipient of letters." Bill Richardson of New Mexico said that he had made a mistake the year before in supporting the $27 million on the strength of promises in a letter. He quipped: "Beware of letters that don't mean anything."

So we wrote legislation fully aware that neither the Administration nor the Democratic leadership would agree to amendments.

The principal purpose of our legislation was to divide the Administration's request into two parts, an idea that was common in Washington at the time. My first impulse was a $40 to $60 million split with a thirty-day delay before military aid would become available. Delay was an idea that was attractive to all moderates, including the Nicaraguans. Howard's first draft contained a 120-day delay and required the President to certify that "negotiations based on the Contadora Document of Objectives have failed to produce an agreement," before military aid could become available (only if Congress did not block the release).

Howard and I also inserted other provisions into the draft legislation. First, on the Administration: "The President, through the Secretary of State, shall designate one official to coordinate U.S. government activities involved in aiding the resistance."

This was an effort to force the Administration to designate one person to run everything. It could have been written by anyone who had ever been close to management of the Contra program, including two Senate aides, Ollie's top assistant outside government, Rob Owen, or aides to Elliott Abrams. All any of them ever saw was chaos, with no one in charge and no one accountable.

This became law, and Elliott was designated, but no one ever saw any difference.

Second, on training: "Such funds may also be used for training in (1) radio communications, intelligence, logistics, and small unit tactics; (2) democratic values and respect for human rights; (3) provision of health care; and (4) literacy."

This provided the answer to numerous complaints that Contra soldiers were neither trained to fight effectively, nor prepared to carry out serious political work with respect to human rights. This provision provided both reform and modernization.

Third, on unity of purpose: "Each group receiving assistance must agree to support the proposal signed by six Nicaraguan political parties and presented by them to the Government of Nicaragua on January 30, 1986."

This provision called for a ceasefire, an amnesty, and new general elections, in order to end the war. The purpose of this provision was to require the different Contra forces, including the FDN, to commit themselves to something less than a military takeover of the Sandinista government, and in that way to encourage a more serious Contra diplomacy. The idea to put it into legislation came from Arturo Cruz.

Fourth, on the Unified Nicaraguan Opposition (UNO): "All military forces within UNO must be directly responsible to the UNO directorate and not associated with any political party, group or organization."

This provision came straight out of Cruz-Robelo draft language for reform of the Contras. The specific target was Adolfo Calero's iron grip on FDN troops.

Legislation is a difficult vehicle through which to realize one's ideas. But this was a better expression of the McCurdy Group experience and beliefs than any legislation I had ever worked on.

Administration lobbying strategy was true to form: charge ahead and ignore warnings that they were going to lose. In its bare bones, their message was, "Give us $100 million or we'll call you communists." Administration hubris was so huge and their belligerence toward Congress so great that during the first half of March, no Administration official was allowed to talk to McCurdy or his closest congressional associates.

Dave was not intimidated. He held to his position. In fact, he insisted on it in a *Washington Post* opinion piece on March 14, 1986.

> The President has created the impression that support for the Contras is a policy in itself, rather than an instrument of policy.
>
> At the same time, the House Democratic leadership cannot walk away with clean hands; defeating the President is a tactic, not a policy.
>
> Some of us would like to create a bipartisan policy on Central America, but our time and patience are growing short. The Administration has wasted time by not seriously pursuing negotiations, by failing to build public support, by encouraging divisiveness among resistance groups, and by alienating allies on Capitol Hill and in Central America. This cannot be allowed to obscure the fact that repression in Nicaragua has become institutionalized and is getting worse. But it means that if there is to be any aid package, the President will have to live with more, rather than less, legislative direction.

On March 18, two days before the vote, the Administration finally had to admit that defeat was at hand without serious action. Their only option was to talk to McCurdy. That Tuesday, the Administration dispatched five lobbyists, including Ollie North and Elliott Abrams, to meet with Dave, and Rod Chandler of Washington State, who represented the swing Republicans.

Since the bill could not be amended, the Administration suggested substituting an executive order with the force of law. They took the McCurdy draft as the basis for discussion, pointing out what was for them unacceptable, most particularly the Contra reform language.

Dave, suffering a bad case of the flu, kept on nodding his head to indicate he understood their objections, but the Administration officials interpreted his gesture to mean acceptance. McCurdy's aide Howard kept shaking his head. At one point, when the members were not present, Ollie approached Howard.

"You keep on shaking your head. Don't you trust us?"

"No," he said more emphatically than he had ever said anything in his life.

That night, Elliott's top aide, Jim Michel, went back to the State Department to draft the executive order and the presidential statement that would accompany it. When Howard and I looked at that draft the next morning, it included the delay but now only the President could decide whether or not efforts at negotiations had failed. Congress would have no role, and there would be no second vote. In addition, the definition of humanitarian aid had been expanded to include handheld ground-to-air missiles! Finally, the Contra reform language was gutted. It now read, "The Secretary of State shall encourage the democratic resistance to increase its unity and appeal to the Nicaraguan people."

A second vote was key. As was Contra reform. Trust was gone. Dave's draft was accepted, minus its key points. The McCurdy Democrats were now being asked to trust an administration that had always resisted partnership with Congress. They needed something.

And they got it, in a meeting with Tip O'Neill. He promised that if they voted against this bill, they would have an opportunity, by the middle of April, to present an alternative. That cinched it. The McCurdy Democrats would vote no, and they announced that fact in a press conference after their meeting with the Speaker.

Except for one statement I had made in the meeting with congressional aides, I took no public position on the President's bill. And I made no effort to dissuade any of the McCurdy Democrats. I wouldn't have been successful had I tried. Loyalty to their party's position is what most members prefer. The executive order enabled swing Republicans to support the bill. The Speaker's offer of another vote gave the McCurdy Democrats what they needed to oppose the Administration proposal.

The President's package was defeated on March 20 by a vote of 222–210.

SECOND VOTE: APRIL 16, 1986

At the end of March I spent a week in Guatemala meeting with President Vinicio Cerezo and a former Salvadoran guerrilla whose closest friend, also a former guerrilla, had recently disappeared.

Vinicio wanted a briefing on the Contras and the Contra debate in the United States. For an hour and a half I held forth, he and his assistant, Sara Mishaan, asking few questions. Vinicio was at that time preparing for the first summit of the current Central American leaders to be held in Guatemala in May. I found it refreshing that a president, even if it was the Guatemalan president, listened to me. Guatemala had been pursuing a policy of so-called "active neutrality." Successive governments since 1981 had openly opposed the totalitarian and undemocratic nature of the Sandinistas, but equally opposed military efforts to overthrow the Nicaraguan government. Secretly, however, the army of Guatemala had provided military aid to the Contras until September 1985, stopping in the final months of that year's presidential campaign.

My meeting with the Salvadoran was more noteworthy. His friend, Raul Guerra, had disappeared on January 16. Raul had many enemies. The Salvadoran army had imprisoned him more than once, as he was a guerrilla and had fought against the army in his home province of Cabanas. But he had eventually despaired of guerrilla victory, when in 1985 he had seen guerrilla leaders order the execution of fifty-five rebels simply for voicing dissent.

Raul and his friend Francisco then traveled to the United States to take a paramedics course. Together with Leonel Gomez, some Americans including myself had been working to help a doctor in El Salvador set up a clinic that would treat peasants and teach them to provide for their own basic health care. Raul and Francisco were to work with that doctor. But Francisco had a falling out with Leonel before the course was completed and only Raul returned to El Salvador to work.

And one morning, he just never arrived. This had unfortunately become a common pattern in El Salvador. Francisco had been in Guatemala visiting a friend when he learned about his disappearance. When he returned to the United States, he and another of Raul's friends independently set out to do their own investigations.

First, they confirmed that Raul's information about the fifty-five executions was correct. They found someone from inside Raul's former guerrilla group who told them Raul was killed because he had learned that one killing attributed to right-wing death squads had actually been committed by Raul's group.

That killing was widely known. I have since spoken with two other Salvadorans who claim their own special knowledge about the right-wing assassins; thus I was and remain dubious that the rebel group did the killings. Nonetheless, Francisco's report should have been checked by someone. But he chose to give it only to me, in confidence, a report to be released only after his death.

I returned to an extraordinarily complicated congressional situation in Washington. The Senate had passed a Contra aid bill, a legislative version of the executive order, with somewhat stronger Contra reform language.

The House Democratic leadership, as promised, was giving the McCurdy Democrats an opportunity to offer their legislation. The leadership now proposed to attach the Senate bill to a catchall appropriations bill (Reagan had already promised to veto because there was too much pork in it). This of course angered House Republicans, who saw it as a cynical maneuver. Henry Hyde described the procedure as a "fraud," weighing down the Contra aid vote "with a millstone that is of grotesque proportions. We are going to vote on a sensitive life and death issue and combine it with a wild spending bill." Nonetheless, the House Democratic leadership was able to insist on this procedure in a 221–202 vote on the rule.

McCurdy and colleagues worked out an arrangement with the leadership by which they would offer restrictions to the Senate bill. The Senate bill contained $30 million in economic assistance, including training for the Contras. The McCurdy amendment wouldn't change that. Instead the amendment—in which McCurdy was joined by six other Democrats, Mike Andrews (Texas), Alberto Bustamante (Texas), Jim Cooper (Tennessee), Buddy McKay (Florida), Richard Ray (Georgia), and John Spratt (South Carolina)—attached four conditions to the $70 million in military aid. First, it eliminated the ground-to-air missiles. Second, it included strong UNO reform language. Third, it delayed consideration of military aid for ninety days, and required direct bilateral negotiations between the Sandinistas and the United States to help facilitate regional negotiations on a Contadora treaty during that period. Finally, it required a second vote of approval by both House and Senate before military aid could be released. It would be in that second vote, mandated by the McCurdy amendment, that Administration veracity, and the Administration role in facilitating or hindering negotiations, would be judged. The Democratic leadership had given McCurdy and his allies the best possible chance to pass their legislation.

A first vote would consider a substitute for the Senate bill offered by Congressman Lee Hamilton, providing no direct aid to the Contras. Then the House would vote on the McCurdy amendment, if the Hamilton amendment was defeated. Then, after consideration of an unrelated amendment, they would vote on final passage. In essence, three alternative policies were being offered: the liberals' (Hamilton), the moderates' (McCurdy), and the Administration's (the Senate-passed bill). The liberal position claimed between 180 and 190 votes, the Administration position 190 to 200. There were only 30 or 40 in the middle.

But those 30 or 40 represented the margin of difference. Because of the rule governing debate, McCurdy and allies could compromise with the Democratic leadership to support restrictions on the Senate bill. Liberal Democrats at the time could not vote for direct aid to the Contras, an action construed by their peers as commensurate with original sin. They could vote, however, to restrict its use.

On the other hand, McCurdy and allies could compromise with the conservative Republicans to seek their support on final passage, even with restrictions. For Republicans, direct aid was key, a step toward their salvation. I don't use theological allusions idly. The principles guiding both liberals and conservatives were deeply held. The debate was as savage and intense as between Catholics and Lutherans during the Reformation. Moderates had no counterpart in this analogy, except perhaps the Dutch theologian Erasmus, who tried vainly to reconcile the dueling forces of the sixteenth-century religious debate. One man against a continent. But in the twentieth century, about 35 moderates were confronting 400 divided into two irreconcilable groups led by hard-core believers. Democracy in Congress means 50 percent plus one of those voting, and the moderates represented that one. Unlike Erasmus, who was buried by his own era, the moderates eventually would win their theological debate on Contra aid, but not until 1988.

McCurdy made a deal with the assistant minority leader, Trent Lott of Mississippi. If the McCurdy amendment passed, Republicans would support the bill's final passage. Moderates would support the bill's final passage if the McCurdy amendment lost. It was a deal to insure that the Contras would get aid, with conditions or without. On April 10, Dave testified before the Rules Committee on which Trent Lott served, and the subsequent colloquy made clear the deal.

I therefore took my time getting to the House side of the Capitol on April 16. When I did arrive at the Democratic lobby, the doors to the House chambers were open as members went in and out to vote. From the lobby I could see the electronic tally showing the number of votes in favor, and against, and the time remaining.

With about five minutes left, the vote tally was showing 290 votes in favor. I was confused, I couldn't figure out what amendment they were voting for. Even the amendment for the $27 million in economic aid the year before had received only 248 votes. I thought no possible combination of moderates and liberals, or moderates and conservatives, could possibly reach 290.

Finally I determined they must be voting on the Hamilton amendment. But I still couldn't make sense of the number. Then a conservative friend walked by, triumphant. They were indeed voting for Hamilton, in a liberal-conservative alliance. The final tally was 361 to 66. The sole purpose was to stop passage of the McCurdy amendment, which would have forced Republicans to pass aid with McCurdy conditions.

Over the weekend, the White House and Republican House leadership had determined that McCurdy could win, and that was considered unacceptable. Partly, my friend told me, it was personal. They were tired of this small band of Democrats dictating the terms regarding aid for one of their two or three most important programs. But mostly it was substantive. They wanted the bill their way, and no other.

The *Washington Post* described the scene well:

> Gleeful Republicans were clearly delighted by the chance to stun the Democratic leadership with an unexpected parliamentary move. Milling about on the House floor, they laughed and applauded—while the Democrats watched in apparent initial confusion—as the strategy was implemented.

After the vote, Dave McCurdy rose in the House chambers to ask about the parliamentary situation. He was greeted by chuckles, then outright laughter, both sides taking immense pleasure in his discomfort. Later, in an interview, Dave declared: "We're not going to be beaten into submission by either side."

At the time I believed the official view, that Republicans had voted for the Hamilton amendment out of anger at the rule, and frustration over the fact that a small number of moderate Democrats thought they could dictate policy. I no longer believe this. True, either might have been enough to motivate both Republican leadership and rank and file. But I now believe someone in the White House approved or even devised the plan, having deemed the Contra situation as no longer desperate.

On April 1 the resupply operation out of Ilopango had begun, and through April 11 it had operated daily, sometimes twice daily. Even before this, some Contras had reentered Nicaragua and were engaging Sandinista targets. Much of this resupply effort was undoubtedly financed by the $3.7 million profit of the February sale of one thousand TOW missiles to the Iranians. On April 4 Ollie wrote his famous "diversion memo," the discovery of which would bring the covert Iran-Contra operations into public view. He outlined his plans for the anticipated $14 million in profits from the next sale:

> • $2 million will be used to purchase replacement TOW's for the original 508 sold by Israel to Iran for the release of Benjamin Weir. . . .
> • $12 million will be used to purchase critically needed supplies for the Nicaraguan Democratic Resistance Forces. This material is essential to cover shortages in resistance inventories resulting from their current offensives and to "bridge" the period between now and when congressionally-approved lethal assistance (beyond the $25 million in "defensive" arms) can be delivered.[19]

Sabotage of the upcoming vote clearly was not on his mind during the writing of this memo. Ollie's reference to "$25 million in 'defensive arms'" suggests he was assuming that a bill resembling the Senate version, with a delay of lethal assistance, would pass, and that profits from the sale would take care of lethal purchases and deliveries during the interim. Certainly sabotage was not on Trent Lott's mind on April 10, six days later, when he made his agreement with McCurdy. Yet House Republicans did sabotage the vote, without knowing whether there would be another vote in the near future. But on the day after the vote, the Republicans began circulating a discharge petition that would compel a vote later in May, a rarely used procedure that almost always fails. A day later, they knew it had failed.

If that was their only fallback, to suggest the House Republican leadership would have acted without consulting the White House makes no sense. The leadership had no independent way of knowing that restoration of U.S. aid to the Contras was no longer desperately needed. In fact, Hyde had called the issue "life or death," the Administration drumbeat for months.

The only explanation that makes sense is that Ollie (or someone close to him who knew what he knew and could communicate authoritatively to the Republican leadership) let it be known that there was no longer any urgency in passing just any bill in order to obtain Contra funding. The message could have been simple: Don't worry about the Contras, they're okay. It's better to defeat this bill that imposes restrictions we don't like, and wait for a more propitious time for a good bill.

I cannot prove this, but I believe it. More than all the revelations of the Iran-Contra hearings, it is what I believe about this vote that has bothered me most. The Administration lost its preferred bill on March 20. They expected to lose again on April 16. Their response was to kill the legislation. Pronouncements about support for democracy began to ring very hollow.

While waiting for that next vote, the resupply network of seven planes continued operations, but not without problems. By the end of April, a gloomy Ollie told a mutual colleague that without a speedy infusion of additional funds, "there won't be a force to help when the Congress finally acts." But by May 16, the Enterprise accounts had received the final $5 million of a $15 million payment for arms sales to Iran. Ollie wrote Poindexter that the "resistance support organization now has more than $6 million for immediate disbursement."[20] Enterprise planes made twenty-eight resupply flights in May, including eight lethal deliveries. The key operatives in the resupply network were Dick Secord in Arlington, Virginia; Colonel Richard Steele, U.S. military attaché to El Salvador and key contact with General Bustillo, Chief of the Salvadoran Air Force; Joe Fernandez, Station Chief of the CIA in Costa Rica; and Ollie North in the White House.[21] They were all linked by the National Security Agency's top secret transmitter, the KL-43, which allowed them to send messages in secret. There were always problems, the system was inadequate, but it was their edge, allowing the Administration to continue operations Congress had shut down, giving the Administration the breathing room they needed to get the bill they wanted.

THIRD VOTE: JUNE 26, 1986

On June 26, two months and ten days after the second vote, the Administration won a third vote, by 221–209. I did not support this bill, but my actions contributed to Administration victory.

Contra reform was still a key issue. The Miami Accords, though fundamentally flawed, provided a framework in which Cruz and Robelo could exert more authority and begin to modernize and democratize the Contras. Three of the eleven who switched their votes to the Administration position from March 20 did so in part because of the reforms.

In late May I told Dave he should no longer trust anyone's word on the prospect of negotiations leading to a Contadora treaty. He should talk to the Central American leaders themselves. He liked that idea, and immediately began to call his colleagues. Eventually, he led a thirteen-member delegation that visited the five capitals of Central America as well as Contra camps.

Key to the success of that trip, in my judgment, was a meeting with Venicio Cerezo and Guatemala's vice foreign minister, Francisco Villagran. Since I knew the Embassy would likely fail to arrange a meeting with Vinicio, and be unwilling to arrange a meeting with Francisco Villagran, deputy foreign minister, I flew down to arrange those visits myself.

Both Cerezo and Villagran made it clear to the McCurdy congressional delegation (Codel) that they would not support the Contras, that they believed in a negotiated solution. But both obliquely indicated that the Contras's existence was helpful.

Villagran said, "We certainly don't want Nicaragua to support our guerrilla movement, and the fact that they have to fight the Contras consumes their efforts." President Cerezo was asked if the Central American countries could exert pressure for democracy on Nicaragua without the Contras. He replied, "No, not yet. . . . If the Sandinistas don't accept a pluralist system, we are going to have problems."

Oscar Arias, the new president of Costa Rica, summed up the contradictory feelings of the region's politicians: "We will have Contras forever unless Nicaraguans feel they have free elections. . . . But I don't think the Contras have a chance of overthrowing the Sandinistas. I see no light at the end of the tunnel. . . . No, I cannot recommend anything (about providing aid to the Contras)."

Members of the delegation came away with strong feelings that the Sandinistas were a threat to their neighbors. But most also believed there was still a chance to achieve a Contadora treaty. They believed the presidents of the four democracies of Central America represented a new breed of politician, more confident of their own power, more willing to take risks to establish democracy in their own countries and peace in the region.

What Dave observed in their press conference when they returned to Washington was prescient, a new element in the debate: "These are impressive men with proven democratic credentials. We should look to them on how to establish peace and democracy in Central America."

Immediately, Dave added two new sections to his bill. One would provide $2 million to aid the four Central American democracies in the search for regional peace. The second would provide $350 million in additional economic aid to the four Central American democracies. These were major shifts. The year before, the Michel-McCurdy bill had provided just $5 million to the Contadora countries for their efforts. In 1986 the Contadora governments of Mexico, Panama, Colombia, and Venezuela, while well intentioned, viewed the problems of the region at a distance. But these new leaders of Central America had deeply impressed the delegation.

Earlier drafts had endorsed the idea of increasing aid and ordered a study. Now, having seen Central American efforts to institutionalize democracy, the members of the McCurdy delegation unanimously wanted to give the leaders and their peoples tangible economic support.

But the Central American presidents also believed that the Sandinistas were a threat to their democratic neighbors, that the solution was to force accountability on the Sandinistas through the ballot. They believed the Contras were not the solution, but they were still indispensable to achieving one.

When I returned from Guatemala on June 4, I had been off payroll for two weeks. Robelo pleaded my case with Spitz at the end of April, but Spitz just shook his head, agreeing I was a good man but insisting,

"He's a liberal, a Democrat, and he doesn't support the President's program." He was right.

What I had now was independence. I had no resources, but I could think and do what I believed was right with no accountability to anyone but my own conscience. In this new role, I could attend meetings of the so-called McCurdy Group. And I was impressed. This group of men and women was working hard to forge a new policy. They were trying to devise the right mix of aid to the four Central American democracies, military aid to the Contras, economic aid to the Contras, requirements for Contra reform, and accountability to Congress through a second vote that could bring about progress toward concrete goals. After what he had seen and heard on his trip, Dave believed he could and should make another deal with the Administration and the Republican leadership.

But in meetings with the Republican leadership, serious negotiations on the terms of the legislation became impossible. These meetings included the House Republican leadership, defined as any Republican member who felt leaderly that day, southern Democrats who were firm supporters of Contra aid, six or seven Administration representatives, four or five McCurdy Group members, and staff from many congressional members' offices. No one in the Administration or the Republican leadership trusted enough to allow one or two among them to go alone to negotiate with the group.

In retrospect, what seemed at the time arrogant and self-defeating in the Administration posture makes sense. The strategy was to appear reasonable, to talk—but to make no big deals. Large numbers in attendance would insure no one would suddenly succumb to a legislative proposal that implied a policy partnership with Congress. Even the hardest-line members associated with McCurdy did not believe in a policy of overthrow, and Administration lobbyists had to guard against revealing that their policy did. Heavy attendance allowed rhetoric to substitute for discussion of actual program.

The Republicans did stress two issues. They wanted no second vote, and they wanted the authority to provide ground-to-air missiles as soon as the legislation was signed by the president.

On June 8 I received a surprise call from Spitz. He claimed he had just spoken with President Reagan, and the President had asked him to get back into the struggle to win aid for the "freedom fighters." Spitz told me the President had been impressed with reports on the McCurdy trip to Central America. And Spitz revealed his awareness of many details about that trip. He asked me to meet him for lunch three days later. At that lunch, he acted as if there had never been any rupture between us. He said he wanted to help me and asked me to prepare a memo for him about what my organization would need.

For the longest time I believed that Spitz's story about the President's call was just hype, that in reality the caller was Ollie, who had read cables from U.S. embassies in Central America and suddenly saw my association with the McCurdy Group in a new light. I was probably wrong. In Spitz's deposition before the congressional Iran-Contra panel, he was asked if he had ever had a telephone conversation with the President. He replied, "He called me in June of '86 once."

Two days later, Spitz gave me a check for $6,000. I accepted it, but over the weekend I had doubts. That Sunday I went running in Rock Creek Park. As was my custom, I concluded by practicing tai chi, a set of exercises derived from the martial arts, a kind of floating meditation. A man in his mid-thirties stopped to watch me. He was James Grady, author of *Three Days of the Condor*. We began to talk. Coincidentally, I had just finished his latest paperback. I told him I was impressed. *Runner in the Street* was compelling and lyrical.

I also told Grady about my political dilemma. I wanted the money, but I didn't like the politics. Spitz, pleasant as he had been, was reactionary and racist. Grady said this policy of arming a guerrilla army could not be successful without strong public support, which did not exist. He was right, but that argument had no impact on me at the time. I did not want to see the Contras in the field indefinitely.

But Grady did increase my doubts and strengthen my resolve to write out my conditions for accepting the money and the job.

Later that night I watched the movie Harvey, starring Jimmy Stewart as a man by the name of Elwood P. Dowd. Dowd lived in his deceased parents' home in a small town with his sister and her daughter. He had once been the town's darling, brilliant, affable, and loved by all. Then he "struggled with reality and overcame it." His constant companion became a pooka, a six-foot tall, invisible rabbit given to jokes and pranks. His sister, fearing that her daughter will never find a husband so long as Elwood always introduces her suitors to "Harvey," has Elwood placed in a sanatorium.

But Dr. Chumly, founder and owner of the sanatorium, has himself seen, talked with, and been spooked by the pooka. So while everyone else believes Dowd to be crazy, Chumly knows better. He explains to Dowd that his sister has drawn up commitment papers, seized Dowd's power of attorney, and that she has the key to his safety deposit box, and has brought him to be locked up. Dowd remarks with wonder at how much his sister has been able to accomplish in just one afternoon. Chumly responds in angry bewilderment:

"Good heavens man! Haven't you any righteous indignation?" Dowd lowers his head and in a confident voice responds: "Oh, doctor, I . . . years ago, my mother used to say to me, she'd say 'In this world, Elwood, you must be'—she always called me Elwood—'in this world, Elwood, you must be oh so smart or oh so pleasant.' For years I was smart. I recommend pleasant."

I had heard it, but I didn't understand a word. I had to be smart, so I wrote out two major conditions. First, Spitz must understand that I would not oppose McCurdy. Second, I would not make reports or submit to supervision. I also asked him to arrange a meeting with Ollie. Spitz accepted these conditions without a murmur. I wanted to go back to work to fashion a new compromise responsive to the McCurdy Democrats, and to good people like Elliott and Bob Kagan in the Administration.

But I was imagining influence I no longer had. Decisions on the new Contra aid package were being made by Republican and Democratic leadership. McCurdy had resumed discussions with the Democratic leadership, sensible meetings. Dave, Howard, and one other McCurdy Democrat on one side, and Democratic caucus chair Tom Foley and Representative David Bonior of the Rules Committee and their staff on the other.

On June 17 the Democratic leadership offered a deal that Dave and his associates could not turn down. A section of the Defense Appropriations Bill was reserved for Contra aid. Humanitarian aid to the Contras and the McCurdy restrictions would be built into that bill without a vote. Military aid could be released only after a second vote in October. While liberals would not be compelled to support economic aid, they would have to support the rule governing debate on Contra aid, which in essence approved it. This new alliance of liberals and moderates would not fall apart until the second vote on military aid in October.

For his part, Dave dropped the condition that the Administration enter into direct negotiations with the Sandinistas. By doing so, he hoped to attract some votes by Republicans who didn't like to compel the Administration to negotiate against its will.

House Republicans took the McCurdy draft and adopted it as their own, except that their legislation did not provide a real second vote. The Republican bill would allow for a second and third vote, but to stop the next installment of aid would require two-thirds majorities in both House and Senate. Under the McCurdy Bill, the simple majority disapproval of either House or Senate would have stopped further aid. And this made all the difference in the world if one believed the Administration would neither promote a negotiated solution nor pursue Contra reform without the pressure of a second vote. It was the only guarantee we had.

In theory, it should not have bothered me to take Spitz's money and support McCurdy. But it did. I needed the money badly. Spitz had promised $26,000. I didn't think I would get the rest if I continued to support McCurdy. But I would not oppose him without his blessing, so I met with him and he gave it.

I then tried to forge a compromise between Dave's bill and the Administration bill. The latter was sponsored by two House Democrats who had worked with Dave in the past, Ike Skelton from Missouri and Richard Ray from Georgia. Richard had been a cosponsor of Dave's legislation in April and was a clear loss.

I wasn't just being opportunistic. I honestly didn't believe that three months was enough time to test Administration policy on reform and negotiations. I was also wary of a vote less than a month before the 1986 midterm congressional elections.

It was June and it was time for my specialty—a letter from the President to Congress. In that letter, I would have the President pledge to abide by a second vote after February 28, 1987, if majorities in both House and Senate opposed further aid.

It was a genuine compromise. McCurdy's bill would have stopped aid if House or Senate objected in October. The Skelton-Edwards bill would never allow Congress to put a stop to aid; the President could and would veto any such a bill, and it would take a two-thirds majority in both House and Senate to overturn. I would have the President promise not to veto a joint resolution, thereby allowing simple majorities in both House and Senate to stop aid. If the two bodies voted to disapprove, the President would promise to use funds to resettle Contra fighters who quit the battle.

On June 18 I was to have my scheduled meeting with Ollie. I prepared the letter the night before. Noncommittally, Ollie told me the letter was good. He then asked why I hadn't come to him earlier, when I had run out of money. "What are friends for?"

Apparently not for approaching the President to ask him to sign my letter. The Administration had the votes they needed and probably already knew it. A decision had been made at the highest level that serious congressional review during the expenditure of the $100 million would not be acceptable.

The Gang of Four had long since ceased to function as it had in the past. Each of us was still working hard, but each in our separate ways. Penn Kemble organized a conference on the Hill with representatives of the internal opposition in Nicaragua. He held a dinner for Violeta Chamorro, the publisher of *La Prensa*, the leading opposition newspaper in Nicaragua. Bob Leiken played a major role in advising Cruz and me during the Contra meetings in Miami. Bernie Aronson topped us all. He wrote the President's speech for the third and final Contra vote in the House in 1986. Though the March speech was strident and unyielding, this one employed measured rhetoric with strong bipartisan overtures, reaching out to Democrats, asking for national unity.

But there was no longer agreement among us. The issues that were important to the McCurdy Democrats, a second vote and a real chance for negotiations, were still primary for me, while aid to the Contras was now secondary. For Bob, Bernie, and Penn, aid had become primary, and they wanted air-defense weapons delivered to the Contras as soon as aid was signed into law.

On June 26 I climbed to the Speaker's Gallery with my other assistant, Eric Singer, and we sat with about twenty anti-Contra activists. Early on it looked like the Skelton-Edwards bill would lose. I was ambivalent, but feeling pretty good. But in the last few minutes of the fifteen-minute vote, Skelton-Edwards surged ahead and never lost its lead.

After the vote I bolted from my seat; taking three steps at a time, I was out of the gallery in an instant. I sought out the McCurdy group, but failed to find them. In reality, I didn't look too hard. I wanted their company but was embarrassed to be with them. Eventually I found Dave in his office. He told me that losing is always difficult, but the bill as passed was okay and he was satisfied. I agreed, though neither one of us really believed his own words. We had too much experience with Administration duplicity.

From Dave's office, I called my answering machine and found a message from Bob Leiken, "Get your ambivalent soul over here. We're at Penn's." I arrived angry and defensive, but the mood was festive and I embraced it. It was the Gang of Four, plus Eric and Bob Kagan. With my money from Spitz, I paid for the pizza. Then Penn called one of his principal donors to tell her we had won, and the sound of that "we" jarred me. I took Bob Kagan aside and told him I didn't like or trust this at all, but that I liked and trusted him. "Do what you can with this, Bob. The only thing I like about this vote is that you will have a chance to try to make Contra reform work."

I met David Horowitz and Peter Collier, former editors of the premier leftist magazine of the late '60s and early '70s, for the first time the next day. In January 1985 they had announced in an article in the *Washington Post Magazine* they had voted for Reagan. At the time, I was rethinking my worldview. Although I did not share their conclusion—that Reagan was what the nation needed—I thought they understood the true nature of the left very well.

I don't remember much about that meeting. As former leftists with second thoughts, we were happy to be together. What they remember is that I was livid with the Administration. I denounced it for having acted in bad faith, for pursuing a stupid policy, for not allowing the necessary corrections Congress wanted. Nonetheless, I maintained that the difference between the McCurdy Group and myself, on the one hand, and the Administration and the rest of the Gang of Four on the other, was a difference of emphasis, not kind. We were still part of one family. But I didn't feel it anymore. ■

CHAPTER SEVEN

SUMMER OF DEFEAT

July–December 1986

I felt defeated. All my efforts, and those of my Nicaraguan colleagues, to reform the Contras had failed. Twice I had traveled to Miami. We claimed victory. But we knew that the FDN still controlled Honduras, that the secretary general of UNO was a Calero ally. Both were riding high, feeling a new sense of power after the vote.

Our efforts to promote a negotiated solution had failed; we had lost the final vote on June 26. The Administration and its allies had used every piece of legislation I had devised, except what was important, the second vote to hold the Administration accountable on reform and negotiations.

Some would argue the second vote was irrelevant with respect to negotiations. The Contadora talks were dead, finished off by the Sandinistas in early June when they refused to make concessions on the size of their army or the weapons they would maintain in their arsenal. This is true, but also irrelevant.

What McCurdy and his colleagues were attempting to do was assert, for the first time, real control over U.S. policy in Central America. Had their legislation been adopted, Contadora would have been resurrected, and the spotlight would have been redirected from what the Sandinistas had just done to what they would do in the months leading up to a second vote. Liberals, moderates, and Central Americans who favored a diplomatic solution would have descended upon Managua to force a revival, and an acceleration of negotiations. Would the Sandinistas have responded? Would they have seen these three months as an opportunity to end, once and for all, the Contra program? It is impossible to know. But what is certain is in that three-month period there would have been intense focus on the willingness of the Administration, the Sandinistas, and the Contras to compromise for the sake of peace. None could have escaped scrutiny, or put up a false front.

But it was not to be. The Sandinistas scuttled Contadora in early June, and the House vote at the end of the month turned into a virtual declaration of war, abandoning the possibility of a compromise. What we could not know at the time was that a time bomb was ticking, and its explosion five months later would create new opportunity. Had I known, life would not have seemed so bleak.

In April I had turned to alcohol. I went to AA for a while, and reduced my drinking; but the Miami trips increased it again. I rationalized that I needed alcohol because the pain in my neck and shoulders had become fearsome. Most days in Miami I would have breakfast with Alfonso, then wait. I would read, then go running in the middle-class neighborhoods surrounding the Airport Holiday Inn. Toward four o'clock I would begin to get antsy, but that was the beginning of the cocktail hour and I could start drinking. All I had to do was sign my name. At night I would meet Carlos Ulvert and Arturo at Arturo's home and drink some more. Often I would have a couple more drinks when I got back to the hotel, sometimes with Alfonso. I would always end the night with one drink alone.

I now believe that my neck and shoulder pain was in part a consequence of my conflicting emotions about the work I was doing. After we lost the final vote, no amount of alcohol could diminish the pain. I blamed myself, I felt responsible. I didn't realize then that the Administration had always had the edge. The Contra resupply operations, paid for by profits from the illegal arms sales to Iran, allowed them to play congressional hardball to defeat the McCurdy plan. They could afford to drop a hand grenade on the April 16 debate, then pick off one moderate after another, until McCurdy had lost his majority. Worst of all, I had helped them.

I gave a memo to Spitz in July. It would eventually be reprinted in the report of the congressional Iran-Contra panel, along with Spitz's deposition. My assistant Eric and I both wrote parts of a memo; therefore reference in the first person alters throughout. Eric's politics were more conservative than mine even when I adjusted for audience. He wrote things I did not agree with and would never say. As I read this memo now, it seems very strange.

Wednesday's 221–209 victory cannot be attributed wholly to last-minute White House lobbying. The groundwork for this vote was being laid over a period of months. In this regard, three events stand out:

1. The Appointment of Ambassador Phillip Habib: Habib had great credibility among House moderates. . . . By mid-June he had been working Central America for over two months; he made the term "good-faith diplomatic effort," and its exhaustion, more meaningful. . . .

2. In May, three weeks of meetings between Arturo Cruz, Alfonso Robelo, and Adolfo Calero, the three principals of UNO, and the FDN directorate. These meetings set in motion a series of [reforms], yet to be tested, that could give more clout to non-FDN forces . . . , establish democratic procedures within UNO and build a credible international image—something the FDN could never do. [Eric noted three Members who had switched their votes because of the reform issue.] . . . [The] modest reforms that were produced, which the Administration said it would encourage, showed that the Administration could make good on its promise. By [the time of the vote] Members who opposed the Administration] could only disingenuously question the reality of UNO reform.

3. The McCurdy congressional delegation . . . in early June. Bruce convinced McCurdy to lead a delegation in early June in the hope of acquainting swing members with the leaders of Central America's new democracies, letting these Members decide for themselves the viability of Contadora. All 13 Members were horrified by the Sandinistas (they met with Daniel Ortega) and recognized them as the real obstacle to peace in Central America. They also recognized that the Central American four—on their own, rather than under Contadora auspices—were the appropriate managers for any Central American treaty. . . .

Four members of the trip switched their votes in favor of military aid to the Contras—Snowe (R-Maine), Bustamante (D-Texas), Rowland (R-Connecticut), and Ray (D-Georgia). Frenzel (R-Minnesota) also switched, reportedly because of influence from Ray and Snowe. I [Bruce] went to Guatemala to ensure that President Cerezo would meet with the Members.

Against this background the Skelton-Edwards proposal, not the McCurdy bill, made more sense. Both proposals established a Bipartisan Commission to monitor negotiations; both called for more accountability of U.S. funds to the resistance, both gave

large sums of economic aid to Central American democracies. The difference turned on a second vote for military aid.
McCurdy's proposed second vote on October 1, 1986 on military
aid was untenable. Few Members wanted to vote on Contra aid
again so close to the November election. The need of the resistance for anti-air defense up front was imperative; its absence in
the McCurdy bill hardly proved an incentive for the Sandinistas
to consider negotiating. . . .

Skelton-Edwards provided both military aid up front and
another vote on additional military aid, including the delivery of
heavy weapons, next February. Essentially, this was the compromise position Bruce and I [Eric] advanced in May, though with
different figures.

In fairness to McCurdy, it should be noted that Skelton-
Edwards attracted votes by taking whole sections of the basic
McCurdy draft. Also McCurdy succeeded in forcing the House
leadership to hold another vote after the President's first request
was defeated in March, and then after the April vote was aborted
by the Republicans.

Seven of the 11 votes that switched after the March 20th vote
did so in large part because of the claimed Contra reforms and
the economic aid for the four Central American democracies sur-
rounded in the bill by rhetoric supporting negotiations.

How could I have signed this memo? I was on their side, the
Administration's, Spitz's, not emotionally, but objectively. They had paid
me, and I had done the work that allowed them to win. After the vote, Spitz
called me at three in the morning from Paris. He felt that I was on his side.
His money would buy me my freedom for the rest of the year, time to figure
out what to do next.

Where Eric was wrong was in suggesting that giving the air defense
weapons to the Contras would encourage the Sandinistas to negotiate. Contadora died soon after the vote and was never resurrected. But
the memo was prescient. It said that the actors to produce an agreement
would be the Central American governments themselves. That was Dave
McCurdy's insight, gained on the trip, and it proved right. The bill's $300
million for the four Central American democracies was in fact the first step

in creating the regional ambience that would make a peace initiative possible. Two more enabling events were yet to come.

But I could not know the future. All I knew was the painful present. I stopped going to the office. Every day I tried to run, sometimes two or three times. And I would practice tai chi. Nothing helped.

The movie of the summer was *Aliens*. Perfect. There could be no doubt who the enemy was, those almost indestructible reptilian creatures with battery acid for blood, who used human bodies to implant eggs from which little aliens could grow. The hero was a heroine, sexy, but not sexual, sensitive and emotional without being quite human. Sigourney Weaver, who played the female lead, Ripley, was dubbed appropriately "Rombolina" because of her physical exploits.

I saw this movie four times, sometimes between running jags. The real world violence that I was part of made no sense; the movie's violence was simple and neat. You could distinguish the good guys from the bad guys and it was important that the good guys won.

Spitz kept on giving me checks from his tax-deductible organization for my organization which was a political lobby. Under law, I could legally accept his contribution, but he could not legally give me these funds. So while I kept his money, I would not spend it, until one of his lawyers approved it, and two months later one did.

At the office I was only going through the motions.

Penn, Bernie, and I attended a meeting at the White House to discuss the upcoming Senate vote on Contra aid. Ollie was there, along with Pat Buchanan. Bernie, Pat, and Ollie did all the talking. I remember they broached the idea of organizing pro-Contra labor workers and leaders to march on West Virginia, to convince Senate minority leader Robert Byrd to switch his vote. They had another plan to change the vote of Senator Dennis DeConcini of Arizona. But that plan was equally tortured and, like the Byrd plan, never carried out. To them it was a public relations issue. The three of them had worked hard on the President's speech; they thought efforts like that would change votes. But the President's speech, while substantial and elegant, did not win one additional vote.

Policy change wins votes. And we had already tested the limits of the Administration; modest Contra reform and more economic aid for Central America was all they were willing to accept. I wanted to point out that Byrd had made it clear in the last Senate vote that only direct negotiations between the United States and Nicaragua would convince him to support Contra aid. But I didn't. To say that was not only to share privileged information, but to reveal that I agreed with Byrd. Ollie had told me that Reagan himself turned down such a deal with Byrd when it was offered in April, because it violated established U.S. policy. We would not negotiate with Angola. We would not negotiate with Cambodia or Vietnam. And we would not negotiate with Afghanistan or the Soviet Union. In each of those countries, the United States was supporting a guerrilla force opposing either the government or an occupation force. We would not negotiate on behalf of the parties (freedom fighters) we were supporting, because that would lend legitimacy to these countries. They had to negotiate agreements with their opponents for themselves.

By the end of Reagan's second term, his Administration had negotiated the withdrawal of Russian troops from Afghanistan through direct negotiations with the Soviet Union and Pakistan. Similarly, negotiations with Angola, Cuba, South Africa, and the Soviet Union led to agreement on elections in Namibia, and a timetable for the withdrawal of Cuban troops from Angola. But such solutions were unthinkable in 1986. The line had been drawn: the front line was Central America.

I also had another meeting with Alan Fiers of the CIA, just a meeting to maintain contact. Alan presented his idea that Marxist-Leninists throughout the world all tended to do the same things because their leaders had attended Patrice Lumumba University in Moscow. It didn't matter whether they spoke Spanish, Portuguese, Vietnamese, or English. Their local histories didn't matter. What mattered was the uniformity of their training in Moscow, and day-to-day guidance from Moscow or Cuba. Alan didn't know Spanish, but he knew the curriculum of Patrice Lumumba University.

For my part, I had given Fiers copies of articles and the transcript of a film that presented in detail the testimony of Colonel Roberto Santivanez. Fiers said it was still under review, he would soon share the CIA conclusions. Then he changed the subject. If there was ever such a review, I never saw its conclusions.

We also touched on two other cases. There was a kidnapping ring in El Salvador, organized by top military officers who ordered their men to impersonate guerrillas and kidnap wealthy Salvadorans for ransom. One of the top leaders of this ring, Colonel Roberto Staben, had been exonerated by the army, President Duarte, and the CIA. Another, a Colonel Zacapa, had fled.

One of the early Contras (later head of counterintelligence) was a Colonel Ricardo Lau. He had been implicated in killings of Hondurans, Salvadorans, and Nicaraguans, some at the behest of the chief of the Honduran army, General Gustavo Alvarez. Fiers told me a CIA investigation had concluded that thirty-five people had been killed under orders from Alvarez. He then surprised me by asking if I knew the whereabouts of either Colonel Lau or Colonel Zacapa. The question was not preposterous, but it caught me off guard, and I fumbled for an answer. I promised to talk to the Nicaraguans and Salvadorans I knew to see if they had any leads.

Fiers and I had one other meeting together, with Elliott and Ollie and the rest of the Gang of Four, Bob, Bernie, and Penn. It was our only meeting together with Alan. Oddly, there was no celebration about restoring military aid after a twenty-month hiatus.

We discussed how military pressure to bring about democracy in Nicaragua might work. Ollie and Alan speculated on scenarios for Sandinista accommodation, either by approaching the Contras (a la Alan Fiers) or by seeking a deal with the United States (a la Ollie). Elliott disagreed. "The Sandinistas are Marxists. They will not negotiate. It won't be a settlement that brings democracy to Nicaragua." His implication was clear. I heard it, but I didn't repeat it or acknowledge it myself. I was on the side of people who favored a policy with which I totally disagreed, thought would not work, believed would lead to the needless deaths of thousands.

In my writings about Central America and the Administration that summer, I now see clarity on the facts but total confusion on policy. Take for instance a small paper titled "Sixteen Theses."

No. 4. The Sandinistas' first priority is consolidation of its totalitarian control in Nicaragua. Its second priority is expansion of the revolution to its neighbors.

It is a conspiracy on a transnational basis—Cuba, the Soviet Union, Nicaragua, and the rest of the Soviet bloc—to spread their system to Nicaragua's neighbors.

No. 11. The transnational character of Marxism-Leninism is not in doubt. The transnational reality of the cooperating efforts of the Guatemalan, Honduran, Nicaraguan (under Somoza), and

Salvadoran armies and intelligence units from the 1950s until the 1980s (including the FDN's counterintelligence unit for Nicaragua in the 1980s) is also not in doubt. They have worked together to repress popular movements, and in certain cases have cooperated in the assassination of each other's left-of-center politicians. There is also no question that U.S. governmental entities in the past have trained and equipped these units, and have in some cases worked directly with the murderers. What is in doubt is the level of cooperation today among these armies in repressing the left and the U.S. role, if any—even by averting its gaze from more hidden horrors.

No. 13. The Reagan Administration rushed headlong into an embrace of the Salvadoran military in 1981 and with the National Guard–led Contras in 1982, as the vehicles to solve those countries' problems.

Congress and the reality in El Salvador forced the Administration to reassess its policy in El Salvador in 1983 and to shift its policy towards greater emphasis on human rights, civilian control, and reform of the military.

Congress alone forced the Administration to rethink its strategy in Nicaragua in 1985 and in 1986.

No. 14. Under Elliott Abrams, the new leadership in the Administration for Latin America is equally, if not more fervently, anti-communist, but also recognizes the necessity of joining its anti-communism with concern for building democracy and protecting human rights.

No. 15. Contadora is a joke, but if the Sandinistas ever desire to negotiate seriously—and it is the Sandinistas who are the obstacle, not the United States—Contadora is the vehicle; the four democracies of Central America are the negotiators.

It is now remarkable to me how consistent I could be about the possibility of negotiations led by Central Americans, but how blind I could be to Elliott's real policy, despite having heard him state it twice.

Our ambassador to Honduras at the time, John Ferch, believed the same thing. He told me that as late as May 1986 he had assured President Azcona that the U.S. had a two-track policy. "I assumed we meant what we said. We wanted pressure so that we could negotiate." Ferch was fired.

"You have to find what makes you happy," Corinne told me one day. "Not the big things in life, but the little ones. And they must be things that are not destructive."

"The beach," I told her, "that makes me happy," and within an hour I was gone.

It was beautiful. Every day I bodysurfed in the ocean for two or three hours. Later I would run. But I was still on edge, and every night I drank.

Corinne knew how to take great pleasure in a simple glass of water after the long ride to my house, in sitting and listening to me prattle or in prattling herself, in baking a loaf of bread; that was enough for a day. Like everyone I know who has found happiness, she had simplified. Her only complication was me. And in the summer of 1986, she had decided that I would never fall in love with her. I have often wished she was right. But when we were finished we were finished, and I wanted to be . . . I don't know what I wanted to be, maybe someone else.

On September 6, I left the past, forswore the future, and flew to Guatemala. I did not know what I was looking for. I only knew I was fleeing my own country. I could not live there anymore.

The Magic of Guatemala: Fall 1986

My only life goals at that time were to learn Spanish and forget politics. I was still having trouble walking without stumbling, but within two weeks I began to regain a sense of body again. In addition to my other physical problems, I had sprained my ankle the week before I left Washington, so I couldn't run. Instead I would swim for at least fifty minutes every day. And every day I attended six hours of Spanish classes. I studied another three or four hours at night.

In my fifth week, I had a terror for a teacher. She didn't let up. She would put a book of cartoons in front of me and tell me to put it into words, Spanish words. She would then read my words back to me, correcting errors, making me list them in my notebook. When I couldn't find a word, she would make me describe it. Every one of those words, she would write down, and I would enter in my notebook. Over and over again. By mid-week, I wanted her dead. But that weekend, sitting in the central park of Antigua, I heard two little girls whisper to their mother, "Gringo!" She and I spent the next two hours talking, in Spanish.

In those days, the most difficult decisions I had to make were where to have dinner and how much time to spend studying the subjunctive. When the Sandinistas shot down a resupply plane (a C123K cargo plane) on October 5, killing three crewmen and landing one in Sandinista custody, I cared, I wondered, but it seemed so far away. That was something to worry about in Washington, not in Central America. With respect to information, Nicaragua is much closer to Washington than it is to Guatemala, only a few hundred miles away.

Bob Kagan visited me that Thursday. He assured me there had been no U.S. involvement in the incident. Although he worked with Ollie, Bob knew nothing about the Enterprise. But even if he had told me the plane was CIA, I don't think I would have cared. We played basketball, halfway up the mountain. We played tennis, with ball boys. The charm of Antigua brought him back another day.

I had become a figure of some controversy at my school. I had hinted at my recent past, but basically I held my tongue. The orientation of the politically active at the school was left, very left, far, far left. Often I talk too much. I am always trying to justify myself. But in Antigua, Guatemala, I enjoyed anonymity. The only things I had to do to justify my existence were to make progress in Spanish and be a good friend to my fellow students. Mostly I succeeded.

I began to understand what it was to live in the moment, to find joy in the way clouds hugged the volcano, in a beer with friends after school, in a quick jog at lunchtime, in haggling over the price of a Guatemalan weaving. When I reached the Spanish subjunctive, I was in heaven. You use the subjunctive when there is doubt about an action or when you have no control over that action. Such a lovely thought.

When I sometimes thought about sex in Antigua, I thought about Corinne. I missed her in other ways, too, and I kept thinking about the happiness she experienced. If I could only understand how she found it maybe I could begin to live in the moment, too. But I didn't understand. And I found my own way to live in the moment. ■

CHAPTER EIGHT

TWO NOVEMBER SURPRISES

After two months, it was time for a break from Spanish. I would return to Guatemala, but I wanted to be home for the 1986 midterm elections. And it was time to look toward the future.

I reentered the United States on the very day the Iran part of the scandal broke. A Lebanese weekly published stories claiming that Oliver North and former National Security Advisor Bud McFarlane had visited Tehran in May, and that the United States was selling arms to the Iranian government.

I was not ready to absorb this, so I ignored it. This was just short of a month after the resupply plane was shot down in Nicaragua. There had been much press speculation about Ollie's involvement in that case. Now Ollie was known to have been involved in Iran. The Nicaragua issue still nagged at reporters and members of Congress. But no one had yet put arms for Iran and Nicaragua together.

I visited Ollie the night before Attorney General Edwin Meese held a press conference that triggered the investigation of the Iran-Contra scandal. Ollie told me and my friend Rob Owen (who had brought me to the National Security Council on another matter) that he expected to become the scapegoat for Iran. But when he talked about the Contras, he expressed faith that the program would continue, well managed by Elliott Abrams.

On my way back from Guatemala, I had had a two-hour layover in Miami during which I was regaled with terrible stories about infighting within the Contra movement by the demoralized resistance staff, supporters of Arturo Cruz. One staffer had been told by an FDN leader that he was a target of the Guatemalan death squads. Another had been warned that the Honduran death squads would get him if he came to do his job in Honduras. These were indirect threats, but they made their point; morale was low among the new Contras.

But I didn't tell that to Ollie. What I felt during our thirty minutes that day was sadness for Ollie. I liked the man. He had opposed reform and negotiations during the first six months of 1986. Still, I liked him.

His energy was infective, and everyone who knew him sensed that energy in one way or another. Some were drawn to him, others repulsed. No one was neutral about Ollie.

But that day, the phones in his office were silent; no one was on hold. It was very strange. Finally Rob and I left, not because Fawn ushered us out, but because there was nothing left to say.

Corinne had called me once while I was in Antigua because she was lonely. She caught me napping, and it wasn't a good conversation. But the call created the expectation that our affair would begin anew when I returned.

She came to my apartment the day after the election. I had a cold, but I was filled with lust. I wanted to make love. She didn't. It didn't feel right to her anymore.

That Friday she was to come to my apartment to go over our proposal one more time, to correct mistakes. I woke early. My passion was greater than ever. But I didn't want it to be a problem, so I dined alone and fantasized about the affair I had had with a woman less than half my age, a woman born after the death of John F. Kennedy. Among men my age (and even those ten years younger), women born after Kennedy's death are considered forbidden. It is a good rule. I should have followed it, as well as certain Commandments, like the sixth.

I was still dressing when Corinne let herself in. When I walked into the living room, I found her lying on the coach—not ready for work, but naked and ready for love. "I changed my mind," she said. She was a witch.

Imperceptibly, but totally, I changed that weekend. I fell in love with Corinne. When I woke up Monday morning, I was amazed by what I was feeling. There is a line that I once transmogrified from the Dick Van Dyke Show, "All your life, you look at a plate and all you see is chopped liver. Then, one day, it's pâté."

We traveled to and from New York for lunch by train. Corinne had been a friend for so long, now she was also my love. It was so easy to be together. On the way back in the train a raincoat covered our laps and our mischievous hands. But nothing could hide our smiles.

When we disembarked I told her I felt as if we were married. In the days that followed, however, she made it clear that our affair was just that and could be no more. We had talked about her coming to Guatemala if I had meetings with Vinicio to discuss our shared representation of Guatemala in Congress. But now I said no. If we had no future, she shouldn't come.

Rob called me on Tuesday, November 25, the day after, to tell me that the President would hold a news conference and Ollie would be fired. Rob and I didn't talk long. Later, another friend called to tell me to turn on the television. It took a while for me to understand what I was hearing, but eventually I understood. Profits from the Iranian arms sales (somewhere between $10 and $30 million) had gone to the Contras. I was surprised, but not stunned.

I wouldn't be enjoying the luxury of anonymity when a few days later I returned to Guatemala. . . . My name surfaced for the first time in the press as a recipient of Spitz Channell's funds. Reporters were trying to link Ollie with Spitz Channell's empire of organizations.

National Public Radio sent a telegram entreating me to call collect. I didn't call. Penn, I called back. He told me I should call *Newsweek*, so I did.

The *Newsweek* reporter told a tale so fanciful that I forget the core. His sidebars included lists of UNO meetings and FDN meetings I allegedly attended. During a single phone call that cost me $120, I explained how I became involved, how it came about that I was funded, and what I had done. Apparently he believed me. No story ran.

I also told my story to Victor Peira, a Guatemalan-American writer. To him, I recounted in detail the stories I had recently heard about FDN threats to Cruz partisans. He said, "The United States should not support thugs. That is a simple and unbreakable rule." At some point I would have to tell my story publicly. He cautioned me: "You must be patient. Wait for the right time and the right reporter."

I left Guatemala on December 23, stopping in Washington only long enough to leave my bags at my apartment, make a few calls, and catch a taxi back to the airport. I then flew to Detroit to spend Christmas with my parents and brother. On Christmas Eve I received a call from John McAward in Boston. The *Boston Globe* had run a story alleging Ollie North had told Spitz Channell to provide funds to an organization run by his friend Rob Owen.

Rob Owen had played a vital role during the period when the Boland Amendment was in full effect. He was Ollie's eyes and ears in Central America, attending the meetings Ollie could not and, at times, passing on military advice and intelligence to the Contras. I had been introduced to him on November 30, 1985, by Chris Arcos, then deputy director of the Nicaraguan Humanitarian Aid Organization of the State Department. Rob was on contract with the organization to help facilitate the delivery of aid to the Contras in Honduras. While Rob was a movement conservative, committed to the Contra cause, he was open to change. Eventually he decided the Contras could not win without fundamental internal change.

Twice after that we met by chance when I was invited to attend conservative functions organized by a friend from the antiwar movement, Rich Pollack. According to the *Boston Globe*, Rob hired me after receiving Spitz's money.

The story was wrong. The second time Rich brought me together with Rob was on February 1, 1986. Spitz had already provided me with $10,000 and had promised $30,000 more. But I had no organization that could take the money, then pay salaries to myself. Rob, on the other hand, had an idle organization and no money. I asked if I could have the organization, and he gave it to me. I insisted he relinquish all ties, since he was already the subject of minor press speculation about his work for Ollie. By Christmas, eleven months later, he was big news. Given all the connections between Ollie, Spitz, and Rob, the *Globe* story seemed to make sense. But it just wasn't true.

Before I left Guatemala I wrote to Ned Crosby, a liberal philanthropist who had funded ADA during my tenure there. Of all my liberal friends, he knew the most about my activities and associates, for the simple reason that he bothered to ask. In a letter after he had visited me in August, Ned had urged me, for my own sake, to quit supporting the Contras. I wrote to him, but I wrote for myself, not for him, so I never sent the letter. In part it reads:

> First, let me say this. On the essential moral question—is it moral to try to pressure the Sandinistas, even by force—I say yes unequivocally. What they have done to their own people, what they have done and would do to their neighbors are not to me questions at issue.
>
> The Sandinistas are venal, power-bent, Marxist-Leninists who by their own choice have tied their fortunes to the Soviet Union. And the Soviets, albeit not in the blitzkrieg fashion of the Nazis, are an expansionist power. They work subtly through an ideology of liberation, which is not liberation, through talk of peace which sometimes is genuine, sometimes not, through

terror usually applied by surrogates, through an international network of all the above which is sometimes directed by Moscow, sometimes not, but all these elements taken together form a system for domination.

On the other hand I am extremely disturbed by the way the United States confronts this challenge. I am not particularly disturbed by what Ollie is alleged to have done, that is, I am not disturbed by the results in the region. But I feel that what he has done is a great tragedy for our democracy.

What is to me most troubling is the arrogance and stupidity of the Reagan Administration. With respect to the Contras, there was their premature formation of the Contras, the choice of the National Guard-led Fifteenth-of-September Legion as the base, its defense of the FDN as "freedom fighters," whose leadership think and act like Mafiosi. With respect to El Salvador, it is their seemingly endless tolerance of Salvadoran officers who are killers and corrupters, even when other Salvadorans officers would like to rid themselves of such vermin. With respect to negotiations, it is the Administration's inability to prove to me and other Democrats that they have allowed the Contadora process to succeed or fail; Administration officials simply act to block it, so we don't know if it can or cannot succeed.

But I am also sick of the left, who use Contadora as a mantra to fend off the troubling questions of who are the Sandinistas, who are their patrons, and what are their intentions for their people and their neighbors.

To be sure I despair. I see few in this debate who care for the truth, few who seek to find a consensus policy that is good for us and good for the Central Americans.

I am plagued by my own doubts, my lack of home and wife, and my continuing ill health. I must get out. I know that. But I don't know how.

In this way I left 1986 behind. ■

CHAPTER NINE

PROPOSALS, PLANS, AND RESIGNATION

January–March 1987

The year 1987 was "the worst year of my life." When I first wrote these words in an early fragment of what would become this book, I believed them. But 1987 was also the best year of my life.

I had been frightened before, felt panic before. Despair, hopelessness, they were old friends. But in 1987, these old companions turned into new devils that sought my immediate ruin.

In that year things happened, many things happened, things didn't stop happening. Events often drove me deep into despair, and I nursed that despair with large doses of scotch. But enough events can also provoke action.

And then for a while, there was love as if for the first time. In 1987 I would soar; there were no barriers to lust, passion, and exhilaration. And there were no depths below which I would not plummet.

Life in January assumed a fast pace. Elizabeth Drew wrote this in the *New Yorker* about the unfolding scandal of Iran-Contragate:

> Among the mysteries that remain as of now are who did handle the money, whose money it was, how much money there was, and where it went.
>
> This is a most complicated, tangled story: each disclosure raises new questions, new figures keep being introduced, and even the most diligent people here find it hard to keep it all straight.

I was one of those figures, albeit a minor one. The specter of Ollie loomed large, but the American public did not know and would not know for months that he and others had created a separate nongovernmental entity (the Enterprise), which had both directed a Contra resupply operation, and conducted the sale of arms to Iran and negotiations with Iranian government officials.

Rich Miller and Spitz Channell had already been linked to Ollie in the press. And reporters had linked me to them. But it was not yet known that Rich and Spitz had raised and diverted funds to an account in Geneva (Lake Resources), controlled by Richard Secord and Albert Hakim, who, together with Ollie, decided how the money was to be spent.

I had expected to have more time to decide how to respond to the press. In the first full week of 1987, James LeMoyne of the *New York Times* came to visit. There are few people I trust more than James on questions of Central America.

From previous interviews James had learned Spitz had given money to UNO's Washington office. He also knew Spitz had given money to Arturo Sr., but Arturo's name was not given to James on the record. Arturo knew only what I knew, what Ollie had told us, that the money to support Arturo would come from a "foreign source." No one, including myself, would confirm on the record that Arturo was the "senior Nicaraguan rebel leader" who had received a stipend. So James had a story, but he wanted the rest.

"What was your relationship with Spitz? All of it!" he demanded.

Today I am amazed at how frightened I was then, how reluctant to answer such a simple question, the answer to which was plain in both House and Senate. Lobbyists are required to file their receipts and expenditures for legislative activities every three months. This I did, and still do today, in relation to my work with Nicaragua.

I had nothing to hide, but in my conversations with James I tried anyway. Eventually I told him about the money Penn had received. He then wrote:

> Mr. Channell provided money to two lobbying groups that have strongly supported aid to the Contras, according to officials of the lobbying groups.
>
> Two organizations controlled by Mr. Channell gave $66,000 to a pro-Contra lobbying group initially known as the Council for Democracy, Education and Assistance, according to the head of the organization, Bruce P. Cameron. The group's name was changed later to the Center for Democracy in the Americas.
>
> Mr. Cameron said he reported the payments from Mr. Channell, as required by law, and spent the money to lobby for congressional support of renewed assistance to the Contras.

This reads to me now like a lawyer's brief, with none of the agony I experienced during that week of conversations with James. But this was also, as I charged at the time, "inaccurate." I did not spend most of the money to lobby Congress. Much more time, salaries, and expenses were spent in meetings and writing memos to promote Contra reform. In fact, because of our repeated failures, I hesitated to lobby. And, my organization did not, I insisted, "strongly support . . . aid to the Contras."

James wrote: "Mr. Channell also gave an undisclosed amount of money to PRODEMCA, another pro-Contra lobbying organization in Washington, according to Penn Kemble, a member of the executive committee of the group." James knew from other sources that I had received funds, but he had known nothing about Penn and PRODEMCA. For this, I was his source. "He got the information from other sources," I lied to Penn when he confronted me.

How do I explain that lie? Certainly I believed we had to be accountable. Technically the funds we had received from Spitz were private funds, but he never would have raised them without the help of President Reagan and Oliver North. To me it was still "government money." The public had a right to know who received it and how it was used.

Perhaps that thought was admirable. But it was far from admirable that I lied to Penn about my being the source. Later all of Penn's records were subpoenaed; he became the target of a major investigation by the House Iran-Contra panel. In time he became my only ally in the Gang of Four on the question of being open with the press. But in the terror of the early days of the scandal, I could not tell him that I was responsible for his first exposure in the press. His death in 2005 prevents me from ever coming clean with him.

Corinne was waiting for me when I returned. We began as though things were normal—an odd choice of words—as though it was understood we would try to rebuild my organization, she would help me think through my position on Contra aid, and we would continue our relationship without talking about the future. That plan lasted about half an hour.

One day Corinne came to work clearly agitated. "Please, I need you to hold me."

"What happened?" Then it was only a question. Later, even today, I might ask, "What happened?" trembling and fearing the worst. But at that time I was not yet accustomed to the worst. For ten years, long after I saw

Corinne for the last time, and long after I stopped fearing the Iran-Contra investigations, I remained afraid. At odd times, my body would thrash around for no apparent reason. I never knew when to expect the next nightmare in which I was chased and would wake up just in time to forestall my own death. And there were times when I would simply mute my answering machine and the ringer on the phone, only to stare at the phone when the answering machine clicked on and the red light went off. Someone was there but I didn't want to know who. On the other hand, when the phone rang when I wasn't expecting a call, I would lunge for the receiver, expecting it might be Corinne. It never was.

What had happened to Corrine this instance? Corinne had told a friend in New England about us and the friend had written a letter referring to Corinne's relationship with "B." Corinne said she tore up the letter and put it in the trash. But her husband still found it, "by accident," he said.

"No," I said to her request to be held. She sat on the couch. I sank deeper into my La-Z-Boy. "Are you prepared to do anything about it, to tell him?" I demanded.

"I can't," she replied, imploring.

"Then I shouldn't hold you. I shouldn't touch you. Corinne, are you sure? What did he say? What did you say?"

"He showed me the letter and asked what it meant. I told him that you thought that you were in love with me."

"Is that all? It was your opportunity."

"I couldn't."

"Don't you know what this means? We have to stop."

But we made love one last time. We made love one last time so many times.

The weekend was horrible for me. I was miserable. I was crazy. I didn't know what to do. I couldn't do anything.

That following Monday I went out. Perhaps I went to the bank, perhaps I went to talk with Rich Miller whose office was just off Dupont Circle.

On my way back I saw a woman who looked like Corinne. I was in the middle of the circle. Washington is filled with them, the convergence of streets with state names, numbers, or letters, in this case "Massachusetts," "New Hampshire," "P," and "19th." In the middle of the circle is a small park, once a meeting place for hippies and antiwar protesters. Everyone uses Dupont Circle as the place to begin a march of protest. I began mine.

I followed her and her companion. One block off the circle, at 18th and Massachusetts, I knew it was she. Deliberately I invaded their space. She introduced me to her friend.

We walked back to my apartment, just five blocks away. Her car was there. I don't know if she planned to see me or why she was downtown. It didn't matter—we were desperately glad to see each other.

Her weekend had been as miserable as mine. She couldn't believe that "we" were over, because she still couldn't see our beginning. We made no plans, we hardly touched. But we smiled and parted, in front of my apartment, together again.

I had to make a decision about the Contras. My good friend Bob Kagan offered to have Elliott write or call the right-wing foundations to which I had applied for support. "No," I responded. "I cannot be beholden to anyone. If they support me, fine. If they don't, fine. But I need to figure out what I am, what I support by myself."

That following Monday, Arturo Cruz Sr. was in town to tell me what he was thinking and planning. Arturo had stories to tell. Stories of his trip to Honduras where he, a Contra leader, found that FDN goons had warned Nicaraguan refugees that he was a communist, that people who talked with him would face fierce reprisals.

There was much more, and Arturo was furious. "The reforms are not working. They are blocked at every turn by the FDN clique." He named fourteen people, including Aristides and Enrique Sanchez, and Adolfo and Mario Calero, and their representative in Washington, Bosco Mantomoros. "The FDN clique has captured control of the Assembly. The Secretariat is not functioning; it is blocked at every turn by the clique."

The Assembly had been created in the summer of 1986 following the June reforms. Arturo believed that through payoffs and the careful seduction of select Assembly members (bringing them to the FDN Contra camps in Honduras, giving them red carpet treatment, complete with wine, women, and the sight of Nicaraguan peasants marching with guns), Adolfo had won a majority of the Assembly to his side.

The reforms had created a secretariat under the direction of UNO leadership. Arturo had succeeded in appointing his people to the political, diplomatic, and military sections. But the heads of "the political and diplomatic sections had both been threatened by members of the 'clique'" the previous fall. The Washington representative of UNO was also systematically undermined by the clique's representative, Bosco Mantomoros.

The clique was made up of men within the FDN who controlled the finances and controlled access to the troops, and monopolized contact with the CIA. In response, Arturo had created his own political group, *Action Democratica*, to mobilize and enlist the support of exiled Nicaraguans in Costa Rica, Honduras, and the United States. His trip to Honduras was to meet with local activists and enlist others.

In response to Action Democratica, the clique had created FODENIC (Fomento Democratico Nicaraguense). Two activists from FODENIC had preceded Arturo to every location he visited in Honduras. At San Marcos de Colon, they told refugees Cruz was a *piricuaco* (a rabid dog), a term used to refer to Sandinistas. They called Cruz an enemy of the Contras. Anyone who met with him would be considered an enemy and face serious consequences. Cruz learned that every thirty days the refugees were required to pay a dollar to the clique in order to remain in Honduras. In El Triumfo, the same two from FODENIC attempted to lead a crowd in chanting: "Kill Cruz, kill Cruz, he's a mad dog Sandinista."

Cruz also reported that he found FDN members who were disgusted with the behavior of the clique. One member of the FDN directorate told him the clique represented "a return to the past," meaning rule in the Somoza fashion, with power in the hands of a small group using terror to repress its opponents.

What we Americans knew at the time was actually just the tip of the iceberg. Accounts of atrocities committed by Contras inside Nicaragua had been told and retold since the beginning of the movement. What neither Cruz, nor I, nor many others knew at the time was that there had been a pattern of ongoing grisly human rights violations committed inside the Contra camps themselves. Michael Massing, in a December 19, 1991, review of Sam Dillon's book, *Commandos: The CIA and Nicaragua's Contra Rebels*, succinctly summarized Sam's findings:

> The Agency was equally unconcerned about the disturbing developments inside the Contra camps. Dillon shows that, while international attention was concentrated on abuses committed inside Nicaragua, far worse ones were taking place across the border. In 1983, he writes, as the war widened in Nicaragua, a "second

front" opened in Honduras, "a largely silent, secret campaign of torture and murder. Hundreds died in and around the rebels' border camps, along Honduran roadsides, and in the back streets of Tegucigalpa. It was a dirty war waged largely by the ex-National Guardsmen commanding the contra army." . . .

"In and around the base camps, there were murders of prisoners and recruits, murders of suspected spies and confirmed rivals, murders of rejected lovers and personal enemies," Dillon reports. Virtually every FDN camp had "its teams of assassins, its clandestine graveyards, its dark stories."

Massing then briefly described the reorganization of the Contras in 1985, leading to the formation of UNO. He noted that Arturo Cruz, a respected liberal committed to human rights, gave reassurance to wavering members of Congress that genuine reform would take place.

Inside the Contra camps, however, the violence continued. "Bermudez's ex-Guardsmen were brutalizing young fighters—especially young women— with the same ferocity as ever," Dillon reports. What's more, he writes, U.S. officials "were working in closer coordination than ever with the ugliest aspect of rebel operations." While there is no evidence that the Americans actually participated in any torture, Dillon writes, the CIA, when faced with evidence of rebel excesses, simply looked the other way.

Later, in 1987, Cruz was angered to the core. He had never easily accepted the fact, but he knew that without him Contra aid would not have passed in 1985 and '86. Yet he was being treated like an enemy. He even heard reports that Calero had told FDN soldiers that he, Cruz, had opposed the aid.

Anger brought clarity. Cruz knew what would have to change for him to continue to support the Contras. The Contra leadership must present a plan for the future. In this, two things were vital. First, the Contras must seek OAU supervised elections in Nicaragua as a way to end the war. Second, they must announce that, should they win by force of arms, the Contra leadership would invite a peacekeeping force to disarm combatants, including their own.

In January 1987, both of these ideas seemed a little farfetched. Today, one observes with some wonder that the OAS did oversee the February 25, 1990, elections, and that both United Nations and OAS helped to disarm and relocate Contra soldiers in the years that followed.[22]

Arturo was also right about Costa Rica. He was bothered by continued U.S. pressure on the Costa Rican government to support the U.S. vision of how to promote democracy in Nicaragua. Specifically, the U.S. pressed Costa Rica to allow the Contras free reign, and to allow Costa Rican territory to be used to resupply Contras inside Nicaragua. Ollie North, in a September 1986 memo to National Security Advisor John Poindexter, wrote that he had personally phoned President Oscar Arias to insist that he rescind his order to close the Enterprise airstrip at Santa Elena. Arias did withdraw his order, then two weeks later he closed the airstrip anyway. But Ollie's report was another lie; he didn't actually call Arias. It was the U.S. ambassador's intervention that stalled the order, and only for a moment.

Arturo was only aware of the pressure on Costa Rica. As a Central American who dreamed one day of real independence for Nicaragua, he resented the pressure, even though it was intended to support his cause. He wanted guarantees that the United States would respect Costa Rican neutrality.

Then, without acknowledging any apparent contradiction, he turned to the question of the Nicaraguan Contras who used Costa Rica as a base. They were not getting any of the supplies that had been approved the previous October, while the FDN was receiving massive amounts, according to Arturo.

Arturo was furious that heads of the UNO commissions created during the June 1986 reforms were being undermined—Wicho Rivas, head of the military commission, Carlos Ulvert, head of the international commission, Alfonso Sandino, head of the political commission, and Ernesto Palazio, UNO's Washington representative. All were Cruz appointees, and all were blocked in the performance of their duties by the clique. Wicho was not allowed to visit the Honduran front. Carlos was told he would be killed if he went to Guatemala. Alfonso was told he would be killed if he went to Honduras, site of the largest concentration of Nicaraguan refugees. Ernesto Palazio had to compete with Bosco Mantomoros, the clique's Washington representative. Bosco clearly had superior contacts in the field, but spent his time trying to undermine anyone who challenged the clique—by spreading (often sexual) rumors to the press.

Arturo ended our discussion by saying, "Wicho must become Supreme Commander of all military forces, and parallel representation by the clique must end. We must change. Decision-making is a laughing matter. Pluralism is a laughing matter."

Tentatively, I told him I didn't think he could succeed. His ideas were sound, but I no longer believed we could force the Administration to support reform.

On the following day I made my decision: I was "out." It was that important, like leaving a secret men's club, a Mafia, like leaving a marriage. In fact, the relationships I had built that year would last a lifetime. But at the time I had to choose that they were not more important than my duty to myself.

Ed King, a consultant to new Senate majority leader Robert Byrd, came to visit me. He was convinced that the time for negotiations was ripe. The Sandinistas would make concessions on the issue of democracy. Ed had visited Oscar Arias in Costa Rica in December, and had received early knowledge of Arias's plan for peace. The logic was simple: the Contras could not defeat the Sandinistas, but a united front of Western democracies could force the Sandinistas to make real concessions on pluralism and democracy, as long as Contra aid was stopped.

I had already ended my relationship with the Administration because of its unwillingness to confront and overcome the thuggery of the clique. Now I saw a formula for negotiations that might achieve our goals for democracy in Nicaragua.

That same week, the *Miami Herald* reported some details:

The Costa Rican leader said Wednesday that his proposed timetable for democratization in Nicaragua would start with an amnesty law and a ceasefire between government and rebel troops. Arias said the process would end with new national elections, possibly at the end of President Daniel Ortega's five-year term.

A crucial part of the Arias formula was that negotiations about democracy and national reconciliation would be conducted by the government and the internal opposition, not the rebel force (in Nicaragua's case, the Contras). This idea was by no means unique. Arturo Cruz had been the first person, the first Contra leader, to give it currency (during the debate on the $100 million U.S. aid package the year before).

I arranged for Arturo and Alfonso to each meet with the McCurdy Group separately. I remember just three things about their meetings.

In the meeting with Alfonso, Representative John Spratt was clear and direct. John has a tendency to agonize over controversial questions. Before the first vote on military aid in 1986, he could not make up his mind. He stewed, and hashed and rehashed the issue with his staff right up to the time of the vote. He even flipped a coin, but the coin did not determine his vote. He finally decided to oppose the President's package.

But John was not indecisive this time. "Alfonso, you have got to realize that it is no longer a question of settling for second best. Now you will have to settle for third, fourth, or even fifth best."[23]

Representative Richard Ray, a stalwart Democratic supporter of the Contras, told Arturo: "The situation is very discouraging. I think Calero should have been gone a long time ago. I think it will be very hard to get additional aid, and maybe we should begin to think about shutting down the program. I am sorry to say this, but I must. Calero says what he says for the convenience of the moment. He has too many warts."

In response to one member, Arturo said: "But Mr. Habib is very good." (Philip Habib was the President's negotiator whose assignment was to explore possible diplomatic outcomes.) "Yes," responded the member. "But we haven't seen much of him recently. They only send him around when there's a vote."

None of them mentioned the Arias proposal; it was too fresh. But everyone in those meetings revealed a willingness to support something new.

Shortly after the meetings, Arturo removed all his belongings from the UNO headquarters in Miami. Suddenly everything he said or did was news. Two days later, he was in Washington to tell Elliott Abrams that he would resign. Elliott asked only that he be given enough time to argue that Cruz's resignation would not injure Contra chances in Congress. Cruz agreed. But his agreement to keep silent became meaningless; suddenly he was conspicuous in newspapers in the United States.

From the *Miami Herald*, on January 30:

[Cruz] remembers visiting Contra troops in Central America and being introduced as a "guest of the FDN," not as one of the three UNO co-leaders. He remembers an article depicting him and Robelo as the 'true enemies' of a free Nicaragua. . . .

Cruz's presence in [the Contra ranks] gave credence to the anti-Sandinista coalition's democratic credentials. His departure will impair the movement's credibility, particularly with Congress and Social Democrats throughout the world.

From the *Washington Post*, on February 4:

An agreement on internal reforms that kept Cruz in UNO during a similar disagreement last May "was all window dressing. Nothing was done," McCurdy said. "When he leaves, they might as well kiss good-bye to aid [in Congress]."

From a *New York Times* editorial, on February 10:

Mr. Cruz, a left-of-center democrat, carried the most weight. Yet now, he seems ready to break with other Nicaraguan rebel leaders. Without him, the Contras lose much of their political credibility.

From the *Los Angeles Times*, on February 15:

The two factions also differed over what the Contras basic strategy should be: Calero and his organization, the Nicaraguan Democratic Force, aimed at overthrowing Nicaragua's Marxist-led Sandinista regime by force, while Cruz and Robelo, both of whom served with the Sandinistas in coalition governments, put more emphasis on negotiations with the regime. . . .

Abrams publicly appealed to Cruz to stay, praising him as a "symbol of the Contras' commitment to democracy."

Elliott's words were repeatedly reprinted:

There is no single leader that has more credibility than Arturo Cruz, certainly in this country and I would say in Nicaragua. Nobody is irreplaceable, but he comes as close as you can get.

Before he had his second meeting with Elliott on January 30, I spent several days with Arturo and his wife in Miami. On the night I arrived, he gave me this speech:

My wife and I have decided to call it quits. Any other decision would be a sacrifice of our feelings and the frustrations we have already suffered.

I am still wrestling with how to tell Elliott. It is difficult, because in part I am acting out of bitterness. But I will tell him that I will wait to give him time to implement reforms. I would even wait two months, but I will make no more public appearances for UNO.

I reaffirm the justice of our cause, the authenticity of our fighters, and their democratic aspirations. Then why am I leaving?

I do not believe in low-intensity warfare.[24] I cannot take the practices of the clique anymore. I will not fight for a free Nicaragua only to see the Sandinistas replaced by yet another tyranny.

I congratulated him on becoming a free man. I told him I had made the same decision ten days before, and freedom felt wonderful. Arturo spoke more the next day when he gave me a set of messages for Alfonso:

You must initiate the proposal for a peace-keeping force. All finances must be centrally controlled. Wicho Rivas must become Minister of Defense. The Southern Front must become a reality. It is the litmus test of the Administration's intentions. If it does not become a reality, it means the Administration has decided that the FDN and the National Guard are the future.

All partisan political activities by groups within UNO must be frozen so that UNO can be the sole political force. It was a mistake to give the Assembly precedence over the Directorate, and that must change. The Directorate must not be enlarged.

There must be a real peace initiative. The clique must be put in its place.

I met with Alfonso to give him Arturo's message. I was the medium of communication; they would not meet together. Alfonso seemed equally discouraged, but he was not prepared to resign.

I returned to Washington with Arturo and his wife, and we went directly to a meeting with Elliott. Arturo began by reaffirming his desire to resign. Elliott responded by saying that while he had accepted Arturo's earlier decision to leave, he could no longer do so. Arturo had become indispensable. The Congress and the media had made him the symbol of all that was decent and democratic in the Contras. "You cannot quit, Arturo. You must stay."

Though this was a major meeting, I cannot remember many details. I remember neither Arturo nor myself objecting. In fact, Arturo left agreeing to reconsider. Elliott asked him to provide a list of the reforms he believed to be necessary.

Bob Leiken was closer to Arturo than I was, but he didn't want him to resign. He wanted to use his threat of resignation as a way to pressure for reform. But Bob did not know Alfonso well. He asked me to arrange a meeting with him that night. This was an easy meeting to arrange, as Alfonso had originated the term "Gang of Four," and he believed that our group was responsible for pressuring the Administration to achieve the 1986 reforms.

Alfonso reported on his meeting with the new National Security Advisor Frank Carlucci, who had visited him in Costa Rica. Carlucci said he wanted a new directorate formed by 100 Nicaraguan exiled notables who would choose eleven new members. Alfonso dismissed the proposal with a wave of his hand. "Carlucci is completely out of his element; he is an irrelevancy." Events began to move quickly.

At ten o'clock the next morning Ernesto Palazio, Carlos Ulvert, and Arturo Cruz Jr. gathered in my living room to put on paper some of our demands for reform. In my basement were two men from the Internal Revenue Service. They were there to go over papers to determine whether I had violated the tax-exempt status of my organization. Between ten and three I shuttled back and forth between my apartment and the basement. Then the IRS left with a promise to get back to me with more questions. We happy few liberal Contras left for the State Department to discuss some of our ideas with Elliott.

I was home at around 6:00 P.M., exhausted. At 6:30 I turned on the ABC nightly news, something I seldom did. ABC was reporting a new break in the Iran-Contra scandal: Jane McLaughlin, who had worked for Spitz Channell, had gone to the network with purloined documents, and stories to tell. The biggest story was that one of Spitz's accounts, the "Toys" account, was really a fund to supply arms to the Contras (with playthings indeed, but not for children).

While introducing the story, various pictures of Ollie North and his associates flashed across the screen. Among these there was a picture of Ollie and me. It was only there for a second, but in that second every organ tried to jump from my body. First I felt drained and exhausted, then I felt full-scale panic. I hit the phones and the phones hit me back. I was surprised to learn how many people actually watch the ABC Nightly News.

The next night Arturo came by my apartment with the same group of liberal Contras. He arrived late, but happy for the first time in many years.

"I saw green pastures today. I can feel clean again." He proceeded to describe a dinner he had with an American businessman who gave him some ideas about work he might find in the private sector. In reality, that man could do nothing for Arturo, and Arturo knew that. But just the idea of being free had brought him to life again.

That night Arturo would not discuss any of our many proposals. He wanted us to listen to him, and listen we did, for three hours. First he talked about his anger at the Administration, and at himself.

> You [he meant the Administration, all Americans, but I was the only one present to represent them] have given nine rocket launchers [that could be used to shoot down Sandinista helicopters] to the FDN and not one to the Southern Front or the Indians.
>
> Naio [the executive director of UNO] agreed to pay me a salary. But he had to check with the "allies" [he meant the CIA, sometimes called the Jesuits, when one was feeling playful and a little contemptuous, or the allies when one wanted to convey anger and a sense of irony] and the allies said no.
>
> And I found out it was Casey, himself, who informed the Intelligence Committees [in 1985] that I had received CIA money.
>
> I look at myself in the mirror, and I don't like what I see.
>
> If I had a dime's worth of credibility in 1985, I don't have a penny's worth today.

What was most on Arturo's mind was the past, what he saw as his constant failures, all of which were due, he insisted, to those times when he heeded his mind and not his heart.

In 1977, Arturo had been asked to join the Group of Twelve, a dozen intellectuals and other men of stature united to oppose the Somoza dictatorship. It was right, he thought. We could bear witness to the horrors of Somoza and have an impact on world opinion. But he sensed that some of the others were communists, their agenda not his agenda, and not the agenda they proclaimed. Nevertheless, Arturo overcame his doubts and joined. By 1979, most of the group had revealed themselves to be members of or collaborators with the Sandinista Front.

In San Jose, Costa Rica, in 1979, as Somoza's government was disintegrating, Arturo and other real democrats met with the Sandinistas to work out a common program and a new ruling junta. He recalled one moment when Violeta Chamorro and he were going down some steps. She stopped him. "Don Arturo," she began. "This is not right. We cannot trust the Sandinistas. I shouldn't join them. It won't work." Violeta Chamorro and Alfonso Robelo were to become the only two democrats in the five-member junta.

Arturo responded, "They're young. We must give them a chance." But in his heart, he wanted to tell her, "Yes, you are right. We will go to Tomas Borge (a Sandinista leader) and tell him no. We will have no part of this. We will flee this place." But Arturo did not listen to his heart.

Only three days after they returned to Nicaragua with the Sandinistas in triumph, to begin a new government, Alfonso had come to Arturo and said, "This won't fly." But neither man did anything.

Finally, in 1981, Arturo did leave the government. Only then did he feel free to speak his mind. But in 1984, a delegation came to him and asked him to run for president. Yes, he thought, though his heart told him to wait until the Sandinistas had made all the concessions necessary for a genuinely free election. Despite his misgivings (and despite the fact that his conditions had not been met), he left his job at the Inter-American Development Bank and pursued his candidacy. In the end, he did not run. Later he regretted that he had not. But what bothered him most that night in my apartment was that he could have ended his gradual movement into the Contras before it had begun—by saying no to the delegation. He had not done so.

Then Arturo told the oddest story of all. After the elections took place (without him) and the Sandinistas had won, he said, he wrote that Daniel Ortega should be given breathing room, time to determine whether he would be president of Nicaragua or president of the Sandinista Front. Shortly thereafter, the Sandinistas reimposed censorship and began to limit the travel of opposition politicians.

Arturo felt betrayed again, and he was in a quandary, being urged to support and join the Contras. He didn't want to, but the pressure from one American organization was unrelenting. He refused to name the organization. I said, "Come on, Arturo. It's obvious. It has to have been PRODEMCA." It was a full year later that he told me the pressure had come from Penn, William Doherty of the American Institute for Free Labor Development, and Mary Temple, executive director of PRODEMCA in New York. They argued that after the elections and crackdown, peaceful alternatives were nonexistent; the Contras were the only option. Arturo understood their arguments, they were logical enough, but again his heart said no. In early January 1985, he participated in a press conference to inaugurate PRODEMCA, and announced his support for the Contras.

But that was the past, he now insisted. He would now listen to his heart, and it wanted out. Still, he made no clear decision before he returned to Miami. The rest of us continued writing up a reform program, a compilation of all the demands that Arturo himself had outlined since his return from Honduras.

What we did not know until the next day was that Elliott had already met with Adolfo Calero. Elliott did not try to convince Adolfo to resign, but he made it unmistakably clear that Contra political fortunes in the United States could not afford Arturo's resignation in the climate of the Iran-Contra scandals.

That Sunday the president of every Central American country except Nicaragua met in Costa Rica to consider Arias's proposal. The formula remained the same: in exchange for an end to insurgencies, governments would grant amnesty and begin a process of national reconciliation leading to elections. The four presidents did not sign the ten-point agreement, but agreed to discuss the proposal at a summer meeting to be held in Guatemala.

Three American senators were also present: one liberal Democrat, Chris Dodd of Connecticut, one moderate Democrat, Terry Sanford of North Carolina, and one conservative Republican, Paul Trible of Virginia. All saw the plan as an alternative to a policy of overthrow. Trible referred to the need for a two-track policy, and said the Arias formula could offer the second track of negotiations. His message was directed at the Administration.

The Sandinistas were not invited to the meeting; they had already announced their opposition to the Arias plan. They perceived the plan and the meeting as ways to isolate them, and to undermine the Contadora process. In one sense, they were right. Contadora placed emphasis on regional military issues and shunted democracy to the side. The Arias formula reversed this.

On the same day, word leaked out that Adolfo would resign his position as director of UNO, while retaining his position as president of FDN. The next day he did so, nominating Pedro Joaquin Chamorro, son of the martyred newspaper publisher and his wife Violeta, as his replacement.

Now Arturo was trapped. There was no way he could leave. And there was an immediate backlash among Calero supporters. One told the *Washington Times*: "We were being blackmailed by Cruz. He wanted some kind of power. He wanted an opportunity to negotiate with the Sandinistas."

Adolfo had said he thought the directorate should be expanded to five or seven members. Elliott said that in addition to reform, there should be an expansion of the directorate. Adolfo suggested he might return as a new member of an expanded directorate. And he finally endorsed the idea of merging all the Contra organizations, including the FDN, into a single force.

Another rebel leader told the *Washington Times*: "I think Calero laid a careful trap for Cruz and Robelo. It leaves them in a polarized position vis-a-vis the Nicaraguan exiles in general. And it leaves them in a very, very polarized position regarding the troops in the field."

FDN sources also began circulating a plan for a new directorate. It would have seven members, one each from the Liberal, Conservative, Christian Democratic, and Social Democratic parties in exile, one from labor, one from among the Indians, and one from the Southern Opposition Bloc (BOS). Calero could easily regain his seat as the Conservative Party representative, while Cruz, Robelo, and the new Directorate member, Chamorro, all represented the Social Democratic tendency.

Surprisingly, opposition to Calero's resignation came from BOS. BOS, in theory, represented the most liberal of the Contras, under the leadership of Alfredo Cesar. BOS's criticism of the FDN and Calero's leadership was the same as ours. They knew the same members of Congress and were sensitive to the same streams of international opinion, especially the

Social Democrats. Cesar's chief deputy, Alvaro Jerez, called to tell me that Cruz's resignation was urgent if the reforms BOS contemplated were to be implemented.

But in this case, family was more important than politics. Cesar and Calero were related through their wives, who were cousins; they had been negotiating for some months. What motivated Cesar was the desire to be the premier liberal Contra. Cruz was competition. Calero was not, and the family connection made negotiations between them easier. Cesar was also close to the CIA. He could make a deal with Adolfo, replace Arturo as the bright shining liberal light of the Contras, and please the Administration, too. Arturo had to be disposed of.

That was not my deal. My commitment was to Arturo. I thought he should leave, but if he stayed I would try to help him get the best deal he could. I even suggested that once he was firmly back in the organization, we should work out a formal relationship by which I could assist him.

I had worked with Arturo's aides for the last month, trying to put his proposals on paper. And Arturo was speaking to the press. He told James LeMoyne of the *New York Times* that he "contemplated . . . a new, expanded civilian directorate with complete control of the movement's funds; the forced retirement of several far-right rebel officials; and integration of the main rebel army in Honduras into a new overall insurgent force headed by civilian officials and under an expanded military command."

Arturo planned to announce his decision to stay in the movement at a press conference at the Carnegie Endowment on February 19. But he had never actually made a firm decision. There was just the time in which he said he was resigning and the time he was not, with nothing in between. His aides and I scrambled to put on paper all his demands before he went to meet with Elliott Abrams to announce his nondecision to stay.

At the last moment, Arturo refused to take any of our papers—even the one written the night before, reducing his demands to two. Instead, Arturo proposed to tell Elliott his needs in person. They were two: First, the Assembly had to be dissolved and a group of Nicaraguan lawyers appointed to make recommendations on how to create a new Assembly. Second, Enrique Bermudez must come to Miami and explain to the civilian directorate his statements to a PBS camera crew in 1985 deriding the UNO agreement.

All of us were dumbfounded as we sat listening to this in Arturo's hotel room. He was ignoring all our advice and refusing to explain his plan. But none of us shouted, demanded, or screamed. Except his son, who had been doing that for weeks. Junior believed his father lacked the will and desire to make reform work. "He wants out. Don't you see that?" he screamed. "Let him go!" And he walked out.

When we were about to leave, I pulled Arturo aside and said, "I can't go with you. You have to go to them, but they are not my friends." This might seem as if I was personally hostile to the people Arturo would meet in Elliott's office. To the contrary, I liked all of them, including Elliott. But in the midst of the divisive Contra debate emotions often became extreme, normal civility too often was lost. At that moment, I saw the men waiting for Arturo as the enemy, not as my friends. But Arturo, too, felt a bit of fire. He said, "I don't want you to go there for them. I want you there with me." So of course I went.

Almost as soon as we went in, Elliott was called up to the seventh floor. That is where power resides in the State Department, where the Secretary of State and his or her immediate aides have their offices. We were meeting on the sixth, the floor for the assistant secretaries. We should have seen the significance of this logistical fact long ago, that the Secretary of State never met with Nicaraguans to discuss reform.

Arturo said nothing about his two remaining demands. So, during the break, I forced the issue, raising the question of the Assembly. Arturo laid out his position. He immediately encountered opposition from Bob Kagan. Kagan did not think that what Arturo wanted could be done and began to explain why. I went to the phone and called the hotel to see if Alfonso had arrived. He, too, opposed the idea of calling for abolition of the Assembly. "Arturo and I already have too many enemies. This would isolate us completely."

When I left the office, Arturo and Bob were still talking, Bob no longer opposing the proposal but pointing out problems.

I left the office to call Corinne. Excitedly, I described the interplay. Truthfully, I loved it. I didn't know what was going to happen, but I had created some tension and I reveled in it.

I wonder now if this was not the kind of Bruce that she didn't like, the Bruce that would cause her to flee fourteen months later. I was too intense. I was allowing the world to pour into our life. I reveled in the tension—but I was not decisive.

When Elliott and I returned, we learned that Arturo had again resigned. Pressure mounted from all sides for Arturo to change his decision. Bob Leiken said, in a belligerent voice: "Arturo, there is not one other person in the room that agrees with your decision." I could have protested, but I did not. Everyone else nodded in assent.

Finally I said, "You know I never say anything in these meetings." Elliott said quizzically, "No, you don't." I went on. "But now I have a question, Arturo. What made you change? And when?"

Arturo was uncharacteristically straightforward. "When I had the discussion with Bob about the Assembly, I knew it wouldn't work. The will isn't there."

His remark threw the meeting into chaos. Bob Kagan was overwhelmed and embarrassed, thrust into the role of spoiler to a project (keeping Cruz) to which (almost) everyone was committed. Private conversations replaced general discussion. These I don't remember, but at one point Elliott was left standing alone, looking utterly forlorn. And a second later, Arturo announced, "Okay, I'll do it."

I should have intervened. But I could not. My moment would come, but the courage to defy those with more power is difficult to acquire, and neither Arturo nor I had yet acquired it that night.

At his press conference the next day, Arturo was once again in his element. He had not told Elliott he wanted Wicho Rivas to become the supreme commander of the Contras's armed forces. But at the press conference he announced it, to the surprise of Wicho and the whole world. Wicho realized immediately that the announcement had probably damaged, not enhanced, his authority.

Arturo continued: "In the past we have pleaded; this time we're going to fight. If (the reforms) cannot be implemented, . . . I will denounce that." He ended on a tough note. He appeared strong. The day was not over, however.

Joe Pichirallo of the *Washington Post* had been given the story that Arturo had received $6,000 a month since the beginning of 1986 in an arrangement worked out by Oliver North. Doyle McManus of the *Los Angeles Times* called soon after. Arturo wondered aloud, when I contacted him, "What next? Will I never have any peace?" He didn't want to deal with the press anymore, so I volunteered to do it for him. I relished being a source in the discussion of other people's problems as demonstrated in the quotes (of "the aide") in the below piece by Doyle McManus.

> "He had no other source of support," the aide said. "He's not try-ing to hide it. But he didn't know where Ollie got the money. All he knew was that it was from a foreign source."
>
> "This is all coming from the intelligence community," one [Cruz ally] charged. "Someone in the intelligence community is trying to destroy him.
>
> "It isn't serious money, either," he added. "Calero's got mil-lions that are missing, and people are worried about a couple of thousand that were given to Arturo Cruz."

What I did is what Washington insiders like to call "damage control" or "spin." But to Arturo the whole episode became another humiliation in his long association with the Contras.

I had assumed that the source of the story was somebody in the Administration, probably the CIA. Years later I ran into Bosco Mantomoros in front of my apartment building, and he admitted that he was the source, after being tipped off by friends in the CIA.

Doyle also wrote: "A former Nicaraguan banker, Cruz has no job and had only a modest family fortune when he went into opposition politics in 1983. At first, the CIA paid him a salary through a dummy foundation but halted the payments after the arrangements became known and Members of Congress objected."

Arturo knew that in the United States close scrutiny is the rule and political figures must expect it. But negative attention is always demoraliz-ing. Arturo needed a stipend to participate in politics. On the other hand, Alfonso was rich, and Adolfo . . . well, we always thought he was stealing, but we never had the evidence. Only Arturo received close scrutiny. And it hurt.

Pichirallo called me a week later. The *Post* had a source who linked me to Spitz Channell and Richard Miller. I didn't want to talk. I was talking for others. Why should I have to reveal anything about myself? In addition to handling much of Arturo's press, I also flacked for his son and Fawn Hall when their affair became a big issue.

But Joe made me talk; he appealed to my sense of morality—an unfair tactic that always works. He put me on the phone with his colleague Tom Edsall. I asked Edsall what I should say. "The truth. It generally works better." Right. Now, from the distance of time, that article seems irrelevant.

> The council was taken over last February by Bruce P. Cameron, a pro-Contra liberal Democrat. Channell paid the council $66,000 to lobby Congress in support of the Contras. The payments were made by the NEPL and Sentinel [Spitz's organizations], a lobby run by Channell.

But I have gotten ahead of myself. When Arturo left that night of February 19, he marked the end of my operational role with the Contras. On paper, we had won, but I knew better. The next week I had lunch with five liberal friends, congressional aides in Congress. They were furious because Arturo had decided to stay with the Contras. They knew his resignation would have won them votes, and they blamed me for his staying.

I said, "Wait. I don't know how or when, but he will leave and it will be soon." ■

CHAPTER TEN

DESPAIR AND DETERMINATION

February–April 1987

*J*ournal entries chronicle a level of emotional pain now thankfully forgotten:
   March 18, 1987, 11:34 P.M.

I am once again suicidal. But I don't know why. Corinne? Scandal? Joblessness—which is a way of saying: I don't belong anywhere on this earth.

   March 20, 10:47 P.M.

I've been here before. It's hard to say. The letter was a clear signal that . . . The message was an affirmation of the sensitive person I know Corinne to be. Her silence tonight (she was to have returned from Florida) is an enormous contradiction. She builds me up and tears me down. She does not know it but I can die over her.

I called the friend with whom I have an anti-suicide pact. She wasn't home.

   March 22, 3:23 P.M.

Corinne is back. She called six times that I know about. I sense nothing in her voice except a desire to continue the past. Her wonderful message.

I need desperately to make love with her. It is the fastest way to get close in a short period of time.

A nice day. Though I smoked too many cigarettes, I suppose because I decided to quit.

   March 28, 11:45 P.M.

Despair and mild drunkenness. Am determined to prepare my will before I die. Spent much time trying to remember what I did last year. Listened endlessly to Mario Lanza singing, "This Nearly was Mine." Two and a half hours of him put me in serious pain.

I hate Corinne with all my heart.

   March 29, 11:30 P.M.

And I will certainly hate her if I continue to see her. I already hate her for being with him. He is bad for being stupid and ignorant about her, and she for being with him. (I promise I don't write or even think sentences like this anymore.)

I have mentioned before a chronic illness. In my entire life I have never felt well. I continually feel a kind of bodily unease. My father suffers from something similar.

Chronic pain began in 1977. It started in my neck and shoulders and, over the next several years, spread to my lower back and legs. For most of the period about which I write, it was debilitating. Most doctors suggested I stop all athletic activity that required hard contact with the earth or a floor. I played no tennis, no basketball. I stopped jogging. In 1978 I had a farewell nine-mile run. I didn't run again until 1985.

During those early years I was often so incapacitated I couldn't work for months. In 1979, I lost four months, in 1980 five. The pain never goes away.

What I wasn't able to stop was an ever-growing dependence on alcohol, tobacco, and food as mood regulators. I have smoked since I was twenty, although I have quit many times, sometimes for years. I learned to enjoy drink at a very early age (sixteen), but it wasn't until 1985 that alcohol became a problem for me. I do not eat out of hunger or for nutrition. I eat to be happy, or at least less unhappy.

I am an addict. When I was in Guatemala, I stopped smoking cigarettes and my drinking lessened. But when I returned to a scandal in Washington in 1987, I drank heavily (a pint of scotch most days), and I chain-smoked cigarettes. But it was still controllable. I could stop (and start) smoking or drinking with relative ease. It was not yet a nightmare. The greater problem was the chronic pain. I was to learn three sets of exercises that year that gained me more control, but I was months mastering them.

During this time, worst was Corinne. Worst? Best was Corinne.

Spurred on by many friends and well-wishers, I proposed to Corinne in February and she conditionally accepted. After I proposed, Corinne and I began a new life together, one that would last four months. We would see each other three or four times a week. If she was coming she would call at 8:30 in the morning. If she was not, she would call at 9:30. If she was coming she would call as soon as her husband left for work. If she was not, she would call an hour later.

If she was coming, I would furiously prepare. Neaten the apartment; give the bathroom a scrub. Sometimes we began with a treat, cookies or croissants.

Sometimes we began the moment she walked in the door. Sometimes we used every room in my apartment. Each day we had only two hours.

For so long, what had drawn her to me was my work. Now my work consisted of responding to the IRS, the House Iran-Contra Committee, and the Special Prosecutor. When I wasn't answering questions, I was trying to convince congressional conservatives to force the Administration into negotiations with the Sandinistas. But Corinne and I didn't talk about such things anymore. We talked only about us, if we talked at all. Mainly, we made love. We had very little time. She went to work at twelve. So often did I doubt her that I was surprised when she actually arrived. At other times, we tried to live more normal lives. When she had an extra hour, we would visit the park near Dumbarton Oaks. We would sit on rocks overlooking Rock Creek. I would talk about a life in which we would be together whenever we wished. She would smile and nod. Then she would be gone.

Always she was gone. We would struggle even to find time to talk by phone.

I began a journal, on the day I saw Tom Edsall's *Washington Post* article, which made me feel even more vulnerable than before. Yet my journal makes no reference to that article. It does provide some insight into my fears while being investigated, but I have never been able to find adequate words to describe those fears.

One day I received a call from someone at the front door. "Does Mr. Bruce Cameron live at this address?" "Yes," I responded. "I am he. How can I help you?" "It's nothing, we're just filming the building for the BBC."

I raced down the hall to the lobby of my building and, together with the building manager and maintenance man, peered from behind curtains to see the film crew. Damn it, I wanted to know why. But when I asked, the crew didn't know. Their assignment was to film the home of that Contra monster, Bruce Cameron. They didn't say that, but that is how it felt.

On Monday, March 9, 1987, at 10:19 P.M., I wrote in my journal:

I keep on talking to all sides in the Nicaragua debate—with the conservatives as if I don't disagree with them, with the liberals as if I do agree with them.

March 7, 1987, 9:40 A.M.

I do believe she has made a firm decision to separate. She did not call last night or this morning.

Not that she had said she would. But in the past she's been driven to it anyway, like the night of my last meeting at State, when she called and left a message and then called twenty or thirty times more, hoping I would be home.

Fortunately I've figured out just the right amount of scotch to drink, enough to leave me deadened, not so much that I have a hangover.

March 9, 1987, 7:38 P.M.

Then she changed her mind.

But it is important for me to remember her call:

"I love you very much. But that doesn't help you, because I can't do anything about it."

Monday, March 9, 1987, 10:19 P.M.

The emotional pain lifted about ninety minutes ago.

It was like a vice that holds my emotions in a desperate panic, and tendrils that spread the panic throughout the whole of me.

During the first three months of our affair, my emotions on Friday would acquire a desperate, hysterical quality. It was more than being on edge, it was like razors scraping at the skin, but from the inside, thereby cutting twice. Nothing could stop this pain except large doses of alcohol. Over time, I saw the pattern. The more I saw Corinne during the week, the longer it would last. I had never experienced anything like it before, nor have I since.

What a remarkable entry. Not for what it says, but for what it doesn't say. Arturo Sr.'s wife, Consuelo, had called me that morning to tell me Arturo had finally resigned, that he was on his way to Costa Rica to give his statement to the press. He had asked her to tell me and Bob Leiken. She asked me to call Bob.

That weekend Arturo had taken counsel with his wife and eldest daughter, shutting out everyone else. They finished drafting his statement at about five o'clock. At six, Bob and Arturo Jr. had called Arturo

Sr. to make plans for the coming week. He talked with them as if every-thing were normal. But after a year and a half of indecision, his mind and heart at last were one, and he dared not communicate, even with those like me who might support his decision, let alone those who would not.

When Consuelo called, I was overjoyed. I stood up and high-fived the air. Mimicking Matthew Broderick at the end of *War Games*, after he stopped World War III, I yelled, "Allll right. Allllll right!!"

In retrospect, when I look back to the time between February 17 and Arturo's decision to leave on March 8, I believe he acted rationally and appropriately. He had laid down three ultimatums: (1) the abolition of the Assembly, (2) a meeting with Enrique Bermudez to insure his loyalty to the Directorate, and (3) the installation of Wicho Rivas as Supreme Military Commander.

The press, Congress, and the State Department had established him as the Contra good guy, their savior. Now he decided to see if he did have a mandate.

Robelo, consistent with what he had told me on the seventeenth, refused to support Cruz about the Assembly. Bermudez first agreed to a meeting with the Directorate, then cancelled. Between that meeting and the one scheduled for March 12, Cruz received two envoys from the U.S. government, one from the CIA and one from the State Department. The message from both was the same: go easy on the Colonel. The military struggle is fundamental and he is the leader. Cruz told Tim Golden of the *Miami Herald* that CIA officials told him, "We can't bother the FDN" as it geared up for its first major offensive in nearly three years.

It was the same rationale he had heard for two years. Cruz said, "Either we have to take the bull by the horns or we stop with this idiocy."

"If you see that what you have is an irresolvable conflict, then step aside," he said. "Because of the ambivalence of the United States, I was convinced that these reforms weren't going to happen."

In those two weeks, Cruz received no help from Elliott or anyone in the State Department. Perhaps help was too much to expect, the CIA with agents stationed in Miami, the State Department with none. Cruz always defined the issue clearly, as he did in his resignation: "The United Nicaraguan Opposition was either to be a pluralistic structure in the service of a goal equally pluralistic" or "an instrument of a small, exclusive clique." Elliott had supported Cruz's vision, but could do nothing to help him implement it, and may even have sent the State Department envoy to tell him to avoid confrontation with Bermudez.

In his final interview with the *Christian Science Monitor* (with the great reporter Dennis Volman, who died some months later), Cruz made a prediction that turned out to be right on target:

> I don't think that [the Contras] can get money directly to buy arms, or that we can get another $100 million. But I believe that we can hope for another $27 million or $40 million to buy non-lethal aid. But I also think that, politically speaking, the Democrats [in Congress] would have to tie any such aid in with a peace plan like Arias' plan to show that serious efforts to resolve the conflict were being made.

He reiterated his belief that the Contras could not overthrow the Sandinistas, or alone force the Sandinistas to seriously negotiate.

In a side bar to Tim Golden's piece in the *Miami Herald*, Sam Dillon and Alfonso Chardy had an article entitled "Cruz Exit May Doom Contra Aid":

> Since 1985, the Reagan Administration's hopes to transform the Nicaraguan rebels from a CIA-created mercenary force into a genuine liberation movement have depended on Arturo Cruz. . . . His withdrawal, coupled with the Iran-Contra scandal, leaves the Contra program in confusion and his reforms in doubt.

Throughout the article the authors argued that the Administration's use of Cruz was only tactical, to win votes in Congress. That had succeeded in 1985 and 1986. They concluded:

> But Cruz's vision was always larger than that of his American allies. He gathered around him an influential group of liberals that included Bruce P. Cameron, a human rights activist; Robert

Leiken, a specialist on Soviet influence in Latin America; and his own son Arturo Jr., a scholar at Johns Hopkins University.

After I resigned, Bob Leiken and Arturo Jr. stayed with the program. Junior found a new patron in Aristides Sanchez. Bob maintained hope in the Administration alliance with progressive Contras, and the imposition of reform on the clique.

Over the next three weeks, two other events convinced me that the Contra movement was terminally ill. On March 23, the leader of the UNO military forces in the south, El Negro Chamarro, resigned. He, too, cited the power and dominance of the clique among his reasons.

That same week, Alfonso and Pedro Chamorro were forced to make a choice. Both were committed to play greater roles in Contra military activities, and both lived in Costa Rica. The Costa Rican government, when made aware of their intentions, informed them that if they took a military route they would no longer be welcome in that country. Both chose to stay in Costa Rica and said they would monitor military efforts "through reports supplied by the United States."[25]

My favorite article of all those inspired by Cruz's resignation was written by the insufferable Jean Kirkpatrick for the *Washington Post* on March 16:

Cruz has long seemed to evoke more intense admiration among North Americans than Nicaraguans. UNO, the organization of which Cruz was a part, was created in Washington by a handful of liberal Democrats who persuaded Lt. Colonel Oliver North and certain State Department officials that there would be a better chance of winning congressional support for the Contras if they were part of a "civilian" political structure headed by "Social Democrats." . . .

During the past year, Cruz and his band of American supporters moved to take personal control of the Contra fighting forces by eliminating Calero from the directorate. . . .

Some even thought Cruz and his supporters had sought control over the Contras in order to negotiate their surrender to Managua. We will never know.

Figure 13: Ambassador Jean Kirkpatrick, Reagan's U.N. ambassador and hard-line opponent of seeing human rights violations in communist and noncommunist nations as equivalent, and Ambassador Ernest Palazio of Nicaragua, first for the contras and later for President Violeta Chamorro. Photo courtesy of Rebecca Hammel.

The "liberal Democrats" had to refer to Leiken and myself; there were no other Americans that close to Cruz. But the rest was nonsense. Neither Bob nor I had anything to do with discussions leading to the formation of UNO. That decision was essentially in place before either of us ever met Ollie. We thought the Contra armies should be under the control of Nicaraguan civilians. As to Kirkpatrick's fantasy about some dream to seize control of the army, then surrender, it was a neat idea, but not ours.

Jean Kirkpatrick never appeared to believe that the facts should strongly influence her writings. This article was no different.

Arturo's daughter, Consuelo Cruz, took issue, in print, with Kirkpatrick's assertion of our alleged plan for surrender:

This is sheer character assassination of a man who, along with many other Nicaraguans and American moderates . . . has tried to break the vicious circle of Nicaraguan history in which liberators become tyrants.

Nicaraguans with a sense of history realize that our experiences with Somocismo and Sandinismo force us to go beyond simple support for Ambassador Kirkpatrick's theoretical fixation of the late '70s in which she draws a distinction between authoritarian and totalitarian regimes. . . .

From an American realpolitik perspective, the goal is to replace the Sandinista regime with a friendly one. The Nicaraguan opposition, however, must strive for much more that this: it must forge a substantive alternative to the programs of the past, and it must acquire the political habits of pluralism that would set it apart from the intolerance that characterizes the Sandinistas, some groups in the present U.S. Administration, and the hegemonic faction within the Nicaraguan rebel movement.

Corinne was leaving for Florida. She was adamant that she would never leave her husband, and that we should use the coming holiday as a way to begin to separate from me. As she left, she said, "Perhaps, it would have been better had we not."

I left the apartment at the same time, to run in Rock Creek Park. Her final words haunted me. When I arrived, I went to the automobile trunk to find something to write on—all I could find was an old AAA triptik. I ran over to the "P Street Beach," sat down in the middle, and scribbled out the first love poem of my life. I know nothing of poetry. I don't read it or understand it. But the words poured out in five minutes.

How Could We Not?

You say it would have been better
Had we not.
It wouldn't've
There is a storm brewing now
For both of us.
The lightning—shocks of reality
That we are alone.
The thunder—the silencing of
The loved one's voice.
And the dark clouds of despair.

One day, the sun will show again.
And we will remember that
We loved each other.
We soared.
When embracing, we touched the sky,
Zoomed through the Magellanic cloud,
Whispering lover louder than the explosions of a supernova.
And when we loved, we swam, mermaid and merman,
Across the ocean floor six miles deep.
How could we not?
How could we not know,
How could we not find
New ways of being human,
New paths of being man and woman,
Coupled into one,
A one we had not known was there.
Duty now requires that we bring on the storm—
But how could we not?

I'm still not sure if it was a good idea to have an affair with Corinne. But I am absolutely sure it would have been better had I not written this poem. It is much too close and grandiose.

Some months later, her husband found it and confronted her. She said, "Oh, that's just a poem a friend wrote in college. How can you be so suspicious?"

That poem was purely a child of the movies. The image of a storm brewing comes from the final scene of The Terminator, *with Arnold Schwarzenegger and Linda Hamilton. A Mexican boy points to the clouds and tells Linda that a big storm is coming. But she knows it is a nuclear war. Mermaid and merman are from* Splash, *from Tom Hanks and Darryl Hannah swimming together as he leaves the world above to join her forever in the great undersea city. Giving up Corinne is the dramatic gesture of Humphrey Bogart in* Casablanca *when he tells Paul Henreid that Ingrid Bergman loves him, and had only pretended to rekindle her romance with Bogart to get the letters of transit to Portugal en route to America.*

I subsequently helped arrange for Arturo to appear on John McLaughlin's "One on One." With Arturo I still felt wonderfully relaxed. I picked him up at the airport and we drove to WNBC on Nebraska Avenue in upper northwest

Washington. His appearance on the show was uneventful; he added nothing to his previous statements. And that afternoon, he gave a small press conference in my apartment, an appropriate ending place. We had made so many plans in that room, most of which came to naught. Arturo told me, "we began this journey as liberals, and now at its end, we are liberals once more." It made me feel good—for a moment.

That next week I received a message. A friend from college was visiting. Her husband had committed suicide when she left him. I had been the person closest to him in the last months before he slashed his wrists, bled for a few hours, and then threw himself through a window and fell six stories to his death. When the police called to tell me he was dead, my concern and loyalty focused on Val. Would she survive this?

I insisted that mutual friends drive thirty miles in the middle of the night to stay with her. Then I insisted she leave her home in the Midwest and fly to Washington to be with John's friends and family (who inevitably would blame her for his death; it was her leaving that had catapulted him into despair). She came, and it proved to have been the wise choice.

Three days later a friend from my antiwar days came to visit. Jeff Malachowsky was eighteen when I met him in 1974, a freshman at the University of Michigan. Within a month of joining the Ann Arbor Indochina Peace Campaign (IPC), he had made a commitment to work with us full time. He dropped out of school and joined a Maoist collective that was a part of our organization. Two months after the war ended, he quit and returned to his home in New Jersey.

When I went to work for ADA in Washington five months later, I resolved to reclaim the best of our movement's people. For the last months of the IPC, the Michigan organization had been taken over by the collective, which turned most of us much of the time into mindless robots parroting the third world anti-imperialist line. And we didn't know how to fight back. We were manipulated by the collective leader who claimed to lead on the basis of antiracist, antisexist, and antielitist philosophies. Until their takeover I had led. I was capable of pragmatic compromise, and under my leadership, IPC was effective, we could talk with the wider community. But the collective never compromised, and our rhetoric isolated us, even on the Ann Arbor campus. And still we could not fight back. Instead, one by one, we quit.

Jeff was the first I reclaimed; I arranged for him to work for a foreign

policy organization in Washington. Eventually I found work for six others,
the last in 1984, nine years after the war ended.

Jeff sharply disagreed with my work with the Contras, but never severed
relations. He was now glad to learn I had changed my position.

Then we discussed Corinne. Jeff told me of his long campaign to reclaim his
love, whom he eventually married. His story strengthened my determination.

That Friday Corinne came to my apartment. After sex, in my bed, I said,
"I will not give you up, but I will be resolutely patient even to the point of let-
ting you go. And I have remade my will; I am leaving everything to you, and
I have taken care to make sure that if I were to die, Allan would never need to
know that you were my beneficiary. You are not even mentioned in the will.
Your name is in a notarized letter I have left with my lawyer."

She cried; she said that no one had ever said or done anything so kind.
But it changed nothing about her decision to stay in her marriage. I could act,
she could not.

My mood lifted because I turned my energies to looking for a job. I was
perhaps no healthier in mind or body, but I was less tormented. The journal
stops abruptly.

The Iran-Contra hearings would soon appear on television, and I
still hadn't told my story to the public. The House Iran Contra panel had
asked me to come in for a relatively short meeting of an hour and a half.
Eventually, they asked me to sign a notarized statement about one thing
Ollie had told me in 1985. It was of little consequence.

In the summer of 1985, there had been much speculation on the source
of private funding for the Contras. Retired General John Singlaub was
presented in most stories as the American most active in getting equipment and funds to the Contras. I volunteered that Ollie had once told me,
"General Singlaub serves a useful role. He diverts attention from someone
more important." I simply affirmed in my affidavit that he had said those
words to me.

I spent much more time with the special prosecutor's office, a unique
invention created in the wake of Watergate. When the Attorney General
finds that a high government official is suspected of serious wrongdoing,
he appoints a three-judge panel. The panel then appoints a special prosecutor to investigate the case, and to prosecute it, if he or she finds sufficient
grounds. The prosecutor is thus insulated from political pressures inside
the Administration.

I was not subpoenaed, but spoke voluntarily with a lawyer and an FBI agent. The interrogation (that's what it felt like) consumed a total of eight hours, spread over the course of a month. The lawyer, Jeffrey Stewart, was part of a unit investigating the "secret war" conducted by high government officials. I turned over all my papers, a task made easy because I had already assembled them for the IRS.

Questions centered on my relations with Ollie, Elliott, and Alan Fiers. But Jeff went further, asking about all my initial contacts with Contra leaders, as well as the work I did with the Gang of Four. But I was only a sideshow. By our last meeting, Jeff was listless and had little to ask; it was over in an hour and a half. Months later, when the list of potential witnesses was made public, I was not on it.

Throughout our meetings, the most memorable comment Jeff made was this: "You must give some remarkable parties. More people we've interviewed here have told us that the first time they met someone was at your home." He also asked if I believed I was guilty of violating any law. My answer was more or less truthful. "Look, I feel guilty of something. But no, I don't think I violated any law."

The investigations left me drained and frightened. Fear was the principal reason I was not more public about my disagreements with the Administration. I didn't feel I could afford to alienate anybody. I had resolved to remain active in the debates. I communicated my doubts about current policy to many of my conservative friends, and tried to convince them to support negotiations. But I was too conflicted to take a clear, determined, public stand.

What is striking in retrospect is that three men were entirely clear and knew exactly what they were doing: Elliott Abrams, Adolfo Calero, and Oscar Arias.

Elliott held a consistent line, oddly enough close to Adolfo in policy terms. But he liked Arturo better and knew he was key to winning the moderates. In an interview on the television program *American Interests*, sponsored by the U.S. Chamber of Commerce, Elliott made his case:

> The case (for the Contras) is really this, that it is in our moral interests and our security interests to prevent the establishment of a Cuba on the mainland of the Americas in Nicaragua. . . .
>
> [The Contras] have prevented the final consolidation. They

Figure 14: Elliott Abrams, then assistant secretary of state for Latin America, now special assistant to the President on the Middle East and Democracy. Photo courtesy of Rebecca Hammel.

have held open, for Nicaraguans and for us, the chance that there can be a reversal of Nicaragua's fortunes. . . .

But what happens . . . if we junk the Contras, that is, if Congress abandons the Contras? First of all, the Sandinistas are triumphant. I mean they have beaten the Yankees. Think of the morale boost to the FMLN, the Communist guerrillas in El Salvador, and think of what it means to the morale of the [Salvadoran government].

It seems to me that for Honduras and El Salvador, there's an immediate shift in fortunes. And when there is a step-up in guerrilla activity—and surely, there will be, they will not immediately win. What I fear is that they'll be ripe for military coups in those countries. And then liberals in Congress will react by saying, "Ah, [inaudible] military coups, cut off aid." And when we cut off aid, the guerrillas will do better and better.

Elliott knew that he could not call for a straight military victory. That was an unacceptable position in Washington in 1987. But he handled the issue deftly when he went before the Senate Foreign Relations Committee in early January.

"Outright military victory has never been part of U.S. policy," Abrams asserted. The goal, he said, was for a "political victory" as a result of military pressure. He further defined the victory as one in which President Daniel Ortega would be compelled "to open up [Nicaragua to democracy]."

Abrams then had this exchange with Senator Joseph Biden, a Democrat from Delaware.

Biden: According to your definition . . . how long do you think it will take to win?

Abrams: We hate to be pinned down on time, but I'll give you an answer. I think you're talking about something like two to four years.[26]

In a speech that spring, Abrams was more specific on how the policy might work, and succeed:

We do not have to face a choice between direct U.S. intervention and containment. An alternative is available. It is to follow our current policy, to continue to help the thousands of Nicaraguans who are fighting to bring democracy to their nation. Freedom may not come in a few months; it may not come this year, but it will come. One day the Nicaraguan democratic resistance will be so strong that the Sandinistas will face a choice: to live up to their democratic promises or yield to a movement that will end their dictatorship and put more representative leaders in charge.

Abrams was ruling out serious negotiations in the short term. In two years, he thought, it might be possible, when and if the Contras were stronger. But the task at hand was building the Contras and defeating efforts (that included negotiations, including the Arias plan) to sidetrack that task.

Figure 15: Adolfo Calero, a leading Conservative Party figure for years who was also head of the local Coca-Cola franchise and later became the head of the largest Nicaraguan guerrilla group, the Fuerza Democratica Nicaraguense (FDN). Photo courtesy of Rebecca Hammel.

Calero, too, knew exactly what he was doing. After he resigned, he continued (as if nothing had changed) to negotiate with Alfredo Cesar on the complexion of a new directorate. His followers released his plan to the press: an expanded directorate based on representatives of the four political groups, plus one from labor, one from BOS, and one from the Indians. Calero's aide, Bosco Mantomoros, leaked the story about Arturo's finances just when Arturo had decided to stay in. And Adolfo stepped up the campaign (in the exile movement) against both Cruz and Robelo, pushing Cruz to become more stubborn and Robelo more fearful of offending Nicaraguans. Calero had done this before, in 1985 when UNO was founded, and again after the Miami reforms of 1986. Either through agents in camps in Honduras or through friendly journalists in Miami and San Jose, Costa Rica, Calero launched attacks on his putative allies.

He had not always behaved this way. Before he left Nicaragua in 1982, Calero had built a record of strong opposition to Somoza, working closely with the business opposition. After the Sandinista triumph he became a major leader of the conservative party. When Arturo and Cordaba Rivas replaced Alfonso and Violeta Chamorro on the ruling government junta in 1980, Adolfo was positively jubilant, because the former were members of his party. But his years as leader of a military movement totally dependent on the United States had turned him into a stubborn bully who admitted no vision but his own. Unlike Arturo, Alfonso, and Alfredo Cesar, Adolfo had no support or rapport among moderates or liberals in the United States, and no support in other international circles, except the Paris-based International League of Resistance and the conservative minority coalition in Spain.

Calero's vision was tunnel: maintain the boys in the field until they won or until the United States invaded and installed them in power. He believed he was Reagan's chosen leader. He had already been through countless battles with Congress over supporting his forces, and he had always prevailed. Nor did he doubt himself at that time; in the short term he was right.

In May, an expanded Contra assembly met in Miami to elect a new directorate. Adolfo was the first to be elected and received the largest number of votes. After agonizing over his decision, Alfonso had decided to stay.

Alfredo Cesar had been negotiating with Adolfo for three months; his target for removal was Cruz. But in the aftermath of Cruz's resignation, Adolfo became stronger than ever. It was time to switch alliances. Until the new Assembly meeting, Alfredo had maintained his alliance with Adolfo; once inside the meeting, Alfredo shifted his support to Aristides Sanchez, elected representative of the liberal parties, and Alfonso. Alfonso received the fewest votes (twenty-seven), only one more than required, and only because Aristides forced his brother (long accustomed to following Calero) to switch his vote. The other two members of the UNO directorate were Pedro Joaquin Chamorro, an independent, and Azucena Ferrey, a fiery leader of the Christian Democrats, who announced she had left Nicaragua to join the Contras. The new leadership agreed to form one organization, the National Resistance, and to abolish the FDN as a separate organization.

Adolfo had won, but his winning was the second nail in the coffin of Contra fortunes on Capitol Hill. The first, of course, was the Iran-Contra scandal. Although many facts were still unknown in the first quarter of 1987, the Administration had already lost a test vote in the House and had won only narrowly in the Senate. Now Cruz was gone, and these new reforms seemed hollow. Cruz had set a higher standard. Chris Hedges of the *Dallas Morning News* summed it up well in an article on May 11.

> To many who had supported Cruz, the reorganization will fall short of the reforms they had struggled to enact. Cruz had tried to oust at least two of the three most powerful Contra leaders—Calero, Enrique Bermudez, and Aristides Sanchez—from the movement. These men control the Nicaraguan Democratic Force, which runs the principal Contra army, and have dominated the Contra movement since its inception in 1981. . . .
>
> Cruz resigned in March after his attempt to place a military commander over Bermudez and dissolve the FDN-dominated civilian assembly failed.
>
> "I don't think this current reorganization is significant," said Bruce Cameron, an influential Democratic lobbyist with close ties to Cruz. "Any agreement which leaves the FDN political mafia untouched cannot produce significant reforms."

While Cruz's story won big headlines in major newspapers and the close attention of Congress, this new reorganization (in many respects positive) received little coverage. It was too little too late.

The scandal and failure of the Cruz-led reforms were two counts against Administration policy. The Democrats, however, still lacked an alternative. Enter Oscar Arias.

Arias formally unveiled his plan in February. The Sandinistas had initially rejected it, then later agreed to discuss it. The U.S. Senate gave its principles nearly unanimous support, 97–3. The Contadora Group, concerned that it not be left out of Central American negotiations altogether, gave the plan its qualified support in April.

More so than Abrams, Arias claimed moral authority in the long-held peaceful and democratic traditions of Costa Rica. He placed emphasis on democracy: "I believe there can be no peace without democracy." There were six points to his plan.

(1) A general amnesty within 60 days in those countries where there were armed conflicts. A national commission for reconcilia- tion would also be established in those countries.

(2) A dialogue between the government and the internal opposition groups in countries where an armed insurgency was operating.

(3) A cease-fire to be declared simultaneously with the begin- ning of the dialogue.

(4) Democratization to be introduced within six months, and press liberty reestablished within 60 days.

(5) A suspension of support to insurgent forces from any out- side force or government.

(6) Verification by the secretary generals of the United Nations and the Organization of American States.

This was the alternative the Democrats were looking for.

Building on the Arias plan, Representative Jim Slattery from Kansas, assisted by his indefatigable aide, Brent Budowski, created a proposal spe- cific to Nicaragua. In addition to the six points listed above, the Slattery alternative included direct negotiations between the United States and Nicaragua once a cease-fire was in place and the Sandinistas had begun negotiations with the internal opposition.

I saw this as a real opportunity. I began to work with Brent to col- lect signatures on a letter to the President calling for adoption of the plan. My job was to seek out Republicans and conservative Democrats (amazing since just three years earlier I knew only liberals). Some 111 members signed that letter. Almost half of them had supported Contra aid in the 1986 vote.

Jim and Brent spent hours discussing this proposal with Elliott and his top aides, who always made time for these discussions. I tried to enlist the support of two specific conservative Republicans, Representative Henry Hyde and Senator John McCain. Both knew Administration policy was in trouble and seemed interested. John had already written an article in which he argued that the goal of U.S. Nicaraguan policy should be to establish democracy (with no other criteria). Though neither Hyde nor McCain said no at our initial meeting, both declined to sign the letter, after conversations with colleagues.

An answer to the Slattery letter was drafted and redrafted in the State Department and White House. Brent was always being told, "just a few more days." By the time Reagan left office twenty months later, there had still been no response.

Elliott knew what he was doing. The political context of the scandal and the Cruz resignation combined with American belief in negotiations to make it impossible for the Administration to say no. But Abrams's belief in his policy, which ruled out negotiations, required that he never say yes.

By the end of April, the Slattery initiative was dead. It was my last insider effort to promote a solution to the Nicaragua problem. ■

CHAPTER ELEVEN

FIRST CONVICTIONS

April–June 1987

A holistic, osteopathic Indian guru, Shyam Singa, whom I had seen off and on for the past ten years, was in town to conduct a weekend workshop.

My principal doctors were his disciples, and much that I had learned from them helped me to cope with my now almost constant physical pain. But I don't like Singa. And he doesn't approve of me.

In 1982 my doctor and friend Jim Gordon decided that Shyam should attend a political rally at which all three of my bosses from the early '80s were speaking—the congressman now Senator Tom Harkin of Iowa, former congressman Father Bob Drinan, president of ADA (who did not seek reelection when ordered to withdraw by Pope John Paul II), and Joan Baez. It was a rally to oppose Reagan Administration policy on El Salvador.

Shyam began his workshop the next evening with a direct attack on political activity. "You can't help the world. You can only help yourself. I attended meetings of the Congress Party in India for years, and life is worse there than it was 40 years ago." Then he described the rally the night before and declared that all involved had simply been wasting their time.

I was outraged. I still believed firmly in collective political action, though by 1987 I had become less certain about this. But since that most difficult year I have become more optimistic again.

On April 28 I made a decision. Freelance reporter Michael Massing had been commissioned by the *New York Times Magazine* to write an article on Spitz Channell and his network. I did not know Michael, but I knew his work. In 1985, he had written an article in the leftist journal *The Nation* criticizing the Sandinistas for their undemocratic rule. He noted the simple equation that if the Sandinistas wanted the private sector to participate in the development of Nicaragua, there must be freedom of the press, freedom of association, and freedom of electoral process. Today this seems undeniable. But in 1985 Mikhail Gorbachev had not yet caused the shibboleths of the old and new left to be tossed aside. There were still those who argued that pursuit of social justice for the poor and the disenfranchised justified limitations on the irresponsible reporting of bourgeois press. *The Nation* published nine responses to Massing's article, eight opposed and one neutral. For a man of the left, who has stayed on the left, his writing was an act of courage. He was the reporter I had been looking for.

In the next month, I would spend more than sixty hours with Massing and would ultimately give him access to all my papers (but not all at once). Some questions I would not answer for days, sometimes weeks. We spent hours discussing the exact wording of quotes that would be published. Months later, when the whole process was over, I asked Michael if I had been his most difficult subject. "No," he responded, "not the most difficult, but certainly the most complex."

On April 29 Spitz Channell pled guilty to one count of conspiracy to solicit tax-deductible contributions for arms, contrary to the charitable and educational purposes and the tax-exempt status of his organization, NEPL (which had given my organization $26,000). In his guilty plea, he named Ollie North and Richard Miller as coconspirators. The next day the IRS revoked NEPL's tax-exempt status.

This was the first ever conviction under the 1978 Special Prosecutor Law. Rich Miller immediately responded, "I categorically deny that I conspired with Mr. Channell or anyone else for that purpose or any illegal purpose."

The *Philadelphia Inquirer* in a May 1 editorial explained the significance of the indictment:

> With his first indictment, Mr. Walsh (the Special Prosecutor) has netted no run-of-the-mill right-wing fundraiser, but an agent in the service (and not so indirectly, either) of the President of the United States.
>
> Channell's fund-raising—and the phony tax deductions underpinning it—was orchestrated by none other than Lt. Colonel Oliver North, apparently acting with the full knowledge and authority of the White House.
>
> It was not simply "humanitarian" aid that he was raising, Channell finally admitted, but guns—shamelessly listed as "toys"—for the Contra rebels. . . .

Nor were Channell's foundations charitable, educational or non-partisan, the cover under which Col. North and others stumped for donations to replace military aid that, at the time, was forbidden by law.

My closest friend and confidant during this period was reporter Doyle McManus of the *Los Angeles Times*. He, more than any other person, knew the terrors that I experienced. In fact, I don't remember them as well as he does. By November the terror was gone and forgotten. But Doyle remembers the time I was not sure I would not be indicted and convicted. At one point I had asked him to come to my home and listen to everything I thought might be of consequence. After fifteen minutes he told me, "You have nothing to worry about." But when he wrote about one of my secrets (with permission), it read differently:

> However a Contra source and a U.S. official said that Abrams did ask (Richard) Miller to direct some of Channell's funds to Bruce Cameron, a liberal lobbyist working on behalf of moderate Contra leaders. Cameron received $66,000 from two of Channell's organizations for his lobbying activities.
>
> An Internal Revenue Service spokesman said it is illegal to use tax-deductible funds to purchase arms or to support a political lobbying effort. In linking Cameron's lobbying effort, none of the officials have suggested that Abrams knew Channell's funds were from a tax-exempt foundation.

On May 6 Rich Miller pled guilty to the same charge as Channell. Two of my closest associates of the year before had now pled guilty to a felony charge. The same day, Congress began televised broadcasting of the Iran-Contra hearings.

During that first month, I missed only twenty of more than one hundred hours of television devoted to the hearings. I had no job, and I wanted to know everything I didn't already know about what had really happened. And I was waiting, of course, to see if my name and activities would enter the deliberations.

I was mentioned three times. My good friend Rob Owen, who had bequeathed me the organization that received the Channell money, mentioned me twice. He reported that I had taken over his organization and that I had been with him on his last visit to Ollie North, the night before he was fired.

During Rob's testimony, memos he wrote to Ollie were introduced into evidence. It was his hope to bolster the Contra cause through his public appearance, but his memos were what people remembered. The *Philadelphia Inquirer* summarized these on May 20:

> He said Calero's subordinates "are not first-rate people; in fact they are liars and greed- and power-motivated. They are not the people to build a new Nicaragua. In fact, the FDN has done a good job of keeping competent people out of the organization.
>
> "None of these people can stand Robelo or Cruz. At every turn they will undermine them and do all in their power to see they are not given any power," said Owen in the March 1986 memo.
>
> "There are few of the so-called leaders of the movement who really care about the boys in the field," Owen said in the memo. Then to add emphasis, he wrote in capital letters: "THIS WAR HAS BECOME A BUSINESS TO MANY OF THEM: THERE IS STILL A BELIEF THAT THE MARINES ARE GOING TO HAVE TO INVADE. SO LET'S GET SET SO WE WILL AUTOMATICALLY BE THE ONES PUT INTO POWER."

In subsequent testimony, Calero was asked why Owen, who had once worked for him directly, had turned against him. Calero ascribed this change of mind to the evil influence of Americans he did not name. In the small world of Contra politics, it was well known that Rob and I had become good friends. But what turned Rob against Calero was not me but the testimony of countless Nicaraguans he spent time with in Honduras and Costa Rica. Following different paths with similar experiences, we had come to the same conclusions, and then become friends. Calero, like his friend, Jean Kirkpatrick, was always clear and determined, but rarely accurate.

In his testimony Rob attempted to justify circumventing the Boland Amendment banning military aid to the Contras. He characterized his work with Ollie and the Contras as a "story of courage and compassion, caring and sharing, of doing what is right and dying for a cause."

I once spent an afternoon in Costa Rica with a Misquito Indian from the Atlantic Coast. He had served in the Sandinista Air Force, but later defected to Pastora's cause. He died when his plane bombed the Managua airport and the concussion knocked him out of the sky. He was a decent man animated by his desire to see the people of the Atlantic Coast live free from Sandinista oppression. And he died for that cause. It was men like him whom Rob was talking about. I agreed with him then and agree with him now.

But Senator Sam Nunn, a conservative Democrat from Georgia and consistent Contra supporter, described what was wrong with Rob's position in his commentary as a member of the Iran-Contra panel in the Senate: "All of us would like to see democracy in Central America. But we cannot abuse democracy at home in the pursuit of democracy abroad. The central issue thus becomes whether this Administration upheld the law or flouted the law."

At the conclusion of testimony from the first set of witnesses in the Iran-Contra scandal, Congressman Lee Hamilton, chairman of the House panel, summarized his findings:

> The President was involved in private and third-country fund-raising for the Contras. Wealthy private contributors were courted at the White House, solicited in coordination with government officials and given what they were told was secret information. American policy became dependent on the contributions of private individuals and third parties.
>
> Privatization of foreign policy is a prescription for confusion and failure. The advance of the American national interest depends on the full use of the many resources of the United States government. We are ill-served when it is otherwise. The use of private parties to carry out the high purposes of governments makes us the subject of puzzlement and ridicule.

The privatization argument bothered me, and I shared my concern with Michael Massing. All of what he said in his article has its place in this narrative, and what he says about privatization is most appropriate here:

[The Gang of Four's] activities highlight the extent to which foreign policy making in the Reagan Administration has been delegated to private individuals. On the military front, people like Richard Secord and Albert Hakim helped set up a covert arms network. In the political sphere Cameron and his colleagues built congressional support. "Republicans in general are not good at dealing with Democrats," says Robert Kagan, head of the State Department's office of public diplomacy. "There had to be a reaching out to Democrats. That was something that neither Spitz Channell nor the conservative movement were capable of doing. . . . These four were instrumental in providing it." The New Republic has gone further. "When the history of the American debates over Nicaragua is written," an editorial declared last year, the group "will be found to have transformed both public discussion and public policy."

I had been the legislative point man, paid out of funds controlled by Spitz Channell, raised through the direct intervention of the President and Ollie North. That is how I thought of myself when the first session of the Iran-Contra panel completed its deliberations on Tuesday, June 9.

For me, the bombshell would be the collection of exhibits prepared by the committee for Adolfo Calero's hearings. By that time we already knew that many of the funds for the FDN and Secord resupply operations came from foreign governments or the Channell-Miller network. What the exhibits revealed was that *all* the money came from those sources. The FDN had no funding source independent of the U.S. government. An exchange between Calero and Senator William Cohen (R-Maine) dramatically revealed the overwhelming political weakness of the Contra effort.

Cohen: But as a practical matter, he was the man controlling the funds and controlling your ability to acquire weapons during this time, from 1984 through 1986. As a practical matter—

Calero: Well, let's say one thing, I had very high respect for Colonel North, and he was very respectful with me, and we had a very, very good relationship. Yes, sir.

Cohen: But the point was that you were in fact indebted to the United States, a country that was helping arrange the financing.

Without the United States government and Colonel North, you would not have been in a position to continue the war effort.

That night I received a call from Corinne, on the eve of her trip to Paris to try to rekindle her relationship with Allan. I was not home to take it, my machine did.

She said, "Hello, darling. I just wanted to call you to let you know that everything you feel, I feel. I wish I were with you. I miss you very much. I love you very much. I'll talk to you tomorrow. Sleep tight, sweetheart."

The next day she called again: "It is ten of one. And oh, I miss you so much. And I will just try to call later and hope that I will catch you in. We will be leaving for the airport, I don't know, probably around four or something like that. Goodbye, darling. I love you very much."

She left for Paris with her husband.

On Friday, I met with Elliott Abrams for the first time since the last meeting that Abrams and colleagues at the State Department would have with Arturo Cruz. It was my fourth attempt to meet with Abrams in three months; the other meetings had been cancelled due to the exigencies of Iran-Contra or Latin America in general. I wanted to let him know before I went public that I now opposed the Administration. A State Department lawyer was present at the meeting, as at all his meetings with people caught up in the scandal at that time.

Abrams said he was surprised I had changed my position. Referring to the Gang of Four, he said, "I thought you were the Four Horsemen whom we could always count on." Though the meeting was generally amicable, Abrams raised his eyebrows when I bitterly complained about what I called the legislative trick the Republicans had pulled in the April 16 vote the year before. "Trick?" he queried, appearing to have no idea what I was talking about. I explained what I called my three "anti-Ds" that had come to characterize Administration policy toward Nicaragua.

"The Nicaraguan Democratic Resistance is not democratic. It is ruled by thugs. The Administration's illegal funding of the Contras in 1985 and 1986 violated democratic principles. And finally, the Administration's approach to Congress was antidemocratic, most evidenced in the April 16 vote. It wanted Contra aid on its terms, and it would cheat and lie to get it. That is not democracy." Maybe I said all that but I bet Elliot said a lot more and got the better of the argument. That was to be my last meeting with a high-level Administration official on the issue of Nicaragua.

The congressional hearings were in recess. I had ten job interviews but only the President of Guatemala had made an offer. It was to his country I fled once again. But I was not fleeing the hearings, my joblessness, or even my physical pain. I was fleeing Corinne in Paris. ■

CHAPTER TWELVE

GUATEMALA AGAIN

June 1987

Antigua, Guatemala. It was time for renewal and it came. My plan was simple: to exercise, diet, and begin the writing that would become this book.

June 13 was magical. In December I had become friends with a girl and her family—sister, little brother, Nicaraguan mother, and Norwegian father. The little girl, Gypsy, was turning seven, and her sister Joisie threw her a birthday party at the hotel where I was staying. I was invited. I couldn't say no. Gypsy had become precious to me, though I didn't want to be there. But the gathering of exuberant youth and elders (growing younger by the minute) pulled me in despite myself.

Someone hung a piñata. A wire was strung between trees and a rope thrown over the wire, the piñata attached to one end. There were other wires to move the piñata back and forth, up and down, away from the blindfolded, trying to smack the piñata with a stick, at other times driving it straight toward them.

Afterward Gypsy decided to investigate my room. There, for the first time in her life, she discovered room service. Soon there was a waitress coming from the kitchen just ninety feet away to deliver four bottles of red soda pop. In the days that followed, Gypsy took to ordering cheeseburgers.

Every day Gypsy and Joisie would come to swim. Joisie tried to stop her sister from ordering burgers, but happily joined her in eating them when she failed. They would stay in the pool for hours, Gypsy demanding I watch her every dive and comment on it. How could I comment on a child's activity in a language I barely knew? I learned it was not what I said, but the fact that I was there and that I said something. My journal entry for that day reads: "So I will take them swimming every day and enjoy their joy."

The next day, the family flew back to Norway. With Gypsy gone, I resumed my journal.

June 24

I am running every day.

Saturday, Sunday, Monday, Tuesday, Wednesday.

50, 45, 80, 85, 72 minutes.

My overall plan is to launch an attack on my belly. And I continue to feel terrible. Run at it, kick it, beat it into condition so you can face whatever it is you will face.

I am coming alive again slowly. I just wish I could be more sure that Vinicio [Vinicio Cerezo, the president of Guatemala] will hire me to be his lobbyist in Washington.

Bob [Leiken] called. He wants me to try to stop or at least change the Massing article. But it is too late. I've done the best I could, I can't maneuver out of it. What's left is to let it come out and take the consequences, good, bad, or indifferent.

The week before I left for Guatemala, I had been summoned by the other members of the Gang of Four to a lunch meeting at the Four Seasons Hotel. When I had begun to talk to Massing, one of the ground rules I established was that anything I said about the other three was off the record. He could not even use information I provided to seek corroboration later. But it was easier to talk about what I had done if I included them in the narrative. As it turned out, the *Times* rejected the original piece focused on Spitz Channell. The *Post Outlook* section was subsequently willing to run something about the four of us.

When we had worked closely together, the dynamics had always been challenging, with Bob and Bernie monopolizing conversation, Penn and I struggling to make our points. But there was real give and take, and generally we reached a consensus.

Despite our agreement, Michael began talking to them and to their friends. Bob and Bernie saw this as an invasion of their privacy; they wanted me to stop talking to the press about our activities, which meant I couldn't talk about my own. Penn was more understanding; he had also worked closely with Spitz and Rich and had been in the papers. They summoned me to lunch.

My liberal friends urged me not to go. I insisted that to duck the meeting would be dishonorable. I swore I would not yield on anything. Since the hearings (especially the Calero evidence), I was convinced I had been used, and used badly.

That was not how the others felt. To them, it was I who had broken faith. They continued to support Contra aid and to insist on the justice of their cause. I don't remember which it was, Bob or Bernie, but one insisted that while the means were wrong, the end (the policy) was right. I quoted Sam Nunn to them: "We cannot abuse democracy at home in the pursuit of democracy abroad."

Penn asked if I had thought he was trying to manipulate me as part of a conspiracy with Ollie North and others. At that time, there was belief in certain circles among the press and Congress that coincident with the secret arms resupply network there was a secret network of State Department, White House, and CIA officials. Independents such as Penn were thought to have carried out a media operation devised to build up the Contras and tear down their opponents.

But, no, I didn't think so then, and I don't think so now. Penn may have sometimes seemed furtive, but in reality he was simply diffident. He was one of Washington's most transparent and accessible people.

June 26

I saw *Prince of the City*, that is, I watched it up to the point where the policeman, talking with a New York Commission investigating police corruption, had to betray his partners to save himself.

I had to talk. I was more involved. I was closer to so many of the principal players: to Ollie, to Cliff, to Spitz, to Rich, and to Rob. I touched (even if I was not involved with) all the key aspects of the Contra part of the scandal.

Rob Owen: had given me his organization so I could raise money and was Ollie's eyes and ears in Central America during the Boland Amendment.

Spitz: raised funds for arms and for me.

Ollie: who touched everything was a master manipulator of many, including me, and provided funds to Arturo.

Allan Fiers: with whom I had secret meetings in Washington hotels, on street corners.

I was an obvious target of the media, the Special Prosecutor, the IRS, the committees, and rightly so. And when I was called, my partners were not there to help me. It was inevitable that when I talked, I would talk about them.

I wrote that in the evening. That day was another step back into life. I had been adopted again—this time by a family whose son was marrying a Guatemalan girl the next day. We sat around the pool drinking beers, talking of home in the United States and Guatemala. I showed them the best places to shop in Antigua. I steered them toward Lake Atitlán. What struck me was the normality of their lives, the simple joys of family.

The next day I learned much more about them, my *ideal* family. Sam and Nancy were only recently married. Sam's first wife, and the mother of his children, had also come to the wedding. You could cut the tension with a knife. Both daughters had two children, one already divorced and the other looking forward to it. Sitting at a table after the wedding, I had never before heard so much antimarriage conversation. Kim, who was still married, was most adamant.

Then my whole world turned around. (Thankfully, I don't use phrases like this anymore.)

On a whim, after that dinner I decided to stop by another dinner I had been invited to attend. Antigua had about a hundred full-time American residents and perhaps another two or three hundred who visited regularly at that time. But Veh Smithers was unusual, having lived in Antigua for eleven years. A woman my own age, she came from a wealthy Virginia family. She could afford to do nothing, but she instead operated a small weaving business. She contracted with Indian women in the highlands to make weavings of modern design, and she sold them in her store in Antigua and to distributors in the United States. Veh once told me, "The sky of Antigua is new and different every day, but always the same." I don't know how much Veh could actually see then, but now she is almost totally blind.

Veh's dinner included Eddie, an American who supervised a family-owned rug factory; "the Bug Man," who found and exported rare Guatemalan insects; an American who ran a million-dollar-a-year firm importing Latin American handicrafts, and the latter's companion; and a Peruvian woman.

Conversation turned to politics, specifically to the Contras. The Peruvian woman, Amalia, spoke passionately against U.S. armed intervention in Nicaragua, arguing for Latin Americans defining their own future, supporting Sandinista efforts to raise their own people out of poverty and illiteracy before demanding perfect democracy.

She was attacked by both the rug man and bug man, who insisted there was no "Latin America," but only a divided and jealously nationalistic and fractious set of Latin neighbors. Her view of a Latin consciousness was called elitist, one held by only a small number of powerless intellectuals. Latin America was in fact a fiction. And Latins (being Latins) always failed at negotiations because they were incapable of real decision and compromise.

Debra, the millionaire importer's companion, said, "I'm really enjoying this. What about you?" I replied, "I am waiting, then I will pounce."

Then I did. "There is a Latin American consciousness. It may reside only in the elites, but it is real, and these Latin Americans, many of whom are presidents and foreign ministers, resent our arrogance and unwillingness to listen to their wishes. They want to try negotiations, but the United States has blocked them over and over." I quoted Alfonso Robelo, "I, as a Latin American, want to give negotiations a fair chance before we begin the war anew." I went on to explain the thinness of the Contra movement, its total reliance on the United States, and its lack of real support anywhere else in the hemisphere.

Amalia, overjoyed, shouted "Bravo!"

I kept quiet for another ten minutes, perhaps twenty.

"Now," I said, looking at Amalia, "You are my next target."

"You want to see the lives of the Nicaraguan people improve. But you place your confidence in a vanguard responsible to no one. Who says they have the capacity?

"They do, the Sandinistas.

"Who says their program is right?

"They do.

"What gives them the right to rule?

"Their monopoly of arms.

"The Sandinistas enjoyed the support of the most progressive bourgeoisie in the hemisphere, and they squandered its trust. Nicaraguans are poorer than ever, and the war is only the second reason. It is your unelected, undemocratic, arrogant Sandinista vanguard that destroyed the economy."

Amalia, shaken by the ferocity of her former rescuer, quietly nodded.

Sometime during the evening, I discovered that Amalia was flying to Miami the next morning. Upon leaving, I regretted aloud that we didn't have time to have a drink together. It was an outlandish suggestion at 3:30 in the morning, with her plane's departure scheduled in just six hours. More outlandish, she immediately agreed.

On the way back to the hotel, Amalia shed all pretenses and began waxing ridiculous: "I have never been so attracted to a man. I want you. I love you." A hundreds times she said, "I love you." The next morning, to her horror, I recounted what she had said.

We had climbed into bed at 4:30 and got up at 7 so she could make her flight to Miami. While we were having breakfast she suggested we go right back to bed. Amalia possessed a fearsome sexuality. I thought she was the devil herself. How could I say no?

We spent the next day together, on horses and on each other. She liked me to tell her stories, and I regaled her with them—about Congress, the Vietnam War, my friend John, the long battles over Nicaragua, and Corinne. About Corinne, she said I was crazy, but otherwise she said I was a sane, interesting man whom she liked very much.

Later that night I received a call from Washington. The Massing article had been published in the *Post*. The caller could not read the entire article over the phone, but it was enough to hear its ending.

> Finally, the group itself splintered. Leikin, Aronson, and Kemble have reaffirmed their full support for the Contras, a position that has severely damaged their influence on the Hill. Cameron, at considerable emotional cost, has broken with his colleagues. The Iran-Contra hearings, he says, have shown that the Administration's Nicaragua policy "has not enjoyed the support of the American people, of Congress . . . even of the Nicaraguans themselves." He adds, "Unless the Administration negotiates directly with the Sandinistas, and the Sandinistas show themselves to be totally inflexible, I do not believe Congress will support aid again—and I don't think it should."

On the front page of the *Washington Post Outlook* section, the political persona of one Bruce P. Cameron was finally made public.

THE RISE AND FALL OF "OLLIE'S LIBERALS"

In late January 1986, conservative fundraiser Carl "Spitz" Channell held a dinner at the elegant Hay Adams Hotel in Washington to honor the Nicaraguan rebels, or "Contras." Anxious to impress some potential donors, Channell had put together a sparkling program. The speakers included Elliott Abrams, Assistant Secretary of State for Inter-American Affairs, and Colonel Oliver North of the National Security Council. Their impassioned pleas on behalf of the "freedom fighters" struck a chord with the staunchly conservative crowd.

Sitting among the well-heeled givers, movement activists, and White House officials was Bruce Cameron, a longtime lobbyist for Americans for Democratic Action, a bastion of Washington liberalism. In recent months, Cameron's politics had taken a sudden turn. Once a determined antagonist of the Administration, Cameron was now escorting Contra leaders around Congress and drafting legislation to provide them aid.

Cameron was one of an unlikely group of veteran Democrats—including Robert Leiken, Penn Kemble, and Bernard Aronson—who might be called "Ollie's Liberals." Although there is no evidence that the quartet was involved in any illegal activi-ties, it played an intriguing role in the unfolding of the Iran-Contra affair. At a time when the Reagan Administration was at the high-water mark of its political power and liberal forces were most disoriented, these four men acted as couriers across the ideological divide, helping make the Contra case to fellow Democrats. . . .

In the spring of 1985, a handful of Democrats began meeting to discuss how to convince congressional moderates to restore aid to Contra forces. The group was brought together by Penn Kemble, a leading figure in the Henry Jackson wing of the Democratic Party and the head of PRODEMCA (Friends of the Democratic Center in Central America). PRODEMCA, whose board members included Jeane Kirkpatrick, John Silber, and Ben Watenberg, sought to build public support for U.S. policy in Central America. Bruce Cameron and Robert Leiken attended the meeting. So did political consultant Bernard Aronson, a one-time speechwriter for Jimmy Carter and an adviser to the Mondale-Ferraro campaign. The foursome was in great demand that spring. Like pollinating bees, they carried information among all the parties to the debate. Recalls Representative Dave McCurdy, an Oklahoma Democrat, "They acted as go-betweens, helping take the edge off the adversarial relationship that had developed between us and the Administration." The four also became close to Oliver North. In meetings at the old Executive Office Building, North listened to their views and, in return, offered sensitive intelligence on Nicaragua. It was an odd relationship—the gung-ho marine colonel and the veteran liberals. Nonetheless, each side realized that the other could help it, and a symbiotic bond developed. After the House approved $27 million in non-military aid for the Contras in June, North invited Bruce Cameron to his office for a victory cigar. But Cameron's role dismayed many of his former liberal colleagues, and he resigned from the ADA.

In 1986, the President announced he would seek $100 million in aid for the Contras, portending another bruising battle with Congress. For all its fervor, the Administration was still unable to sell its policy to the American public. For conservative activists, that failure was a fact of unending frustration. Spitz Channell decided to do something about it. A relative unknown, the conservative fundraiser saw in the Contra cause a way to boost the profile of his National Endowment for the Preservation of Liberty. With the blessing of Oliver North, Channell conceived an elaborate $2-million PR campaign While preparing the campaign, he met with Penn Kemble and encouraged him to participate. Kemble was reluctant, he had never heard of Channell and couldn't find anyone else who had—but he put Channell in touch with Bruce Cameron, who was looking for a job. Soon after, Channell agreed to fund Cameron's lobbying activities.

All that Cameron lacked was a tax-exempt organization to receive the money. He got it from his friend Robert Owen, who had been Oliver North's "courier" to the Contras. Owen had a mostly inactive lobbying organization that he deeded over to Cameron who renamed it the Center for Democracy in the Americas. Cameron was now in business. In the coming months he and the center would receive $66,000 from Channell. Eventually Kemble, too, came on board, his doubts laid to rest by Channell's close ties to the Administration and conservative donors. (Both Kemble and Cameron say that, at the time, they had no knowledge of Channell's role in supplying weapons to the Contras.) . . .

Cameron and the others decided that the only way to reverse the vote was to win over moderates—and that would require cleaning up the Contras. Seeking to overcome Administration indifference to Contra reform, members of the group strenuously lobbied Elliott Abrams. At one of many meetings an exasperated Abrams admonished the four for becoming so enmeshed in Contra affairs. The "meddlers," he called them.

The foursome's involvement with the rebels indeed ran deep. Cameron and Leiken became confidants of Arturo Cruz and Alfonso Robelo, leaders of the United Nicaraguan Opposition (UNO), the principal Contra group. The two Americans counseled Cruz on his efforts to reform UNO, guided him on dealings with the Administration, and, when Cruz contemplated resigning—which was almost all the time, they were there to dissuade him. Leiken's opinion, says Cruz, "had tremendous influence on my decision to stay." Leiken went so far as to visit a Contra camp in Honduras, telling field commanders and common soldiers of Washington's interest in human rights. Not everyone appreciated his concern. A few weeks later, a congressional delegation visiting the camp saw a soldier bearing a sign that declared, "Robert Leiken es non grato."

Meanwhile there were sessions with Senator Sam Nunn and Dave McCurdy and appearances before the foreign affairs committees. Special attention was directed at Representative Les Aspin. The Wisconsin Democrat had voted against Contra aid in March, but was not entirely comfortable with that position. Impressed by articles that Leiken had written, Aspin contacted him and longtime acquaintance Bernard Aronson. In April, both accompanied Aspin on a fact-finding trip to Nicaragua. Eventually Aspin voted for Contra aid. "The Congressman is no expert on Central America," an aide observes. "People like Leiken and Aronson . . . had considerable input into his decision."

As the vote approached in the House, President Reagan delivered a last-minute address to the nation. His speechwriter: Bernard Aronson. White House Communications Director Pat Buchanan sent a preliminary draft to Aronson for a look. "It didn't strike the right tone," Aronson recalls. In rewriting it, Aronson took pains to address Democratic concerns. His draft contained the Administration's first admission of Contra human rights abuses and a presidential pledge to stop them. In the end it is unclear how much influence the speech had. It was delivered at an odd hour—noon—and the networks refused to carry it. Nonetheless, the President's accommodating approach was widely noted during the debate the next day (June 25). The final tally: 221 to 209 in favor of aid. The Contras would get $100 million, including the first lethal aid in two years.

In early August, Oliver North invited Cameron to his office for another cigar. North presented him with a letter from President Reagan. "Your contribution to forging a bipartisan policy of democratic renewal in Central America has been of profound importance," it stated. "While the struggle is not yet over, with your help we have taken an important step in the right direction."

Four months later, Oliver North was out. Later, Spitz Channell pled guilty to conspiracy charges. The IRS began investigating Cameron's tax-exempt organization. PRODEMCA, stung by the reports on Channell, reimbursed the money it had received from his organization. On top of it all, in March, Arturo Cruz resigned from UNO. The man whom the liberal foursome had made the centerpiece of its reform efforts had finally called it quits.

Finally, the group itself splintered. Leiken, Aronson and Kemble have reaffirmed their full support for the Contras, a position that has severely damaged their influence on the Hill. Cameron, at considerable emotional cost, has broken with his colleagues. The Iran-Contra hearings, he says, have shown that the Administration's Nicaraguan policy "has not enjoyed the support of the American people, of Congress . . . even of the Nicaraguans themselves." He adds, "Unless the Administration negotiates directly with the Sandinistas, and the Sandinistas show themselves to be totally inflexible, I do not believe Congress will support aid again—and I don't think it should."

Two days later I met with Vinicio. I had the job. And he had a vision:

There must be another way to fight the communists in Nicaragua. We must build the democratic forces both inside and outside. Inside the leaders must be willing to go to jail. Nicaraguans have no leaders to inspire them to resistance. The Contras have no program for them. They don't try to explain any vision of tomorrow. Military pressure is necessary, but it is not the principal key. Your job is to be a Christian among the lions.

My army needs more, it needs U.S. assistance. My job has been to give everybody a part of the Guatemalan political system, the private sector, the unions, and the political parties. We must give the army something, to show them their contribution to the democratic way of life is valued. ■

Chapter Thirteen

Heroes Jim Wright and Oscar Arias

July–August 1987

A few days after my meeting with Vinicio, I traveled to Miami. I visited friends from Peru and my Contra friends, many of whom had retired from the movement after Arturo's resignation. I met Aristides Sanchez, whom I had blasted so many times in the press and Congress. Surprisingly, I found him delightful. Sanchez recalled that I had labeled the ruling threesome of the FDN—Calero, Bermudez, and himself—the "iron triangle" of Contra power. Calero, he reported, had reacted with fury. But he had remonstrated with Calero:

"It is true," he said. "You control politics in Miami and our relations with Washington, I run our operations in Honduras, and Enrique is in charge of the war. How can you fault that description?"

I complained that in the Contra debate the Administration had ignored one obvious alternative: strengthening the internal opposition. Sanchez nodded. "That was true, but the Administration has destroyed that option by pulling out so many of our leaders and telling us to put our energies in the military front."

That argument made some sense, but Arturo had consistently argued that the aim of the Contras should be to strengthen the internal opposition. I pointed out that the whole point of the Arias plan was to reverse the priorities of the U.S. Administration. Sanchez predicted that the Arias plan had no chance.

Toward the end of my stay in Miami, I called my answering machine. I had been away for a month, and there were many messages, including one from Bob Leiken. He said Michael Massing was writing an expanded article on the Gang of Four for the magazine *Mother Jones*. Bob knew that would violate my agreement with Michael, and he wanted me to withdraw all my quotes, which, he believed, would kill the article. But the article was printed, and I was quoted.

When I returned to Washington, I decided to research the conduct of the war between Contras and Sandinistas, believing that by this time the effects of the $100 million should have become visible. The State Department had a clipping service which copied from the U.S. press all the articles on Central America. Diligently I went through the first seven months of 1987.

Steve Kinzer, a reporter I met in Guatemala in 1980 while he was researching the 1954 CIA-sponsored military coup against the government of Jacobo Arbenz, gave this account in May in the *New York Times*:

> American operatives, free from earlier congressional restrictions that limited their contact with rebel leaders, consider the success of the clandestine air re-supply operations during the first months of 1987 to have been one of the major achievements of the entire war.
>
> By one estimate, since January more than 100 plane loads of weapons, ammunition, medicine and other supplies have been dropped to the Contras by pilots flying secretly at night. And in a new tactic, the Americans have lately begun sending some supplies by boat to Contra units operating near the Atlantic Coast.
>
> The Contras' success at moving into Nicaragua reflects the value of the training and financing they received from the United States during the second half of 1986. To keep the war going, they needed continued American help.

A week later William Branigan, writing in the *Washington Post*, described how the Contras were conducting renewed warfare, along with the criticism expressed by foreign diplomats in Managua.[27]

> "This is one of the problems in getting them to stop hitting cooperatives," the diplomat said. "These guys love to go against cooperatives. Those are the symbols of the deprivation of their land." Although the cooperatives are usually defended by militiamen, he added, the attacks often result in civilian casualties.
>
> Other failings in the Contra strategies, diplomats said, lie in what the rebels are not doing. There is no evidence that the Contras are engaged in any of the painstaking political work that has to be done if they are to build a dependable base of support among peasants in the countryside. Rather, the entire effort is a

military one that relies almost entirely on U.S. aid.

In hitting military targets relatively rarely, the Contras seem to be doing little to weaken the Sandinistas' control over the country, the diplomats said. In particular, they noted, there has been no visible effort to strike at such instruments of state control as the General Directorate of State Security, the secret police.

James LeMoyne documented additional criticisms in a June 1 article:

[T]hey are . . . repeating serious political and tactical mistakes that greatly lengthen the odds against them in their uphill struggle against the Sandinistas.

Defending fixed positions easily reached by the Government's Soviet-provided rockets and artillery, the Contras were taking steady casualties in a pitched battle that broke all the rules of the hit and run guerrilla war they must wage if they are to weaken the far stronger Nicaraguan army.

Rebel commanders admit that the Government is fighting very effectively against them . . . inflicting as many casualties as they are receiving.

Their most serious errors include the practice of kidnapping civilians in Nicaragua and forcing them to join the rebel ranks.

Two weeks later, in another article, LeMoyne expanded on Contra problems:

In a similar war in El Salvador, leftist rebels treat any village that forms an armed defense unit as a legitimate target. There, the rebels have kidnapped mayors, burned down offices, and executed hundreds of people suspected of being informers.

The war in northern Nicaragua has a similar bitter texture, but its conduct has raised serious questions about whether such tactics, either here or in El Salvador, can win wider popular support for the rebels.

The war seems more brutal here because the Contras appear more prone to kill suspected opponents, to be far less disciplined than the Salvadoran rebels, and to lack political direction and sophistication.

In recent months, in other parts of the country, the Contras have attacked several small cooperatives that appear to have no military importance, killing civilians and alienating their friends and families.

The Sandinistas were also violating human rights, and some of these violations made Contra operations more difficult. Wilson Ring reported the following in the *Christian Science Monitor* on July 23:

Contra operations inside Nicaragua have been hindered by the Sandinistas forcibly removing civilians from some war zones, Contra and informed sources say . . .

Partly as a result of the relocations, rebel recruitment is barely keeping up with casualties because the Contras draw new soldiers from the civilian population. . . . And a record number of deserters is showing up in UN refugee camps. . . .

The relocation effort has also made it difficult to find food inside Nicaragua. Contra doctrine calls for troops to buy food from civilians. But the dearth of civilians is forcing Contra columns to spend more and more time locating food.

The Sandinistas' gross mismanagement of the economy and the war was having a disastrous effect on life in the cities. Glenn Garvin reported this for the *Washington Times* on June 18:

"Nicaragua," [a foreign visitor] declared, "is going back into the 19th century."

Almost every kind of food is in short supply. A pound of butter costs $150 dollars at the official exchange rate. Bread, tortillas, butter, cheese, coffee, meat, chicken, propane gas, and cooking oil are all but impossible to find.

In Managua, the city cuts the water off at least two days a week in a desperate attempt to keep the ancient water mains functioning. Power failures are a daily event. Epidemics of typhoid and rabies afflict rural Nicaragua. Here in the capital, pregnant women are crammed two and three to a bed in maternity wards.

"People are beginning to feel hunger now," says a small businessman. "The situation has come down so low. I don't know how we're going to get out of this. There's money, but there's nothing to buy."

The official exchange rate is 70 cordobas to the dollar. The black market rate is 7,200 to the dollar, and that's expected to jump to 9,000 any day now.

The Contras, however, were never able to organize discontent to create an urban base. Andres Oppenheimer reported on that failure in the *Chicago Tribune* on May 31:

> The U.S.-backed Contra rebels are not winning support in Managua and other Nicaraguan cities despite growing dissatisfaction with the leftist Sandinista regime. . . .
>
> "The message of the Contras has not yet found an echo in this part of the country," said Virgilio Godoy Reyes, President of the Independent Liberal party, one of the most vocal opposition groups. "Support for the Contras is basically limited to the rural areas."
>
> Part of the Contras' problem . . . is that they have not been able to create a mystique about their cause, or themselves.
>
> The very name Contra, which in Spanish means "against," conveys the rebels' opposition to the Sandinistas . . . but projects no positive message about what they stand for, making it difficult to shed their image as followers of the late strongman Anastacio Somoza.

LeMoyne summed up the situation in an article at the end of June:

> What lies ahead appears to be a debilitating war that the Contras cannot win, but the Sandinistas cannot bring to an end so long as the United States is willing to back the rebels.

There appeared to be no solution for Nicaragua. Arias visited Washington in mid-June to sell his program to President Reagan.

"We might share the same objective—that we want democracy in Central America. We disagree on the means and how to obtain it," Arias told *Long Island Newsday* on June 19. "I don't think the Contras are the answer. I think the Contras are the main excuse by the Sandinistas to abolish individual liberties. I propose to get rid of the Contras so they have no excuses. It is true they cannot have a pluralistic society if there is a war."

Presidential Spokesman Marlin Fitzwater stated the Administration position, a complete reversal of the Arias formula: "The greatest concern is the need for the Sandinistas to act on genuine democratization before pressure on the regime is removed in any way."

My review of the journalists' reports, along with an entire day of discussion with LeMoyne in Guatemala, had convinced me that the war by itself was without purpose. The Contras by that time were the beneficiaries of a well-organized resupply operation. Yet they did not engage the enemy directly, preferring soft targets, principally cooperatives. CIA training was unsuccessful in preparing the Contras to carry out real political work among the peasants, many of whom were sympathetic to their cause. The lack of vision was in large part due to the absence of real connection between the fighters and their political leaders. Aristides Sanchez once told Alfonso that if the two of them ever landed in a rebel camp in Nicaragua without warning, they would be lucky to get away with their lives, because they would most likely be unknown to the fighters. The liberal Contras, as I called them, had contact with Arturo and Alfonso and their immediate aides, and some of the rank-and-file internal opposition. But since they did not know the fighters or their officers, since there was no shared vision, they could forge no link with the Contra fighters.

The Nicaraguan opposition was fragmented into three parts: the Contra fighting force, the bourgeois leaders in exile, and the internal opposition, led by middle-class, bourgeois politicians. The internal opposition saw the Contra fighters at best as an instrument that kept the Sandinistas off balance and at worst as the Sandinista excuse for limiting freedoms. Most disdained the Contra politicians as exiles who lived in Miami comfort, while they faced Sandinista mobs and saw their followers jailed, subjected to psychological and sometimes physical torture.

I concluded that the only purpose that the Contras served was as an instrument for gaining diplomatic goals, while simultaneously shutting them down.

One day, as I was discussing my views on the military situation with my friend Colonel Ed King, who was a consultant to Senate majority leader Robert Byrd, the operator broke in to tell me that she had an emergency call from Scotland.

It was Corinne, of course. She had called the day before and had encountered me when my emotions had shut down. Now she was calling again in search of reassurance. "Do you still love me?" she pleaded. "I do," I lied, plausibly. "It's just that we have not seen each other for so long. It was so hard for me when you were in Paris. It will be fine when you get back." But I didn't mean it. And for reasons known only to the Power that runs the universe, on that same night Amalia called and uncharacteristically asked the same question. I gave her, too, the answer she wanted to hear.

I disapprove of men who play with women, and I like to think that I don't. I felt trapped, in both cases, into giving an answer that was false. In Corinne's case, thousands of miles away and with a long history of intimacy and shared expectations, my response was reasonable. But my behavior lost any pretense of reasonableness when I gave the same answer to Amalia. I had behaved dishonorably.

Corinne's return fell on a weekend, and I didn't mind the fact that she didn't immediately call me. But on Monday she came to my home and flew into my arms. "Oh, I missed you so much."

And then she said she had decided.

"I know now I can't live without you—I will do anything you want me to."

I did not scrutinize her statement. I would have been equally indifferent to an announcement that she had decided to leave Allan and come to me.

And then I told her that because she had gone to Paris with Allan, I first had stopped believing in us, then in her, and finally had lost any feeling at all about our relationship.

"It isn't because of anyone else, is it?" she asked. "If there were someone else, it would mean that all our love had been without meaning or consequence."

It was time to lie again.

"Of course not. It was because of Paris."

She continued to come to see me, and we continued to make love. And even that, for the first time in our relationship, turned stale.

One night I was walking home from the grocery store, a block and a half away from my home. It was raining. I walked in the street; the gutter was filled with debris, a metaphor for the ugliness and chaos of the world. I hated making Corinne unhappy, and every time I saw her, her usual smile—that once could inspire poetry and trigger warmth in sagging muscles—was gone, her mouth now twisted in pain.

I thought about it. Corinne and I were good for each other once; maybe we could be good again. I would take that chance—I shook my head and added a finished cigarette to the debris in the gutter.

The next morning Corinne arrived. I told her what I had been feeling the night before. And in a flash I was in love again.

I took her into my arms, doubling her over until her head almost touched the floor. I had taken a leap of faith; I would try trusting her again.

But now she was not sure. And she insisted that we had to date. She found a way to be free one Wednesday night and then again on a Friday. The man who wrote poetry was back stronger, and weaker, than ever.

She told her mother.

Her mother disapproved. "How could you let this happen?"

Corinne described her problems with Allan, explaining that sex with him hadn't been good for years.

Her mother replied, "Sex is something you just have to do. It doesn't have to be good."

She told her best friend, Mildred.

Mildred disapproved, too. "Marriage is like any other job. You just have to work harder at it. Why don't you keep Bruce as a lover on the side?"

And suddenly there was no decision. We were back to May, back to before the Paris trip—which was supposed to decide everything.

One day in July Tom Loeffler, a former congressman from Texas, stopped by to visit Speaker of the House Jim Wright. Before running for governor of Texas, Loeffler had been a Republican member of Congress and served in the post of chief deputy whip for the minority. He was one of several members of Congress whom I knew and who knew me by sight. I had never before known his name. We had always simply nodded and exchanged greetings. Still, I had recognized in him a certain energy and determination.

Although he held a high post in the Republican leadership, he had become frustrated in the minority. He had run for governor, but lost in the primary. Afterward he had become active in the final effort to secure passage of the 1986 bill that proposed to give $100 million to the Contras. By that time, I had already fled to Guatemala.

Figure 16: Speaker of the U.S. House of Representatives, Jim Wright, with Costa Rican President Oscar Arias, the two people who helped broker the peace agreement between the Sandinistas and the Contras in Nicaragua. Photo courtesy of Jim Wright.

Now Loeffler had returned to Washington to fill a special post in the White House, assigned to coordinate efforts to win new aid for the Contras. Unlike previous White House lobbyists, Loeffler knew the House and could count votes. He determined that the votes just weren't there. This flew in the face of conventional conservative wisdom.

Polls taken the week after Ollie North finished testifying before the Iran-Contra panel had shown that the American public was closely divided over Contra aid, perhaps narrowly in support. That marked the first time in six years of Contra aid that the American people did not register overwhelming opposition. Conservatives believed it was time to forge ahead, to put a new Contra aid proposal to Congress.

Loeffler knew that, while the polls might have changed, members of Congress had not. In his talks with Administration officials, he learned of a plan, devised by Bernie, to put forward a bipartisan peace proposal with the emphasis on steps the Sandinistas would have to take to implement democratic reform. "It would end once and for all the crap about a negotiated settlement," Aronson reportedly had said.[28]

I knew nothing of this. It was the first initiative on Contra policy in two years to which I had not been a party. I was in limbo: no longer part of the Administration network, not trusted by the liberal opposition. Moderates had spent their energy on the unsuccessful Slattery effort.[29]

The steps Loeffler took, from a lobbyist's point of view, were predictable. You have a big problem; you go to someone on the other side whom you trust, who trusts you. As members of the Texas delegation and leaders of their parties, Loeffler and Wright knew and trusted one another.

Loeffler went to Wright. Wright had supported the Administration's El Salvador policy; in the crucial vote in 1984, his support had made the difference. Loeffler probably knew the Sandinistas had broken promises to Wright in 1980, when the Sandinistas were organizing a new ruling junta following the resignations of Robelo and Violeta Chamorro.

According to Barry, their first meeting began with Loeffler establishing his bona fides. He told Wright that the Administration budget called for only $105 million for the Contras in the next fiscal year, but the Administration would probably ask for $200 million. Loeffler said that Reagan was serious about a diplomatic solution. Wright responded by "reviewing the prospects of the (Arias) peace plan."[30]

Then Loeffler improvised, though this is not what Administration lobbyists are supposed to do, especially in foreign relations. But if you possess a strong sense of yourself and your own vision, as well as a willingness to take risks to make good things happen, you act—even without orders.

"They need support," said Loeffler, referring to the four presidents of the Central American democracies. "I've been wondering, would you be willing to make a joint statement with the President in pursuit of a diplomatic effort? . . . What significance for the speakership! The importance to our allies, to the Soviets, to the world, of seeing the United States united in foreign policy—it would be tremendous! It would call the bluff of the Sandinistas."[31]

I recognized the argument; I had used a similar argument in trying to sell the Slattery plan to Congressman Hyde and Senator McCain.

This time Wright agreed, and began a week of intense negotiations with the Administration, at the White House and in the House Democratic Caucus. For the Administration and most of the House Republican Conference, nothing was more important than continuing Contra aid. For the Democratic Caucus, nothing was more important than stopping it. Wright and Loeffler were attempting the impossible.

Members of the Democratic Caucus immediately suspected a trap. Majority Leader Tom Foley (D-Washington) declared in one meeting, "There can be absolutely no linkage between this and Contra aid. No connection. No implication if this [peace plan] fails, the Speaker is expected to support Contra aid."[32]

On July 30 Wright met with George Schultz. The latter reiterated the Administration's standard line: support for negotiations backed by military pressure. Wright insisted that the peace proposal stand alone. Foley repeated his admonition about linkage between the plan's success or failure, and Contra aid. Foley challenged the Administration: Why did they need the Speaker? Why didn't the President make a proposal on his own?[33]

"The President doesn't have any credibility," Loeffler explained. "If the President made the proposal it would be dismissed as empty rhetoric."[34] My personal guess is that Loeffler acted in good faith. But key players in the Administration quickly became familiar with his negotiations with Wright, and what was planned was indeed a trap.

Bear in mind that an Administration never acts as a single entity, with one policy, speaking with one voice, and this was especially true under Reagan. An Administration includes many voices, many policy tendencies, often pulling in different directions. But it is also an organism with one central voice, one central tendency, the President's. And Reagan wanted the Sandinistas gone. He was unwavering in that goal, though never clear about how to achieve it, and he permitted subordinates to convey different messages and put forward contradictory policies.

Hard-liners, led by Elliott Abrams, National Security Advisor Frank Carlucci, and Defense Secretary Caspar Weinberger, would never have let Loeffler's initiative get that far. But, once it had, they came to see it as a convenient trap for the Democrats. It could go forward, the Sandinistas would reject it, then the Administration could have Contra aid. But Carlucci couldn't keep his mouth shut.

Wright met with his own leadership and staff. No one supported the proposal. An aide to Foley pointed to a story in the *Washington Times* where Carlucci was reported to have said that "after Congress adjourns the first week in August" the President would announce a $300 million aid program for the Contras. Wright called Carlucci. Carlucci said it was a misquote. But at the end of the conversation, Wright reported to his colleagues, "[Carlucci] started talking about negotiations with Contra aid too, just in case."[35] The peace plan was dead—shot down again by the Administration.

But Wright had been talking with more than just the Americans. He had spoken with Arias on a number of occasions. He had also met with Arias's brother and Chief of Staff John Beal in Puerto Rico. Over the ten years he had been active on Central American legislation, Wright had developed and personally maintained a large number of contacts in the region. To them he was always accessible, arranging no less than ten meetings from 1981 to 1985.

"An hour [after the call with Carlucci] Costa Rican ambassador Guido Fernandez . . . walked into Wright's office for a final conversation before returning home to prepare for the Central American summit [to be held in Guatemala on August 6 and 7]. . . . Wright showed him a one-page memo that outlined the basic aspects of this proposal. Fernandez was enthusiastic and said if Wright and Reagan jointly endorsed such a plan, it could well spur the Central Americans to an agreement."[36] In that moment, the plan was reborn.

That weekend Wright reworked the proposal in response to White House requests. That Monday, a bipartisan meeting was held that included the Administration, Senate minority leader Robert Dole, and Republican and Democratic House leaders.

In that meeting Foley restated his point, "We must reiterate as we have from the start: this is a peace plan. It has nothing to do with whether Contra aid passes or not. The separation is absolute."

House minority leader Trent Lott of Mississippi responded, "This entails risks for us too. The trap will have trapped us."[37]

And that is exactly what happened.

The plan was announced on Wednesday, August 5, the night before peace talks were to begin in Guatemala. In brief, it called for a simultaneous and immediate cease-fire between the Contras and the Sandinistas, an end to U.S. aid to the Contras and Soviet bloc aid to the Sandinistas, and the restoration of civil and political liberties. The Sandinistas were given until September 30 to agree.

The Administration stabbed Wright in the back. He discovered this reading a memo given to him that morning at the White House as he rode back to the Capitol in his chauffeured limousine (a special perk of the

Speaker). In twenty-one points, it outlined Administration interpretation of the Wright-Reagan plan. Wright called Chief of Staff Howard Baker to complain. He clearly did not agree.

The memo stated that compliance with the plan would require presidential elections in Nicaragua before 1990 when Ortega's term was scheduled to expire. It also stated that the President could begin to criticize the Sandinistas, and call for Contra aid, within two weeks if the Sandinistas did not accept the plan.

Baker said the Administration needed the memo to satisfy its right wing, which was going a bit crazy over the plan. And he promised it would not leak.[38] Both the *Washington Post* and the *New York Times* knew about the memo by the very next day.

Wright did not simply stew. In a phone call to Guido Fernandez, and subsequently through his former aide Richard Pena, his man at the Guatemala City meetings, Wright made it clear that the purpose of his plan was to stimulate a peace settlement, not to dictate its terms. "Costa Rica's most critical question concerned the timetable. Arias envisioned ninety days for compliance, whereas Wright-Reagan spoke of sixty days. Was this rigid? Back came the answer from Wright: No, you can modify it. The plan is meant to complement, not substitute [for the Arias plan]."[39]

At 4:30 Friday morning, Fernandez called Wright at home to tell him there was an agreement in principle. Later that morning Pena called from the airport to confirm that the agreement had held. Wright announced the success at a morning press conference.

According to Gutman, the announcement was premature. Honduras, the country that had given sanctuary to the main Contra bases, whose military helped create the Contras, was holding out. After Wright's announcement, even the Hondurans gave in. The agreement was signed. Gutman also points out that the Administration had not given guidance to its closest allies, El Salvador and Honduras. He suggests they had received a copy of Wright-Reagan without the twenty-one points. Arias, on the other hand, had "an official interpretation," Wright's interpretation, and he "used the opportunity to the fullest."[40] Wright immediately endorsed the agreement: "I cannot conceive of the United States being in a position of upsetting the timetable or doing anything but rejoicing or cooperating."

The Administration was confused. Two days after the signing, Vice President George H. W. Bush charged that the agreement favored the

Sandinistas, saying, "We are not going to leave the Contras twisting in the wind, wondering whether they are going to be done in by a peace plan." The next day, however, Marlin Fitzwater said, "We are encouraged by it. We think it moves in a positive direction. We want a negotiated settlement in Nicaragua, and we just have to see how the process works."[41]

Like Wright-Reagan, the Guatemala City Accord called for a cease-fire, democratization, national dialogue, and an end to aid to rebel forces. It made these proposals binding in all Central American countries where there was conflict, not just Nicaragua. It did not call for an end to Soviet bloc aid to Nicaragua. It left that issue and all regional security issues, except for support to irregular forces, to the Contadora Group talks. Its timetable for the cease-fire, democratization, and an end to aid for irregular forces was ninety, not sixty, days. The extremes were not happy.

William Leogrande, a political science professor at American University in Washington, D.C., and a polemicist for the left-wing position on Central America, complained bitterly in the *Los Angeles Times* on July 13:

> House Democrats emerged from the tumult of the past week looking very clever, albeit largely by luck. But what the Democrats gained in political positioning by their support of Reagan's peace plan, they lost in principle. The vast majority of Democrats have always opposed Contra aid on the simple ground that it is wrong and therefore the United States ought to stop it. . . .
>
> Perhaps without meaning to, the Democrats gave up that principle when they endorsed the Reagan-Wright plan. The essence of the plan was to halt Contra aid in exchange for a series of concessions by Nicaragua. The implicit premise in such a deal is that Contra aid is a legitimate policy instrument that should be given up only if something is received in return. . . .
>
> Whether they want to admit it or not, they have retreated from the position that Contra aid is just plain wrong. That is why Wright's endorsement of the plan was such a political coup for the White House.
>
> The advent of the Arias plan conceals but does not erase the Democratic concession. The Administration's new position is already forming—Reagan will request humanitarian aid for the Contras while the Arias plan is alive, and military aid to be

Figure 17: Ernest Lefever. The author played a key role in 1981 in defeating Lefever's nomination for assistant secretary of state for human rights when the author organized an impromptu press conference outside the Senate Foreign Relations Committee for Jacobo Timermann, a recently released political prisoner from Argentina. Lefever's defeat made legitimate for the first time Republican efforts to go beyond their narrow human rights criticism of Communist dictators to include right-wing dictatorship. Photo courtesy of Rebecca Hammel.

released if the plan dies. He will argue that this incentive will make Sandinista compliance with the plan more likely.

In fact, its effect would be just the opposite. But after supporting the Reagan-Wright plan, it will be hard for liberal Democrats to persuade their moderate colleagues that this is an unreasonable proposal.

Ernest Lefever, President Reagan's first nominee for assistant secretary of state for human rights (who failed to win Senate confirmation because of his opposition to an activist human rights policy toward noncommunist governments) spoke for the ultraright in *USA Today* on August 12:

> But does anyone believe that peace will break out or that democratic reforms will sweep over Nicaragua in the next six months, much less the next six weeks.
>
> The Sandinistas violated basic rights—freedom of speech, press, and religion—before U.S. aid to the Contras. Will an end of U.S. aid to the Contras induce the self-declared Marxist-Leninists in Managua to restore these rights and hold free, multiparty elections?
>
> When the plan fails, will Congress support the President's Central American policy? That is the real test of the USA's commitment to peace with freedom in Central America.

Neither Leogrande nor Lefever examined the plan itself, the political context, the military situation, or Central America. Both wrote as theologians—one for Contra aid as the path to salvation, the other against Contra aid as original sin.

James LeMoyne, writing in the *New York Times* on August 10 and 22, put the Guatemala City Accord into a political and military context:

> The new initiative comes at a time when the rebels have defied their harshest critics by successfully reinfiltrating Nicaragua, where they now appear to pose an enduring problem for the Sandinistas. American training, new anti-aircraft missiles, and regular airlifts to rebel units have finally put the Contras in a position from which they can bleed the Sandinistas indefinitely, even if they cannot defeat them.
>
> Given the disastrous state of the Nicaraguan economy and growing public dissatisfaction with the Sandinistas, the rebels have become a debilitating force that drains the limited financial and political resources. So the Sandinistas would very much like to see the Contras neutralized, a prospect offered by the treaty.
>
> In essence the treaty guarantees political survival to the Sandinistas if they agree to stop running the country like a one-party

revolutionary socialist state. Since the Sandinistas have been a revolutionary party since their founding 25 years ago, such a change would be significant.

A senior Costa Rican official said he felt the Sandinistas had decided to sign the plan because they realized the Contra war would go on and they were worried by apparent bipartisan support in Congress for the far tougher accord put forward by Mr. Reagan.

But if the Sandinistas genuinely permit the restoration of a free press, free organization of political parties and political rallies, as well as a return of exiles and rebels seeking amnesty, they will have made a major shift in the way they exercise power.

Nicaragua could then conceivably enter a much more flexible and pluralistic period of political change, even if the Sandinistas remained in control.

If, however, the Sandinistas do not offer such a political opening, it is likely that Congress will support increased aid to the Contras, and what failed to be decided this week at the negotiating table will again be contested on the battlefield.

In summary, the Contras could not defeat the Sandinistas, but the Sandinistas could not defeat the Contras as long as the United States supported them. Arias had put forth a proposal, but its chances were slim as long as the United States opposed serious negotiations. The Administration had known that it would lose a House vote on military aid in 1987 unless it created a trap for House Democrats. Jim Wright knew that he could win the next vote, but that it would be bloody, and not definitive. Events in Central America itself could affect the five to ten votes that determined whether military aid stopped or flowed.

It was a crucial moment in history, awaiting action. Often there is no one to seize such a moment and mold history to his will. Tom Loeffler's serendipitous call on Wright offered an opportunity and Wright seized it. Leogrande is right that the Wright-Reagan plan implicitly made Contra aid a legitimate policy instrument, to be relinquished only if something were offered in return.

But what was demanded of the Sandinistas, as LeMoyne points out, was not their surrender, but a democratic opening. And that was the only thing that Contra aid as a policy instrument could accomplish. That was not insignificant or impossible. After the accord, all attention was focused on Nicaragua and Sandinista compliance.

Phillip Habib, the President's negotiator, wanted to travel to Central America to make the Arias plan work, to "fill in the gaps" on regional security issues, including Soviet bloc aid. Elliott Abrams was vehemently opposed to Habib's traveling. The only message he wanted to send to Central Americans was that they had made a mistake, and that they should help the United States create a climate conducive to the restoration of military aid to the Contras. He won Caspar Weinberger to his side. Reagan denied Schultz and Habib's wish for the United States to play an active role in negotiating compliance with the accord. Habib resigned.

Former Secretary of State Henry Kissinger summed up the Habib episode in the *Washington Post* on August 16:

> What happened, starting with the Reagan-Wright initiative, was that the Administration altered the terms of debate from the wisdom of pursuing a military course with Nicaragua to a hassle over terms for cutting off aid to the Contras. . . .
>
> The subsequent decision by the Central Americans to come up with their own variation on a peace plan was a logical extension of what the Administration did. . . . Having taken the first step down that road, the administration cannot credibly veer away because it is uneasy about some aspects of the Central American plan and seek to alter it with changes of personnel. . . .
>
> You can't carry water on both shoulders. If the aim of the Administration is to overthrow the Sandinistas, it should say so and get Congress to vote up or down. If the Administration is not prepared to do that, then it needs to seek formulas for an accommodation and cannot allow itself to be pressured into changing course constantly.

In his Saturday radio address on September 12, the President attacked the Arias plan: "We welcome the Guatemalan plan, but it falls short of the safeguards for democracy and our national security contained in the bipartisan plan I worked out with the congressional leadership. That is why . . . there should be no uncertainty about our unswerving commitment to the Contras." Wright responded that such aid would be inappropriate while negotiations were taking place and that any request for military aid would therefore be defeated.

The Democrats now possessed the third arrow in the quiver[42] to defeat Contra military aid forever, a genuine diplomatic alternative. With Habib gone, and facing a hostile Administration, Central American leaders would turn to Wright and the House Democratic leadership to facilitate compliance through diplomacy. This is how the situation looked in December of 1989, when I began this writing; Sandinista intentions were still in doubt. Every move toward compliance was immediately followed by serious backsliding, then limited progress. The Sandinistas and an almost united opposition selected their presidential candidates and their platforms, and began their official campaigns. The Contra forces were still largely intact, but there had been no major fighting since March 1988, although the Sandinistas had recently ended the formal truce. Humanitarian aid continued to flow to the Contras, but there had been no new military aid since February 28. Liberals and moderates were waiting to see if elections scheduled for February 25, 1990, would take place, and whether the Sandinistas would allow an honest counting of votes. The Sandinistas were discovered in 1992 to have delivered surface-to-air missiles to the Salvadoran guerrillas and to have permitted the Salvadoran and Guatemalan guerrillas and others to maintain secret arms caches. The implicit threat of renewed Contra aid hung over the Sandinistas if they cheated in the elections, or were discovered as in 1992 to be continuing aid to the FMLN.

It was messy. But it represented a great change—from stalemated, brutal warfare and a regime that allowed no freedom of the press or association and incarcerated thousands of political dissidents. Meanwhile, President Ortega had signed another agreement with his four Central American colleagues calling on the FMLN guerrillas to lay down their arms and incorporate themselves into the political life of El Salvador.

It was an uneven course of progress, but the only one that offered hope for peace in Central America. More than anyone else in the United States, Jim Wright deserves the credit for setting it in motion.

In 1987, the plan was agreed to. But its strength had yet to be tested in Congress. And I had two more scenes to play. ■

CHAPTER FOURTEEN

MOZAMBIQUE

August–October 1987

*C*orinne's mood in August was like a rubber band in the hands of a five-year-old. She had begun the month by saying, "I cannot stand another minute at home. I want to be with you." But she couldn't decide and she couldn't act. Any feelings she had for "us" were negated by the fierce opposition of her mother and Mildred.

One day she exploded at me, "I must try to see if my marriage can work. I just cannot walk away and say, 'Well, too bad I am wrecking all your lives. Good-bye.'

"And I must do it for you, too. Because I am going to feel guilty anyway. At least I would feel less guilty if I could really know that there is nothing left in my marriage and that I'm justified in leaving it. It's the only way I can proceed."

"What about Paris?" I asked. "I thought that was the test."

"No, all I thought about was you, never about him."

She then informed me that her psychologist had recommended she and Allan see a marriage counselor.

And then, one night in late August or early September, Corinne lifted one of her many moratoriums on our lovemaking. Denial made our coming together explosive. When our passion was spent, our desire for union was not. We ended on the couch in the living room. I ordered her, still naked, to move to the center of the living room. I wanted to look at her, all of her, at once. She was nervous and shy at revealing herself and looked as if she wanted to return to the safety of embrace.

But in that moment I felt the sureness of command and ordered of her an act, never before contemplated, an act of intimacy so close though we did not touch. And in the doing she was no longer shy of being seen, but even proud of her newly revealed depths. We marveled afterwards that though we had never imagined the need, we had been waiting all our lives, she to be asked, I to command. We were never more one than in those moments, never before, never since.

When she left, I sat in my chair for a while, first reliving the experience and then trying to tell myself what it meant.

She has gone, but she is still here, and now she will never leave again. I don't quite understand what happened in that moment, but it was the most transforming moment of my life. We were truly one, and yet we were not touching. Fused. Union. The merging of souls, one a man, the other a woman, and in that unity was the total transcendence of self, and yet the concrete affirmation of our separate flesh.

I am now bound to her so totally that no marriage vows are necessary to affirm our oneness. I want her. If life chooses or if she chooses to unravel what we have just made, I doubt that it will really matter.

Corinne is the one I have been looking for all my life. In that one brief moment of command and obedience, we fused.

I am undone. I am happy, so exhilarated that death itself cannot cheat me of this moment. No, better, only death can guarantee that this moment will last forever. Life, which is change and decay, is now beyond me.

This rush of thoughts that would have embarrassed the young Werther[43] *or in another time Henry Miller made me think I was truly mad. How could I have pulled all that feeling out of such a small act? I seized my coat and dashed out into the dusk. Either a bright sun or a dark sky would have propelled me into further flights of unchecked romanticism or despair—and I wasn't sure which would have done which. But the dusk was comforting, and off to the gym I went, shading from passersby this new light within me.*

When I returned home, I found that if indeed I was mad, I was not alone.

Her voice spoke to me from my answering machine.

"Hi, it's ten o'clock and I'm at the grocery store and I wonder where you are. Are you still at the gym? I'm sorry I didn't find you in. I'll call you in the morning, hopefully before nine o'clock, I don't know, I have a lot of people at my house.

I've just been thinking about you and feeling like I belong to you and it's all yours. I love you. Good night, sweetheart."

Fusion, extravagant romanticism, the total immersion of each in the other. Yes, and I was not alone.

The message the next night was just as passionate.

"Hi, sweetheart. It is 7:15 and I just wanted to tell you (her voice drops and has an edge of desperation), I just wanted you to know that I am thinking about you, and me and us. And I'll call you tomorrow. I love you."

Still, the counseling continued, and Allan moved back into the bedroom. As high as I had flown, I now embraced the depths of despair.

One Saturday in August I went to the gym. When I finished, the thought of returning home (to my desk, to my telephone) made no sense to me. I wanted to see a movie. Two blocks away, the new James Bond was opening. I bought the ticket, but a very long line lay between me and a seat. So I began looking around for someone I might know. And it just so happened that the sixth person in line was an old and dear friend, Jose Ramos Horta from East Timor.

East Timor constitutes half of an island in the Indonesian archipelago just above western Australia. But East Timor was part of the Portuguese colonial empire when Indonesia received its independence from the Netherlands in 1949.

In 1974 the Portuguese armed forces, exhausted by long colonial wars in Mozambique and Angola, rebelled against their civilian rulers and Portugal's new government immediately began decolonization. In August 1975 the left-wing independence movement, FRETILIN, seized power in East Timor with the help of the Portuguese garrison. There followed a brief civil war, which FRETILIN easily won.

On December 7 Indonesian armed forces trained and outfitted by the United States government invaded, driving FRETILIN from the capital and major towns. Over the next three years more than one-third of East Timor's population, some 200,000 people, died in that war and the war-induced famine.

Jose had been sent by FRETILIN to represent his party and his country in the United States and United Nations. I had met him early on during my time at ADA, in 1976. The very first amendment I drafted for consideration on the House floor was to cut military aid to Indonesia because of its invasion of East Timor.

Every year thereafter, until 1985, I worked with Jose or with an American human rights advocate, Arnold Kohen, to raise the issue of East Timor in Congress. In 1980 Jose asked me to address the United Nations Commission on Decolonization about Carter Administration assistance to Indonesia to consolidate control over East Timor. In 1982, during a UN Special Session on Disarmament, I arranged for Jose to be photographed for television standing between Joan Baez and Senator Ted Kennedy. When he came to Washington, he often stayed with me, and when I was in

New York I stayed with him.

Three years since I had last seen him, Jose was in Washington to serve as press attaché for the Mozambican Embassy.

After the movie, we had dinner at La Fonda, a Mexican restaurant near my home. I explained my recent past and my hope for a job with Guatemala. Jose was never a conventional third world revolutionary. He knew little of Marx, Lenin, or Mao—although he pretended. In the Middle East, his sympathies were with Israel, and he thought that I was right to have promoted the views of Pastora and Cruz.

He told me that Mozambique's government was thinking about hiring a lobbyist. Mozambique had a nominally Marxist-Leninist government. It became independent from Portugal in 1975, after the ruling party FRELIMO had fought the Portuguese for thirteen years. But the white minority government of Rhodesia organized a rebel force, recruiting black Africans who had been Portuguese regular or secret police. When Rhodesia became Zimbabwe under black majority rule in 1980, the South African government assumed sponsorship of the rebel group RENAMO. The South Africans expanded RENAMO and changed its fighting strategy. Instead of targeting the FRELIMO army and mobilizing political dissent, the new RENAMO went after soft targets, unleashing a campaign of terror, massacring whole villages, mutilating its opponents, real or imagined.

At FRELIMO's Third Congress in 1977, it officially embraced the "experiences of Marxism-Leninism" as its guide for rule in Mozambique. Emphasis was placed on the state sector, and Jose told me that half a billion dollars was put into state farms, "almost all of it wasted." Nonetheless, the government made dramatic improvements in the health and education of its citizens.

The 1977 decision to embrace Marxism-Leninism was entirely understandable. Those were heady days for third world revolutionaries with close ties to the Soviets. The United States had been defeated in Indochina. Congress would not allow continued CIA support of two movements that were fighting Soviet and Cuban-backed forces in Angola. Later there would be coups by Soviet-backed factions in Ethiopia and South Yemen. In 1979 rulers in Nicaragua and Iran, two close American allies, fell. Meanwhile, the United States, England, France, and Germany all seemed unable to manage their own economies. It was a period of western gloom and self-doubt. "Armed revolution and socialist development" seemed to be the template

Figure 18: Happy, well-fed children internally displaced by the rebels in Dondo, Mozambique. Author photo.

of the future. A Mozambican once told me: "Armed revolution is as natural as breakfast."

The Carter Administration tried to help the new government in Mozambique. However, congressional activism unleashed by the Vietnam War to curb aid to right-wing dictators provoked a conservative response. All aid to nominally left-wing governments like Mozambique was cut off.

By 1982 the South African–backed rebels had destroyed much of Mozambique's rural infrastructure, and reversed earlier gains in health and education. Schools and clinics became constant targets, perceived to be symbols of the government.

The government realized it had to reach out, expand its base both domestically and internationally. It first talked with the churches— Muslim, Catholic, and Protestant, whose property the government had seized in the 1970s.

Relations with the Reagan Administration began badly when the South Africans, emboldened by the prospect of an Administration more sympathetic to their aims, launched a raid into Mozambique's capital, Maputo. Subsequently, the government arrested a number of its citizens identified as CIA agents and expelled American diplomats.

Nonetheless, the Reagan Administration displayed no strong ideological antipathy toward Mozambique, as it had toward Nicaragua and Angola. And in 1984 the United States played a small but important role in facilitating the Nkomti agreement between South Africa and Mozambique, in which each agreed not to aid the rebels fighting against the other. In 1985 when the Reagan doctrine of aiding anticommunist movements to roll back the Soviet empire of client states in the third world had reached its peak, Mozambique was spared. In fact, even as the Administration sought authority to restore funds to guerrillas in Nicaragua and Angola, it requested military aid to enable Mozambique to fight its own nominally anticommunist guerrillas. But that request was defeated, badly. As a lobbyist for ADA in the '70s, I had worked against efforts to restrict aid to Mozambique. But in 1985, absorbed by the anticommunist drumbeat to which I was then marching, I barely noticed the amendment.

During the first six months of 1987, the Administration proposed aid for the rehabilitation of Mozambique's railways. Again it was defeated. Both Mozambique's Administration allies and its liberal congressional allies told the government it was time to get a lobbyist.

"They know they need a lobbyist, but the government is split. The Foreign Ministry does not want to spend funds, funds that would have to come out of its budget, to hire a large law firm. Other departments do; they are feeling the pressure of the Americans," Jose told me.

I told him that I was interested and could do the job. "The key members will be the same members I have been talking to about the Contras for the last three years. I don't know if we can win, but they are the people we have to talk to.

"But I have to ask you a question. Look, I've been associated with difficult causes in the last years; it hasn't worked out too well for me. Is this a government that one can feel good about?"

Jose's answer was simple. "I would not work for the Angolans; they're too bureaucratic. I'm not sure I could have worked for the previous president, but President Chissano I trust completely. He is a pragmatic man looking for real solutions to the terrible problems of his country. And the party? There is nothing corrupt about FRELIMO."

That was enough for me. At the time, Jose was one of only a few people in politics I trusted completely. His word was good, and I trusted his unconventional instincts, which mirrored my own.

I will always remember a story told about Jose, one he never tells of himself. FRETILIN's headquarters in exile were in Maputo, the capital of Mozambique. Recognized by the government of Mozambique as representative of East Timor, the mission had extraterritorial status. In 1980 Jose returned to Mozambique for a visit. When he arrived, he was imprisoned, tried, and sentenced to death by the FRETILIN politburo, by that time completely Marxist-Leninist. Jose was found guilty of trying to make a separate peace with the Indonesian government that would grant autonomy to East Timor; in this alleged conspiracy, Jose would become provincial governor.

According to the story, a representative of FRELIMO visited FRETILIN leadership, stating, "What you do is your decision. You are sovereign here in this building. But if you execute Horta, we will expel you, and no one else in the world will take you in or heed anything you say. He is the only international credibility you possess."

Jose probably did talk with the Indonesians. He talks to everybody. That is his gift. But FRETILIN did let him go and sent him back to New York. That was reason enough to trust FRELIMO. East Timor became the twenty-first century's first new country. Jose Ramos Horta is now prime minister.

In the weeks that followed I researched the Mozambique issue in Congress. Mozambique had a hard core of liberal supporters, particularly Howard Wolpe, chairman of the House Subcommittee on Africa, and members of the Black Caucus. Two moderate Republican senators, Nancy Kassebaum of Kansas and John Danforth of Missouri, also favored aid to Mozambique. But it was the first year of the 1988 presidential campaign, and these seven Republican candidates were all trying to win the hearts of the American right wing. Support for anticommunist movements was a key litmus test. Aid to the Angolans was reestablished in 1986; the big jewel for conservative Republicans remaining was Mozambique. Senate minority leader Robert Dole, together with Senator Jesse Helms, had held up the nomination of Melissa Wells as ambassador to Mozambique for eleven months; she was considered unsympathetic to RENAMO. Aid to Mozambique had been one of the reasons that a supplemental foreign aid bill was defeated in the House in April. The price for reviving the supplemental demanded by Senator Robert Kasten, ranking Republican on the Senate Foreign Operations Subcommittee, was no aid to Mozambique.

But there was another chance for Mozambique. The foreign aid bill for fiscal year 1988 would also be debated that fall in the House. In my talks with the staff director Steve Weisman of the House Africa Subcommittee, whom I had known for ten years, I found I could still forge a close working relationship with a liberal. He instantly saw the potential in my moderate contacts in the House, but Mozambique also needed a major Republican lobbyist, Steve believed.

Based on my research, I made a proposal to the Mozambican government, a strategy to reverse their earlier fortunes. I attached the articles about my career from the *New York Times* and the new Massing article in *Mother Jones*.

I had already waited five and a half months since my first talk with Vinicio to start working for Guatemala. I had other things to do and I could be patient. Now I asked for an audience with Jose. We sat in his house in northeast Washington and drank Johnny Walker Red.

"Can I count on this job?" I asked.

"I think so," he responded, which in fact meant not very much. *Pensu que sim* in Portuguese (*pienso que si* in Spanish) translates to "I think so," but long experience with Guatemalans and Mozambicans has taught me that it actually means "I don't know."

But Jose *was* trying hard to get me the job. I had put forward my proposal, and Jose had arranged for me to submit a joint proposal with a New York firm. He was covering all bets. Meanwhile, I was to take a train to New York, to receive instructions from Vinicio and discuss salary.

The next week Corinne told me that when she had finally made up her mind to come to me she would tell me, "This is never let me go day." Then every year on that day each of us will find a new language in which to say "this is never let me go day."

It was a happy gathering. Vinicio had come to give a speech before the United Nations General Assembly. Attending a party at the Guatemalan mission in New York were Vinicio; his ambassador to the United Nations, Fernando Andrade; his ambassador to the OAS, Paco Villagran; and his ambassador to Canada, Lico Urvella. During Guatemala's transition from dictatorship to democracy, Fernando had been foreign minister, Paco the minister counselor at the Embassy in Washington, and Lico ambassador in Canada. Fernando had worked hard to ensure a smooth transition. Lico explained the transition to an often hostile Canadian parliament that saw Guatemala as an Indian killing field. Paco did the same thing with the U.S. Congress. I had been their key contact. It was a moment of great satisfaction, knowing that I would now become the lobbyist for a democratic Guatemala.

In New York, I called Corinne.

When she answered she went straight to the point. "This is never let me go day."

I was stunned. I had not expected a decision so quickly.

"Allan told me last night he had given up hope that I could ever be in love with him again. He doesn't want to go to any more counseling. We'll be talking tonight about how to make the separation," she said.

Thinking back, I remember I heard no joy in her voice.

"Corinne, you know I will do my best. My God, my job, and my lady all in the same day. I love you. I'll call you tomorrow."

"I love you, too," she told me.

My meeting with Vinicio was routine. I explained to him the current situation in Congress, the pressure by some human rights activists to end military aid. A new OAS report stated that human rights violations in Guatemala had recently increased, although it did not attribute the violence to the central government. I assured Vinicio that he himself and Guatemalan government efforts to strengthen democracy still enjoyed strong congressional support.

After our meeting I left for the restaurant at which Michael Massing was waiting for me. I showed him a speech I was preparing for a conference in October. The 1985 article about me in the *Times* had caught the attention of two former editors of *Ramparts*, the premier journal of the new left. In 1985 David Horowitz and Peter Collier had announced (in a highly controversial article in the *Washington Post*) that they had voted for Reagan. On the day after the June 26, 1986, vote for the $100 million for the Contras, they had asked me to speak at a conference of former leftists who also had "second thoughts." Fifteen months later I had written a speech titled "Third Thoughts," which I showed to Michael for his criticism and suggestions. I had been working on it since early July but it still made me nervous.

Michael read it right there in the restaurant, occasionally nodding in agreement. "This will be a bombshell," he said.

That afternoon I flew to Ann Arbor to give a speech in Rackham Hall at the University of Michigan Graduate School, where thirteen years earlier

I had organized an antiwar rally with Jane Fonda and Daniel Ellsberg. We had packed the auditorium with more than 1,500 people. That night I would be speaking on Central America, the Vietnam of the '80s. I was not invited by the left this time, but a local center-right group. It was a joint appearance with Ron Raddosh (another "second thoughts" guy), and Father Bill Davis for the left.

I had expected that my newly announced opposition to Contra aid would be welcomed on the left. I had badly miscalculated. The audience of 300 (with about fifty exceptions) was packed with true believers. Nicaragua was the new Jerusalem. They did not welcome my criticism of the Sandinistas as a totalitarian party that had built its own mechanisms of social control. To them, the Sandinistas were creating a new society, to replace the fascist Somoza government that was maintained by terror and U.S. government assistance. Most of the audience agreed with one woman who described murders by the Guatemalan army as egregious human rights violations and murders by the Sandinista secret police as justifiable defense against imperialist war.

But there were two moments during which I experienced some satisfaction. First, when one young woman demanded of me and Ron, "I just want to know what you have done to fight the fascist junta in Chile, the Argentine death squads, the Somoza regime, the death squads in El Salvador, and the racist government of South Africa."

I laughed and answered, "It's a good question but you've picked the wrong person." I described the legislation I had drafted and successfully lobbied on all of those issues.

Five people approached me afterwards to say how much they appreciated hearing from someone who refused to simplify complex issues, who tried to negotiate a reasonable position between extremes. One was a Vietnam veteran who had worked with me in Ann Arbor in the old days.

I was not able to see Corinne until Friday. She told me that the night before Allan had come to her and told her he loved her, that he didn't want to leave, that he wanted her to love him again. "Just tell me that everything will be all right," he pleaded.

We talked about it for an hour before she had to leave—but I didn't understand, I didn't get the message. And I didn't get it until the next morning, when she called.

It was back to the old plan.

I was in shock. I did not know what to do. I called Amalia and told her everything. This is what she told me:

You have an image of yourself. It is the way you have adapted to living in this world. It is not a true image, although you are not a fraud. You present yourself to the world as sweet, mellow, oh so understanding. You would never do anything rotten. But being rotten is sometimes fun and you know it.

Behind that sweet facade is a giant ego as large as a cathedral. You don't even care about most of the people you are sweet to. Your friend plays on this because she knows it and, monster that she is, she uses it to manipulate you. But you let it happen, because you don't want to lose the image you have of yourself as Mr. Gentle Sweet. And she twists you, turns you upside down, inside out, and you let it happen. And that's wrong for you and wrong for her. How can she respect you? You show no strength, no sense of survival or self-protection. You don't even know what the new rules are. You let her dictate them to you.

I can't appeal to you on the basis of protecting yourself so let me appeal to the martyr. Define new rules. Tell her you will give her six months. Let her try her marriage. Then go home and cry, torture yourself, but know that you did it for a higher purpose. You will have done it for yourself, but you will have your illusion.

And her marriage will one day end, and she will find someone else, someone with the strength you do not have; those types always survive.

And stop trying to please everyone. You can't do it. And life is no fun when you do.

Every time I read that speech, I wonder how much of it is true. That morning, when Amalia delivered it, what I heard was the ridicule and the hostility, all of which I felt was well deserved. What I still do not know is whether—no, not whether but how much of—that portrait of that poor pathetic creature is me.

At the gym, sometime later, I called my machine. Corinne's message: she would be unable to meet me. I slammed down the phone and started crying. Al Houseman, a friend for twenty years, moved to comfort me. I ran and hid in a toilet stall. When I had composed myself, I went to the racquetball court to meet my regular partner, Peter. In recent weeks, I had already passed him by and was winning regularly. That day in five games, fifteen to win, I gave up only twelve points. I was pure, focused fury, but I could not even feel it. I channeled it all into excellence on the court. And each time thereafter when I would beat Peter badly, he would ask, "Corinne?"

Sunday, Corinne called. I asked meekly, "Are you still coming, Monday?" She responded with enthusiasm, "Wild horses couldn't stop me."

The next day she was unbelievable. She wanted sex everywhere, in every way. In a frenzy of passion we moved from room to room, ending finally with arms, legs, buttocks, breasts all entwined, joined on the bed in a full-throated end to frustration, hate, and bewilderment.

The next day we were to meet at the convenience store near the National Zoo after she had finished her counseling. She said I would need the reassurance.

The next day I arrived thirty minutes early. For forty-five minutes I skulked furtively in the store, downing one small cup of coffee after another, never buying a large cup because she would surely be there soon. Finally I crossed the street with a large cup and waited on a bench near the entrance to the zoo.

Thirty more minutes passed. Then I saw her. She was walking with Allan. I jumped up and turned away from them, joining a group of people from South Dakota talking to a guard.

When the two had passed I began to pace back and forth, back and forth, bench to telephone, telephone to bench, until finally after many calls I found a message on my machine. "I'm sorry! I'm sorry! He surprised me and wanted to have lunch. What could I do? I'll meet you at your home."

When I arrived home, I found a letter from Amalia:

Dear Mr. Cameron:

The following is to state I hereby submit to you my resignation from the post of Head Executioner. I would like to take this opportunity to thank you profusely for the confidence you have deposited in me during the time of my tenure. . . . The reasons for my resignation are purely personal. You see, Mr. Cameron, the fact is I do not really enjoy my work plus I think you need a more experienced person to run the department.

You know very well how complex the job is; really, Mr. Cameron, *at the hour of truth I am a very simple person with simple needs and desires. The qualities of callousness, lack of compassion, and aggressiveness so inherently necessary for aptly performing the job are failing me. Lately I have been repeating myself constantly in a high-pitched voice; definitely my heart is not in it. I honestly think you should look for a replacement in the area. If you permit a suggestion you might look in the yellow pages under S & M services.*

Mr. Cameron, there is something else I want to make very clear. I do not want to leave the organization. If you can think of any other available job let me know. I suggest the post of "Friend," no title attached. I truly believe that I could perform with excellence in such a post. I would be covering amongst others: love, companionship, loyalty, compassion, sadness, happiness, exasperation. As you see I could use my past experiences in a more humane environment. Please consider this possibility. I think we both would enjoy it immensely.

I put down the letter, laughed aloud, and booked a plane to Miami, leaving on Saturday. (I could depart no earlier since we were making preparations for the visit of the president of Mozambique. I did not have the contract, but the Embassy was treating me as if it were likely.)

Corinne arrived shortly thereafter to tell me (1) that she had gotten a new job and (2) that there was no longer a "we." She was going back to her marriage and she would make no further promises. All she would say was, "Let me go, but don't give up on me." And in less than fifteen minutes she was gone.

My friends Ed Long, Steve Daggett, and Mike Fonte came over that night to watch me drink. And it was a good drunk. I finished just one drink short of a fifth of Scotch. In one week I had gone from engaged to a piece of junk.

On Thursday I wrote what I consider to be my best poem.

LIFE WITHOUT CORINNE

The sun will rise,
But the clouds, the clouds—
We'll never see it.
A child will cry,
She'll not be heard.
The roses will go out on strike.

"If this love isn't real, then
There is no love.
We'll wait to see if
Another two will make us smile as much as these."
Poets will put down their pens and
Sail paper airplanes into the sunless void.
God will abolish Sunday,
And they will ache forever—
For they had too much love to lose
And did

The next day both Corinne and I were miserable and we shared our misery on the phone for an hour. When I read the poem to her on Thursday, she asked where I had found it, it was so beautiful. I said I wrote it for "us" and my voice choked. "You really wrote it?" she asked.

I told her that I was leaving for Miami to spend some time with Arturo.

I was getting good at lying, and this one was easy.

On October 2 when I returned to Washington, Mozambique's Ambassador Valeriano Ferrao called, asking me to arrange appointments for the President with Appropriations Committee members. By the end of the next day I had made appointments with the chairs of the Foreign Operations Subcommittees in both House and Senate.

On Saturday the Mozambican foreign minister, the minister of International Cooperation, the ambassador, and Jose would meet to discuss my employment.

On Saturday I flew to Miami. Amalia and I had a good time. She kept me at arms length all of Saturday but on Sunday her body betrayed her will and strengthened mine.

On Monday I confirmed all the appointments I made on Friday, then wrote a memo for the President. That night we had our first meeting. The President was soft-spoken and listened carefully to my presentation. I cautioned him not to ask for aid. But in meetings the next day, he ignored that advice. Instead he was forceful in pointing out how much the people and the country were suffering from South African sanctions and aggression (through the surrogate war of RENAMO) imposed by South Africa. "The rest of the West is responding. Where is the United States?"

I learned something important that day. My advice was correct for foreign ministers and ambassadors. But presidents are accorded a more special place by other politicians. Out of the twenty-five he saw that day, not one representative or senator took offense. His demand was a president's prerogative.

Around lunchtime, as we were entering the Rayburn Building, a man began screaming at Jacinto Veloso, the minister of Cooperation, beside whom I was walking. "How many people did you kill today, Mr. Veloso?" Then pointing at me, he yelled, "How can you accompany murderers?" A couple of capitol police grabbed the man and whisked him away.

Our meetings began at eight in the morning and finished at seven at night. I particularly enjoyed the limousines. Since the President was on an official visit, secret service protection was well provided. The President's motorcade of limousines led by four police motorcycles could even drive through red lights.[44]

Jose and I left the presidential party at 7:30 that night—he for home and I for the whirlpool. When I arrived at my gym, I was accosted by a former colleague of the Coalition for a New Foreign and Military Policy. "How are things with your friends Ollie and the Contras?" he asked. "What you've done is disgusting and terrible. I'm sorry I ever knew you."

It is a good day when one is verbally assaulted by representatives of both the right and left extremes.

On Friday I signed a contract with Mozambique.

The next day Corinne was at work and left a message on my machine in Spanish. We were not to see each other anymore, but she needed to return my typewriter and wanted to bring it to me Friday.

"Hola, mi amor. I am in the office and I am going to leave soon. I have been thinking about you all day. I have been thinking of Friday, too. Sleep well, I love you much, adios." We met Friday and made love "for the last time." The same day I signed a contract with Mozambique.

But I could not leave her alone. I peppered her with phone calls at her new office. Finally she complained to my best friend in the house, who passed the complaint to me.

The disaster I had long expected had come about. She had taken it all away. And though I dogged her, she had nothing more to say. Ever. I kept calling, over a period of two weeks. Calling. Calling. ■

CHAPTER FIFTEEN

THIRD THOUGHTS

October–November 1987

O n October 17 I was scheduled to speak at the Second Thoughts Conference to be held at the Grand Hyatt, one of downtown Washington's most beautiful hotels. I had given a copy of my speech to Bob Kagan. He would not endanger our friendship by discussing it with me. I had sent it to Bob Leiken, as well as Peter Collier and David Horowitz. I had called David a month before, suggesting that I withdraw from the conference. My speech was at great variance with what others would say; it would dilute the impact of the conference. David protested, "This conference will have diversity. We do not have a line."

As leftists, we were always finding reasons to exclude a person, a group, a line. David did not want to do that as a new leader of the right. He wanted diversity and I would be the ultimate proof of that.

On the Thursday three days before my scheduled speech, I visited David at the hotel where the conference was to be held. "David, for Christ's sake," I insisted. "I represent the People's Republic of Mozambique. You don't want me at your conference." My friend, Mark Falcoff, a witty, hard-line conservative, was properly outraged, but David said: "You're participating."

Why didn't I just back out? Because I wanted to give the speech for a variety of complicated reasons. Massing, after sixty hours of interview, had written about me, "He could be ingenuous and cunning at the same time, his sense of principle forever warring with his attraction to the limelight." In this case, the opportunity to speak truth to power (to the Reagan Administration and its followers) propelled me toward the limelight, but friendship and honor required I give David another chance to take me off the program.

At the conference on Friday night, I caught a whiff of what was about to occur. Over cocktails, I saw various liberal and left-wing reporters. Todd Gitlin told me there were great expectations about what I was going to say. They had all read Michael Massing's articles.

While writing my speech, I had spent a lot of time thinking about the end of the war in Vietnam and the terrible events that followed—the imposition of a Stalinist regime in South Vietnam, the hundreds of thousands of people who took to the sea in search of freedom, the tens of thousands who perished. There had been a treaty, the Paris Peace Accords, which recognized two legitimate forces in South Vietnam, the South Vietnamese government of President Thieu and the Provisional Revolutionary government (which we called the Vietcong). That treaty indirectly recognized (and accepted) the presence of some 200,000 North Vietnamese soldiers in South Vietnam. But its emphasis was political; it created a framework for political competition in South Vietnam.

The treaty also called for a cease-fire. But the day after it was signed, the South Vietnamese government mounted a major military campaign against the North Vietnamese and the Vietcong. Kissinger and Nixon backed that effort with massive amounts of military aid.

I was still haunted by that time. I asked the morning panel at the conference if there had been any other way to end the war. Doan Van Toai, a political prisoner under both the Thieu government and the later victorious North Vietnamese, said no. The Saigon generals were too corrupt. After the fall of President Diem in 1963 there was simply no better solution.

In my speech I had written, "I doubt that much could have been done to stem the progress toward eventual domination by the communists." But I also envisioned what might have happened if the United States and Thieu had not resumed operations but abided by the accords. There could have been much less bloodshed. The entire society of South Vietnam would not have suffered the traumatic changes that took place after the North Vietnamese army in April 1975 crushed the South Vietnamese army in total defeat.

And I saw a parallel with the present. Both the Paris Peace Accords and the Guatemala City Accord represented defeat for the maximalist goals of the United States, and both provided a way out, less suffering (and in the case of Nicaragua, some opening of the political system). But the parallel was too tricky so I removed it from my speech.

David and Peter had just returned from a U.S. Information Agency–sponsored tour of Nicaragua; it was their first trip. They had heard countless tales of Sandinista misdeeds, and they had established a quick rapport with opposition politicians, two of whom they brought back to the conference. They also added a last-minute luncheon speaker, Tony Ibarra, a former Nicaraguan Trotskyite, who had joined the Contras as an advisor while still teaching at the University of Dubuque in Iowa.

Ibarra gave the speech the crowd of 300 was waiting to hear. He denounced the Arias plan as the "new Yalta."

> Is this a new Bay of Pigs? Speak out . . . so there do not have to be Second Thoughts about your complicity. . . . We have 15,000 Nicaraguans armed . . . set up to be massacred. Are you going to be silent?

As I listened to Tony Ibarra I realized the conference had become a celebration of the Contras. I decided to strike my conciliatory paragraph about the Reagan Administration, where I credited it with providing a military shield to El Salvador, providing time for Salvadoran democrats to build a foundation for democracy. I had also noted that, albeit under strong Democratic pressure, the Reagan Administration had insisted on democratic renewal and greater respect for human rights in Guatemala and Honduras, as well as El Salvador. I struck that, also. Gone, too, was my acknowledgment that the last installment of $100 million in military aid for the Contras was probably necessary to exert maximum pressure on the Sandinistas. It was no longer time for conciliation.

I had also written a section on Mozambique. But I was unwilling to reveal my thoughts to that audience unless I acknowledged that I was now that nation's lobbyist. So I struck that section while sitting in the audience next to Todd Gitlin. Todd had been perhaps the best of the student leaders in the '60s—always rational, always a mediator. He was writing for the Jewish magazine *Tikkun*. He anticipated the impact of my speech and believed the section to be vital. Okay, I said, but I have to tell the audience about my new job. There must be no concealment of my possible motives.

He began his story by noting that not much had been said "about the embarrassingly clandestine junta of CIA director William Casey, Lt. Colonel Oliver North, and friends. If democracy had to be destroyed to preserve democracy, well, this possibility might be disconcerting enough to occasion a third thought or two."

Third thoughts there were, here and there, and they provided the conference shocker: apostasy's own apostasy. You could hear a leaflet drop as Bruce Cameron . . . declared that he had been "fundamentally in error, both in my support of the Contras and in my understanding of the Reagan Administration." The third-world (counter) revolution kindled in his breast turned out to be another fraud. He decried conservatives' "error of volunteerism, that is, the belief that by sheer force of political will, one can surpass and overcome stubborn and recalcitrant social realities. The right believes that if you call a movement of people 'freedom fighters' often enough, not only are they, but they can win. . . . By denouncing the sins of the Sandinistas, which are legion, and by evoking the suffering of the Nicaraguan people, including those who have joined the Contras, one nonetheless cannot change the stubborn reality that the Contras cannot win in the foreseeable future."

Another case in point: Mozambique, where massacre-making RENAMO, beloved by the hard American right, was founded by unreconciled Portuguese settlers working for Ian Smith and later fronting for South Africa. Having denounced the "fantasy" of the democratic counter-revolution, Cameron administered the coup de grace, announcing that he had just signed on as lobbyist for the People's Republic of Mozambique. Hisses and gasps in the hall! . . . Collier and Horowitz had known for weeks what Cameron was going to say—indeed, they had talked him out of withdrawing from the conference—but most of the audience was astonished and horrified.[45]

When I finished my speech, about fifteen people stood up and applauded wildly; the remainder . . . well, the *Washington Post* describes it best. Such attention I had not expected. Three days before, I had stopped shaving. I do that periodically, when I decide I have to reform. It is a spur to curb my drinking and smoking, a signal to the machine that the mechanic is coming to perform an overhaul. So I was sporting a three-day growth. But the *Post* reporter still asked me to meet him afterward for a photo.

On Sunday, I ran an advertisement in the newspaper, seeking an assistant. Early Monday morning I found my unshaven face on the front page of the *Washington Post Style* section, next to an article titled "Thunder on the

New Right." Little did I know how much attention the two unrelated events would bring me. The key sections of the article follow.

[T]he weekend did not unfold as planned. In the midst of the choreographed conversions, there was a spontaneous conversion—the wrong way.

The apostate was Bruce Cameron, a pro-Contra lobbyist and former associate of Lt. Col. Oliver North, who now bore witness to his new beliefs: the Contras cannot win and they aren't democratic "freedom fighters."

There was dead silence, quickly broken by boos and hisses.

The article moved on to other issues, then returned to the beginning of my speech:

Bruce Cameron arose, visibly shaking, constantly sweeping his hand back across his gray hair. His commitment to the Third World Revolution in the 1960s had, in the 1980s, found the Contras as its object. He had been a crucial player in getting them aid.

Now, he declared, he had "third thoughts." The Contras are "an army without a vision of a future society . . . the Contras cannot win. . . . I have great doubts whether there can be a democratic counterrevolution. . . . There is no wing of the Democratic party soft on Communism. Liberals are not pro-communist and anti-American." And, he announced, he was now a lobbyist for the "People's Republic of Mozambique."

"Boo!" shouted Reed Irvine, the conservative press critic.

And Norman Podhoretz, the conservative editor of *Commentary*, could not stop shaking his ahead.

A break was called. Seated in his chair, Cameron trembled uncontrollably.

"I want to cry," he said.

Arturo Cruz Jr., the Social Democratic Contra leader and exboyfriend of North secretary Fawn Hall, embraced Cameron. Cruz felt a bond of personal emotion that transcended the opinion of the moment.

[Cameron had] traveled [to Nicaragua] and eventually became

disillusioned with the Sandinistas. When he became convinced the Reagan Administration wanted a negotiated settlement, he supported Contra aid on that basis. One of those who convinced him was Oliver North. "I liked him," said Cameron. "His energy was infectious. He was absolutely seductive." . . .

By the end of 1986, after successfully lobbying for $100 million in Contra aid just months before, Cameron had a change of heart. The talk of reforming the Contras, he decided, was a sham. "They were behaving like thugs. There just was no change."

The Iran-Contra scandal stunned him. "I was shocked," he said. "I had a couple of clues, but not enough." Not only were the Contras "undemocratic," but the Reagan Administration was "anti-democratic in its relations with Congress." . . .

Cruz Jr. tried to halt the harsh criticism. "I will always love him," he said, gesticulating with a cigar. . . . But Cruz could not hold back the flood.

"Stale specious arguments," said Leiken, who had been Cameron's comrade in the Contra cause. "I could go on at length about the progress of the Contras. You are an American who works on the Hill . . . another form of imperialism, another form of isolation."

"He's the one who's going to get all the press attention," said Irvine, demonstrating his expertise.

Leiken started attacking the press. "The coverage of the *New York Times* is very depressing. . . . "

"There is a line for this conference!" shouted Horowitz, now at the microphone. "If someone has not come to the conclusion that communism is a threat, then they have not had second thoughts." Referring to Cameron's anti-war lobbying of Congress, he said, "I might have done what Bruce did, pull the plug on the people of Vietnam. The effect of pulling the plug was the death of 3 million people. . . . I'm never going to pull the plug on an anti-communist struggle again!"

The session was over, and walking toward the door Horowitz denounced Cameron for another crime: "He dominated the whole afternoon. It'll probably be the lead!"

That Monday the phone rang off the hook. There were calls about the job, calls from people I hadn't heard from in years, people who wanted to congratulate me on my "courage." By 9:00 A.M. I had already made three appointments with prospective employees. Then I began screening calls.

I answered or returned only calls from old friends. I was particularly proud that both of the Salvadorans who had lived with me when they first went into exile called to congratulate me. One, who knew many stories about terrible deeds of the Salvadoran left, told me, "I could never do what you did." I responded, "But the stakes aren't the same. No one will come to kill me." "That's true," he said. "But that is not what stops me. It is that the culture of the left dominates the exile community, and I would be ostracized. I don't want that. I could not bear to be alone."

I interviewed two young men for the job. It was clear that neither was right, and I politely sent them off. The third, a young woman, intrigued me. We talked for forty-five minutes. I asked her to drop off a writing sample the next morning. Corinne called, too. She had read the story and wanted to know how I was.

"I think I'm nuts," I responded. "That was a damn fool thing I did this weekend.

"It could have cost me my job. The Mozambique Embassy has been getting calls all day. Their loyal supporters of the last two decades have been calling up outraged that they have hired a Contra supporter."

Actually, the embassy's reaction was one hell of an endorsement. Jose asked one caller, "And what have you done in ten years to help Mozambique? Nothing. We like our choice." The ambassador told another, "We've made our decision. If you don't like it, I'd advise you to go to Maputo, raise the flag of revolution, and—if you succeed—you can choose your lobbyist; we've chosen ours."

I had not considered the consequences for my future before I gave that speech. I was acting out all the frustrations of the last few years—in one grand gesture. By the time my best friend from Michigan called, it was clear there would be no major consequences anyway.

The next day the young woman, Merritt Becker, dropped off her writing sample. She told me that she had been unable to sleep the night before, she was so excited about the prospect of working for me.

When she left, I said to myself, "what the hell," and put a message on her machine to call me back. I hired her the next day. It was a totally impulsive decision. I was choosing her because she was an attractive woman and she had spirit. Later I would call her a sentimental leftist. She did not know the philosophical underpinnings of her own political positions. She wanted good things to happen to people, the poor to be helped, those victimized to be saved, and for the thugs of the world to disappear. For here, there was no Marx, no Mao, no Che Gueverra, no Ho Chi Minh, the guides of my generation, just a desire to see things made better, and a conviction that the United States too often sided with the thugs. What she lacked in analysis she made up in charm and enthusiasm.

Merritt started to work for me three days later. There was an article about the conference in the *Village Voice*. I ran out to buy a copy at a store at the corner of Connecticut and K Streets, the true heart of Washington. I had felt frustrated because the *Post* had not quoted me about the Guatemala City Accord. The *Voice* reporter, Jim Ridgeway, an old adversary in the press, had quoted 90 percent of my speech, including that key section:

> "The stubborn reality is that the Contras cannot win. If we could provide them 7 to 10 more years of funding by virtue of their location in the Western Hemisphere, the Sandinistas would probably collapse under the pressure. That would constitute a war of attrition in which tens of thousands more would be added to the already high casualty count. A war of attrition that would not necessarily end in Sandinista overthrow.
>
> "The American Congress has no stomach for it. Nor in my judgement should it. The American people do not believe the Contras are democratic, and this is despite the presence of many, many good democrats in the movement. And they do not believe the Contras could win. If the American people are not willing to openly support the Contras, then the only way to continue supporting them is covertly, and, as we have seen in the Iran-Contragate scandal, lawbreaking by some of the highest officials in the land. The consequences of these acts have been to undermine our own democracy. I believe that what goals are achievable through the Contra policy are achievable now. . . . What we can achieve now through the Guatemala City Accord and the Contadora plan is sufficient both in terms of our

legitimate security interests and perhaps in a meaningful opening of the political process in Nicaragua. . . ."

In his apparent attack on his Contra comrades, Cameron in reality was showing them a way out. Consider Hubert Humphrey. . . . The exotic flower of Reaganite interventionism can be replaced by Humphrey's more subtle, less violent tactics of economic persuasion. . . .

Cameron's latest career move hints at how such political nostalgia may actually be the new wave of [neoconservative] fashion. . . . Looking ahead to eventual revolution in South Africa and the creation of a black state, the U.S., largely on the initiative of the State Department, is attempting to position itself in southern Africa through economic support of Mozambique. . . . This former colony, once abandoned by the American right as an odious outpost of Third World Marxism, may witness the rebirth of Cold War pragmatism and ideological subtleties. And Bruce Cameron may be its wet nurse.[46]

I read the article, bought two copies, and walked outside. It was a beautiful, crisp autumn day. The sun was shining brightly. Life at its best. At last I was free. No Contras. I could begin again. I walked along Connecticut Avenue looking into shop windows, watching girls, looking up at the sky and the sun. For the first time in years in the United States, I noticed the sun. My soul dashed along the street like a leaf in the breeze.

I felt alive again, whole, and it felt good.

. Merritt and I began our work on Mozambique.

Then the nightmare began again.

I called Merritt to get my messages.

There was one from Corinne.

"Corinne who?" I demanded.

"She spoke as if you knew her."

"I do. I do."

I called her. Why did I call her?

Corinne had news. The night before Allan had told her that I was a homosexual.

On Friday Corinne had asked Allan to let her go. But when he said maybe, she backed off. She still wasn't sure.

The following Tuesday we met in the Dirksen Senate Office Building, on the floor outside the cafeteria. From there we found a stairwell below the basement. We stood there kissing and hugging.

"I don't know what to do. I can't do anything. I just want to imagine a future for us, a time when we are together. I just want to see if I can hold that vision and believe in it."

That was enough for me. I left a happy man.

She had lunch with Allan where he told her I was not only a homosexual but a habitual cocaine user, that I had been with six different men, one of whom had given Allan a deposition.

There is a beautiful movie called Starman, *not so much a movie about aliens but about humans, specifically Americans. Toward the end of the movie, Jeff Bridges, the alien who has taken over the body of Karen Allen's deceased husband, is dying. The human body cannot keep his alien spirit alive.*

Jeff and Karen have driven from northern Wisconsin to Arizona to rendezvous with the alien mothership. They are opposed by the Reagan Administration, a formidable foe I knew well.

In one of the final scenes, Jeff Bridges stumbles as Karen Allen struggles to hold him up.

When I met Merritt, I felt like Jeff Bridges's alien. I no longer knew what to believe. Allan was lying, or his informant (of course there was no informant) was lying, or Corinne was lying. The latter thought turned me to alien mush. I was literally stumbling. Merritt was the one to break my fall.

That night I called my lawyer. I told him of my meeting with Corinne and the latest developments. The next day, Corrine and I went to see him together. Corinne told him what Allan had said.

"I've known him for ten years. I no longer love him, but I know when he's lying, and he's not lying now. There really is this man making these charges against Bruce."

I looked at her, then at my lawyer, who surprisingly accepted her word.

I was dead.

Corinne drove me home. I pleaded with her to see what was happening. Allan was lying. There was no man. There were no drugs. I had only seen cocaine once in my life, in Guatemala, and I had refused it. Drugs I was into, but only tobacco and alcohol.

"How can you go back to this man, this liar?"

"I must," she insisted. "But how can I ever give up what we have together when we make love?" And she drove away.

I was defeated, but this time I accepted the situation. There would be no more phone calls, no more meetings. The week of madness had ended. There was no sun, there was no Corinne. There was nothing except a lot of work.

Unexpectedly, there was also some play. On Halloween I was invited to the annual New York Times party. In Washington Halloween is for adults, more than for children. It is a night to dress up, to pretend, in a city of multiple roles. It is fun to play roles you really never had and never could have. I liked to play Timothy Leary, the Harvard professor who embraced LSD in the '60s. "Turn on, tune in, and drop out," he advised my generation. Later he was freed from prison by the Black Panthers and fled to Algeria. I would wear a Nehru jacket, beads, and a peace sign. I was given to blessing people, but I did not pass out drugs.

That year I danced with a new acquaintance. And then we danced again. There was promise, possibility. We had fun.

I was giving a party myself the following week. My new friend would be there. I was interested and I already knew she reciprocated my interest.

But I couldn't really be interested, according to my code, if there was any chance left to be with Corinne. So the Thursday before the party, I called her.

"I was just thinking of calling you," she reported. "Allan has decided. He doesn't want to continue counseling. We've agreed to get a divorce."

I hedged my bets accordingly. The next night, before the party, I told my new friend, "Look, there's another woman, but she's married. If she comes back, I mean, the minute she says she's back, I'm gone."

The next day I met Corinne, we found a quiet spot in Rock Creek Park. For a while, we wandered aimlessly, just holding hands and smiling. Suddenly, I wanted to be rid of all the people on public paths taking their time walking in the warm autumnal afternoon. I grabbed Corinne by the arm and we broke into the forest, finding our own isolation. There were still enough leaves on the trees to protect us from wandering eyes.

We sat down and I looked at her unsmilingly. She returned my gaze with understanding. Then I took her and I was not kind. Afterward, I was overwhelmed by guilt. "I'm sorry. I was too rough."

"No," she answered smiling. "If you were too rough, I would tell you."

That afternoon, I walked through a door into a place from which I have never exited. She was again my willing servant and again showed me there *would be few limits. I may have dominated, but dominance was hers.*

Her body had become no less essential to me than my next breath. Her surrender to my every whim became my life force. If the day before I had thought another woman could break me free of Corinne, that opportunity was now gone, gone in a minute. I had known, lost, regained, lost again, and reclaimed the right, which she gave unconditionally, to embrace her solely for my pleasure, unmindful of hers. Yet hers was a vibrant, living ecstasy that poured liquid joy, glistening on her happy face. Certainly she would be mine forever, even at the end of the corporeal self. Fantasy alone would nourish my unceasing, ever-demanding need. ▪

CHAPTER SIXTEEN

DECISION ON MOZAMBIQUE

October–December 1987

*T*he decision was made, although I knew it had not been hers. I willed myself to believe that at least we could be together, as we were before August. But she had a job, a child, and her house. Merritt and I continued to work out of my home.

Worse, although Allan had made the decision, he resented it and took no real action to implement it. Life became unbearable. Corinne believed he watched her every move.

She called often from a certain grocery store. "Hi, I'm not at home, and it's two o'clock. I just wanted to explain, I know it's absurd, but I just don't trust my phone."

Then one day Allan simply eased up, and the mood in the house went from tense to neutral. They both agreed to get lawyers.

The day before Thanksgiving Corinne visited me at home for the first time in more than a month. She surprised me by taking me to bed.

Later she left a message:

Hi, sweetheart. It's Thanksgiving, and I just couldn't wait until Saturday to leave a message on your machine. Isn't it funny—it's funny, knowing you're not here, and I just miss you and love you. . . . I hope everything is going well for you in Guatemala, and I love you and I can't wait until you get back. Bye-bye, honey.

My assistant had come in to work and heard the message. "I never realized—Can't you hear her? She loves you very much. You're lucky."

I was committed all over again. All doubts vanished.

Allan and Corinne began to have big arguments about custody of their adopted son, Sam. Corinne's lawyers told her that if she left her home at this point it would constitute "desertion" and jeopardize her case for sole custody. They admonished her not to see me, and certainly not to have any more assignations.

Our furtive love began again. For the rest of the year, until Christmas, we would still have lunch together, but we never touched except in basement stairwells in Dirksen. There was also a certain spot in the walkway from the Capitol to the Hart Senate Office Building, alongside the subway, where the tunnel curves.

We planned Christmas. To hell with lawyers, we would be together if we could.

One day at a mall in Montgomery County, we bought Ice Capades tickets for Corinne, her mother, and Sam. We tried to proclaim the real "never let me go day," but our proclamation rang hollow. We agreed we would know when it was the right day. We would wait. And I would continue to wait, for eighteen years.

When I saw Corinne for lunch, and on the momentous occasion when she met my aunt and uncle, I gave her presents. I often gave her presents. Sometimes it was just a knickknack from my collection (a Lenin pin, a coin inscribed "Bruce P. Cameron, Lobbyist and Tap Dancer," or some other trinket); once it was a beautiful red scarf.

My new contract with Mozambique returned me to the halls of Congress and required that I assemble a liberal-moderate alliance to win. At that time, Mozambique was eligible for only humanitarian aid—food and medicines for people displaced by the war, plus a small amount of economic aid for its few private farmers. Direct aid to the government was forbidden. In early 1987 the Administration created a special fund of $50 million to aid projects designed by the Southern African Deveopment Coordination Conference (SADCC).

SADCC was a coalition of eleven southern African states who joined forces to increase economic cooperation, decrease economic dependence on South Africa, and create a vehicle to attract western aid. For planning purposes, SADCC organized itself into functional areas (e.g., agriculture, mining, environmental concerns). Perhaps the most important area was transportation, and the key to SADCC transportation routes, independent of South Africa, was Mozambique. In each region of Mozambique (southern, central, and northern), a railway corridor linked the more developed, former English colonies—Botswana, Zimbabwe, Zambia, and Malawi—to the Indian Ocean. But all three corridors had deteriorated, due in part to economic mismanagement, but also to war. By 1984 western governments (under the leadership of the Nordic countries, and including Great Britain,

Spain, and the United States) began to rebuild the center railway in the Beira corridor.

In the 1980s, despite the expulsion of U.S. Embassy officials thought to be CIA agents, the government of Mozambique began discussions with the Reagan Administration as part of its effort to reach out to the West. State Department officials laid out three requirements for normalization of relations between the two governments: (1) an end to anti-American rhetoric in meetings of international bodies like the United Nations; (2) cooperation with international economic institutions like the IMF and World Bank to develop sound economic policies; and (3) accommodation with South Africa.

By 1985 the Administration was so impressed by Mozambique's progress (major economic reform and an agreement with South Africa) that it used special authority to transfer funds from one account to another, to provide $10 million to repair more than twenty locomotives for the Beira corridor. The U.S. Embassy even hired a Mozambican from the state railway company to supervise what it expected to be a multi-year program. But Congress rejected (247 to 177) a $3 million military aid package initiated by the Administration, and limited economic aid to humanitarian and agricultural assistance, channeled through the private sector. This effectively ended aid to the railway corridors.

Such was the environment in which the Administration proposed to give $50 million to SADCC. The Administration sought these funds in a supplemental appropriations bill, which also included $300 million for the four democracies of Central America.

Normally, but rarely in the last twenty-five years, Congress addresses an Administration request for foreign aid by first considering the foreign aid authorization bill, which originates in both the House Foreign Affairs (now the International Relations) Committee and the Senate Foreign Relations Committee. The authorization bill develops policies to guide foreign aid programs and sets specific policies in certain functional areas, such as arms control or population planning. Following the authorization bill, the appropriations committees in both House and Senate have the job of determining the actual dollars to be spent. When necessary, the Administration will seek a supplemental appropriations bill for programs that are running out of money or for new programs. The supplemental bill the House debated on April 23 contained two new controversial programs: aid for SADCC countries and aid to the four Central American democracies.

Representative Mickey Edwards, a Republican from Oklahoma, the principal sponsor of the $100 million package for the Contras the year before, laid out Republican objections:

> Half of this money is to go to Central America—but in a way that sends a very clear signal to the democracies in Central America that they are better off if they do not support our own policies. Fifty million dollars less for El Salvador. Ten million less for Honduras. . . . And nearly $50 million more for the two countries (Costa Rica and Guatemala) that are the most critical of our policies. . . .
>
> Fifty million dollars of this money goes to help front-line Marxist countries of southern Africa. To Zimbabwe—presumably to help pay the Russians for the 12 new Mig 29s. To Mozambique, which calls itself a Marxist-Leninist country and voted against the United States last year in the United Nations 94.1 percent of the time.

A close look at the debate found Republicans and conservative Democrats opposing money for SADCC because of an almost hysterical fear of supporting "Marxism" in southern Africa. The concern was entirely real in those days, but the language of the debate was excessive. SADCC states were labeled variously as "outright communist states," "front-line Marxist countries," or "communist repressionist governments." One member singled out President Robert Mugabe of Zimbabwe as a "Marxist-Leninist for life," and two additional members insisted that support for his government would in effect subsidize Zimbabwe's purchase of Mig 29s from the Soviet Union.

On the other hand, supporters of the supplemental foreign aid bill argued that the aid was part of an overall U.S. effort to oppose apartheid and promote stability and economic progress in the region. These members argued that a vote eliminating the foreign aid section of the bill would be a vote to strengthen South Africa's policy of internal apartheid and destabilization of its neighbors.

House members were in a surly mood in April 1987. The Administration was at its weakest (due to the Iran-Contra scandal) and House Speaker Jim

Wright had not yet asserted his leadership. Only at such a time could the following comment be left uncontested in the House of Representatives: "What is wrong with not giving aid to Zambia? Zambians, it has been reported, are routinely sodomizing their children in Zambia's prisons."[47] The vote was 209–194, stripping the foreign aid section from the supplemental bill.

The bill was next considered in the Senate. Because Republicans in the House had been almost unanimously opposed, Senate Republican votes were now key. Senator Robert Kasten from Wisconsin, the ranking Republican on the Senate Foreign Operations Subcommittee, became their indispensable leader. He had been an early supporter of rapprochement with Mozambique, but unlike the Administration, had found the degree of change in Mozambique disappointing.[48] Kasten insisted that approval of the SADCC funds be made conditional on a prohibition of their use in Mozambique. And that prohibition was eventually accepted by both House and Senate and signed into law by the President.

Pro-SADCC and pro-aid-to-Mozambique members of the House and Senate got another chance in October 1987 when Congress considered the regular aid request for fiscal year 1988 in the House authorization bill and later continuing resolution (which contained the foreign aid appropriations bill). There was no chance the Senate would pass the House version of the authorization bill, so taking the fight to the conservatives was not a question of changing current law that restricted aid to Mozambique. Rather, pro-aid-to-Mozambique forces would have the opportunity to show their strength on the House floor, a demonstration that could be used in the subsequent debate in the Senate.

I had developed a three-step strategy in my work on the authorization bill:

> (1) It is not possible to lobby the entire 435-member House of Representatives. Fortunately, a lobbyist doesn't have to. On any given vote, it is possible to identify a manageable number of what we call "swing votes." Generally in the 1980s, 90 percent of the swing votes on foreign policy and defense issues were Democrats from the South and Southwest, and border states (between thirty and fifty members), and Republicans from the Northeast and Midwest (between ten and thirty). In the South and adjacent

states, the Democratic Party was less affected by the anti-interventionist sentiments that had fundamentally changed the rest of the party after the Vietnam War. As a result, those Democrats are more vehemently anticommunist, and more willing to consider the use of force in third world conflicts than Democrats from other states. Similarly, Republicans in the Midwest and Northeast were less affected by the conservative movement's gradual domination of the Republican Party (which began with the Goldwater campaign and culminated in the election of Ronald Reagan in 1980). Those Republicans are less stridently anticommunist, and less willing to consider the use of force in third world conflicts. Swing votes, in other words, tend to be members not in harmony with the main tendencies of their party.

On Mozambique votes, I based my swing list on the 1985 vote on military aid to Mozambique. I could safely assume that most northern, midwestern, and western Democrats who had already voted for military aid to Mozambique would continue to support aid to Mozambique (and would oppose crippling amendments). I could safely assume that most southern, western, and mountain-state Republicans who had opposed military aid to Mozambique would again oppose aid and would support crippling amendments. After poring over scores of Nicaragua and El Salvador votes, I was able to make an informed decision about which southern Democrats and northern Republicans it made sense to lobby,[49] either because their affirmative vote was shaky or because their negative vote could be changed with new information or pressure. I put seventy-four members on my swing list: seven northern Republicans, sixty southern and border-state Democrats, and seven who were outside these categories.

(2) My second step was to write counteramendments to the crippling amendments of conservatives trying to stop aid to Mozambique. Under the rule governing debate on the foreign aid authorization bill, members had to submit their amendments well before debate on the House floor.

(3) It would be my task to enlist allies from my Contra days to speak on Mozambique.

The Democratic leadership was well organized. Departing from previous strategies on the authorization bill, in which Chairman Dante Fascell of the House Foreign Affairs Committee would try to find common ground with committee Republicans, this time under the leadership of the chief majority whip Tony Coelho, a Democrat from California, it was liberal Democrats who were encouraged to put their stamp on the bill. In this way, the bill was brought to the floor with tremendous enthusiasm and strong Democratic Caucus support.

From the middle of November until the votes on December 10, I spoke with over forty members on my swing list. My assistant, Merritt, was visiting every office to drop off a long memo I had written. I would not always raise the topic of Mozambique; sometimes we would just talk about developments in Nicaragua, and I would leave the member with a copy of my memo. I saw some members more than once. A few told me not to worry, they could and would vote with me this time.

At ten days before the vote, eight amendments that would have made SADCC aid to Mozambique impossible had been printed in the Congressional Record. A few would impose some insuperable condition; others would strip the SADCC funds from the bill altogether. The most serious threat was proposed by Representative Thomas "Buzz" Lukens, a Republican from Ohio, who wanted to prohibit aid from the SADCC account to any government receiving more than three-quarters of its military aid from the Soviet Union, or employing more than fifty-five Soviet bloc advisors. As law, the Lukens amendment would have denied aid to Mozambique and Zimbabwe. I suggested an amendment to the amendment, to attach a simple presidential waiver: "Unless the President certifies that assistance to such countries is in the national interest and will help promote peaceful resolution of the regional conflicts." Representative Dan Burton, a Republican from Indiana, proposed another amendment—to bar military aid unless certain conditions were met. At that time, my allies in the Administration and Congress weren't even asking for military aid for Mozambique but we felt that we couldn't afford to lose a single amendment; we needed to preserve House negotiators' strongest possible hand in dealing with the Senate. Burton's amendment would have inserted two conditions for military aid: limiting the number of Soviet advisors to fewer than fifty-five, and holding free, multiparty elections in Mozambique. Mozambique could meet neither condition in the foreseeable future. So I drafted alternative language requiring only "continued progress" in reducing the number of Soviet-bloc military advisors, and "movement" toward competitive elections in which amnestied RENAMO soldiers could participate.

I gave these counteramendments to Steve Morrison, Howard Wolpe's aide on Mozambique. Steve encouraged me to secure promises from Representatives Richard Ray, a Democrat from Georgia, and Dave McCurdy, that they would speak out against the Republican amendments, and in favor of aid to Mozambique.

In the remaining few days leading up to the votes, I spent eight hours a day on the second floor of the Capitol, at the several entrances to the House chamber, waiting to stop members willing to spend a few seconds on Mozambique. My records show that I spoke to only nine swing members on December 8, just two days before the vote. That may sound like a lot of wasted time (at slightly more than 1.2 members per hour). But members come and go through three main doors; no matter where you stand, there are always two other exits through which they can escape you. Furthermore, it is easy to miss one member while exchanging information with others. And sometimes when a key member emerges, you simply freeze. Then you have to wait for the next floor vote that will bring him or her back to the House chamber.[50]

Morrison continually urged me to reach McCurdy and Ray. But while I found it easy to ask for a silent vote, I was reluctant to ask anyone to give a speech in support of Mozambique on the floor. Finally Morrison stopped asking and just told me, "Do it, now. Or you will lose. Now, do it." I responded, "Okay." But how would I do it?

That afternoon I met with Representative Richard Ray, who made it easy for me. He knew nothing about Mozambique and doubted that many of his colleagues did, either. Before I could ask, he offered to give a speech about Mozambique, without specifically opposing the Republican amendments or endorsing aid to Mozambique.

Emboldened, Merritt and I walked straight to a friendly office where we could both find typewriters and write draft speeches. She took hers back to Ray's office, I left in search of McCurdy. Normally I would have spoken first to Dave's assistant, Howard Yourman. But in just a few days he was leaving the office and I did not want to impose on him again. He and Doyle McManus of the *Los Angeles Times* had often patiently heard my tales of professional and personal woes over the past year. Besides, I needed to be a little less passive—just this once. So I went to Dave personally, and gave him a copy of my draft speech. He, of course, took it right back to Howard, who chided me for going out of channels.

On December 10, four of the original ten proposed amendments on Mozambique funding were introduced. Three would have eliminated the SADCC earmark altogether, or conditioned it to make Mozambique ineligible. The other was Burton's amendment on military aid to Mozambique. Unlike their performance the previous April, the Democratic leadership appeared forceful, coherent, enthusiastic, well organized. On each of three recorded votes, at least four Democrats stood at both the Republican and Democratic entrances to the House chamber urging opposition to the Republican amendments or, in the case of the Burton Amendment, support for the substitute based on my draft.

Democratic leadership had secured, with my assistance, eleven speakers, including two Republicans and three moderate-to-conservative Democrats who would support SADCC funding and aid to Mozambique. The opposition, on the other hand, could find only three speakers, all extremely conservative Republicans. Our side was clearly more diverse. The third conservative Democrat who spoke was John Murtha from Pennsylvania. Like Ray and McCurdy, Murtha had been a supporter of the Contras and the rebel force in Angola, UNITA.

Opponents of aid were predictable. Representative Dan Burton stated, "Enough is enough. These are communist countries. . . . It is hard to find a group of countries outside the Soviet bloc that attack the United States more than the front-line states."

Richard Ray partially accepted the premise but also challenged it, "I am aware of the communist influence in this country [Mozambique], but, nevertheless, every Western European country, as well as Japan, Brazil and Canada, is providing assistance because there is a possibility that Mozambique can be rescued from the Communist influence." That line was Ray's and it made his speech uniquely effective. Here was a strong partisan of the Contras and a very conservative Georgian, known for his directness, holding out the possibility that Mozambique might change.

McCurdy also acknowledged Mozambique's ideology and foreign ties:

[President] Chissano has not denounced Marxism-Leninism. He has not renounced his ties to the Soviet Union. But in the vitally important southern African region, Mozambique has cooperated with the United States, and its government has the support of the Reagan Administration. Against the wishes of the Soviet Union, Mozambique signed an accord with South Africa by which each government renounced support of irregular forces in the other's country. . . .

Right now in Mozambique, people are debating a revision of the Constitution. Serious consideration is being given to changing the present system from one in which the ruling party chooses the President to an open election with multiple candidates. Where Mozambique will be in 2 or 5 or 10 years is still an open question. But I agree with the Administration that at this critical time it makes sense to work with them and encourage continuing movement toward the West.

"Buzz" Lukens argued in support of his amendment that the United States must have standards if it is not to "be used by the Soviet Union to feed countries they are subjugating and controlling."

Burton's amendment to delete SADCC funding (and create instead a fund for established U.S. allies in Africa) was easily defeated 236 to 172. Regarding Burton's amendment, leadership decided not to oppose it directly, but to offer the substitute I wrote. It passed easily, by 218 to 177. Another amendment to drop the SADCC earmark was also defeated in a voice vote.

For the Lukens amendment, leadership decided on a straight up-or-down vote without amendments. It was narrowly defeated, by 199 to 190. The leadership had to secure a change of vote on the part of four moderate-to-liberal members in order to ensure victory.[51]

By raising the Soviet specter and inserting numbers right in the amendment (no aid to any country receiving more than three-quarters of its military aid from the Soviet Union or having more than fifty-five Soviet advisors), Lukens forced many members to vote against aid to Mozambique as they had in April. This time, however, Tony Coelho, his staff, and other members whipping the bill were right there on the floor watching each vote as it was made. Using good will among Democrats and probably some additional leverage as well, they convinced enough members to ensure victory.

The next day the Senate took up the continuing resolution for fiscal year 1988. At about 10:30 P.M. Kasten offered his amendment. His aide, Jim Bond, a friend of mine from 1977 when I was still a revolutionary anti-imperialist, had made it very clear that Kasten was unhappy with Mozambique's slow pace of progress and that he would consequently offer a crippling amendment, one that would make aid to Mozambique impossible. In the Senate there is no Democratic organization close to the operation in the House. On the contrary, Foreign Operations Subcommittee Chair Daniel Inouye, a Democrat from Hawaii, placed primacy on maintaining a good relationship with Kasten, to guarantee Republican support for foreign aid. Leadership's overwhelming desire was to avoid divisive floor debates, to encourage private deals, and to achieve consensus before amendments came up for a vote. All this strengthened Kasten's hand.

The amendment Kasten offered conditioned the use of SADCC funds in Mozambique on that government's progress in returning church schools and radio stations to their original owners, its guarantee of private property against future expropriation, and a reduction of Soviet-bloc military and security personnel from the levels of 1986. The amendment was adopted by voice vote.

When Jim Bond saw me an hour later, he said (both to mollify and bait me), "You made out like a bandit." An aide to Inouye standing next to us corrected him, "No, you just had your nuts handed to you."

That was Friday night. I finally went home around 2:30 A.M., after the Senate finished debating various provisions on Nicaragua. The next day I took a copy of the Kasten amendment to the State Department, went to the gym, and attended a small dinner party. I had decided to let my mind idle before devising a scheme to defeat Kasten in conference committee.

On Sunday morning I read through both the House and Senate foreign aid appropriations bills in their entirety, to get myself in the mood to write a substitute. Then I called Jose Ramos Horta (I would call him ten times over the course of the day) to ask for specifics about church schools and radio stations, the status of private property, and the number of Soviet-bloc advisors in Mozambique.

By 4:00 P.M. I had actually to admire the artistry of the amendment. It seemed plausible, as American as Main Street. It sought the return of confiscated church schools, guarantees for private property, and a reduction of the Soviet military presence. But in each provision there was mischief.

The confiscated church schools had been run by the Catholic Church for the white Portuguese elite. Most Portuguese, including priests and teachers, fled before, during, and immediately after Mozambique's independence. Had the government not taken over the schools, they could not have functioned. The one church-operated radio station had depended on subsidies from the Portuguese colonial authority. After independence, the subsidies were withdrawn and the radio station ceased to operate. On the other hand, the return of other kinds of church property, especially buildings of worship and a former dormitory for a Catholic seminary, were genuine issues in Mozambique. The schools were not. The Church would be unable to operate them if they were returned.

The second provision (to guarantee private property against future expropriation) was equally mischievous. Such a standard was not acceptable. Governments, even those where private property rights are enshrined in law, always give themselves the right to assert the principle of eminent domain, the right of the state to seize private property for public purposes. Since 1983 Mozambique had been breaking down state farms into small family holdings or private farms. In addition, thirty enterprises had been returned to private hands. What was reasonable was to ask for guarantees that private property be protected against future expropriation without due process and just compensation.

The last provision was sneakiest of all. It required reductions of Soviet-bloc security personnel "from the levels of 1986." I believed the high-water mark for Soviet advisors in Mozambique had been reached in 1981, and a slow reduction had been in process ever since. I argued that it would not be possible in 1988 to certify a significant reduction from the 1986 level. As it happened, my numbers were just wrong, but they were numbers the State Department had given me. Six months later, in a report to Congress (using figures compiled by the intelligence community), the State Department acknowledged that the high-water mark was actually reached in 1984, and numbers had changed little since then. Estimates ranged from 1,500 to 2,000. But in this case, truly, ignorance was bliss. I wouldn't have known how to proceed if I hadn't believed this provision to be mischievous as well.[52]

By 11 that night I had drafted two substitute amendments and a memo to explain them. The gist of the principal substitute was to condition aid to Mozambique on a presidential certification that the government of Mozambique had made "significant progress" toward:

(1) Resolving through dialogue with the Catholic Church the return of church property;

(2) Guaranteeing private property against future expropriations without due process and just compensation; and

(3) Continuing to reduce the number of Soviet bloc military and security personnel from the level of 1981.

The next morning, I met with three officers of the Africa Bureau of the State Department, including Deputy Assistant Secretary of State Roy Stacey. Within forty eight hours, the State Department was circulating a version of my amendment which made aid to Mozambique subject to three conditions:

(1) The Government of Mozambique has entered into a dialogue with the Catholic Church regarding the return of church property;

(2) The Government of Mozambique has taken steps to assure against future expropriation of private property without due process and just compensation; and

(3) The number of Soviet and Eastern bloc military and security personnel are being reduced.

Key supporters of aid to Africa (and specifically to Mozambique) on the House Foreign Operations Subcommittee included Representatives Bill Gray, a Democrat from Pennsylvania, and Julian Dixon, a Democrat from California. Their assistants were given copies of my language, and the language modified by the State Department.

In conference the following Tuesday night, Bill Gray was given the task of negotiating with Kasten. Very quickly, they agreed—on the three points as modified by the State Department. Kasten dropped his more draconian standard. Then they suffered a critical misunderstanding.

The language before them required, as a condition for the release of aid, that the President certify that Mozambique met these three standards. Gray said he wanted to change the certification to a report. Kasten understood him to mean that the word "certify" should be changed to the word "report."

I learned of the misunderstanding on Thursday from Jim Bond. An hour later someone from the Administration told me Jim was "tasked" with preparing the final language. He quite reasonably wrote it the way he understood it, but unfortunately that was not the way Gray intended it. Gray just wanted a report. The difference was enormous. On the one hand, the Administration would be required to merely make a report on three subjects; on the other, it would be required to make assurances that certain standards were met before aid could be released.

My concern was not whether Mozambique could meet the tests. (I, wrongly, believed it could do so in all three cases.) Rather, I was concerned about a lag in the certification process. I was convinced the State Department would be reluctant to take certification for review to Senator Kasten, State's most consistent and skillful defender on questions of foreign aid. I also feared that while State dithered, conservative forces would mount a campaign to block release of the aid.

I rushed to Jim Bond's office and asked to see the draft language. When I read it, the three items were still standards the Mozambican government must meet as a condition of aid. I was in a full-scale panic. I rushed off to find the assistants to Gray and Dixon. It was late and neither was there. That Friday I arrived early, and overplayed my hand. Both assistants were busy and couldn't see me. I insisted to their receptionists that the matter was urgent. They advised me to leave a memo. For once I had none.

I tried to ambush the assistants. I even stopped Bill Gray personally. He told me, quite correctly, that I needed to see his assistant. I had become a pest. I can clearly remember Gwen Brown of Dixon's office walking right by me, refusing to even look let alone talk to me. And Gwen was arguably one of the three or four most agreeable Hill staffers. I had to push pretty hard to make her mad. I had. Finally I realized that and retreated.

That Saturday I meekly sought out my friend Gary Bombardier of Matt McHugh's office and explained how I had screwed up. I showed him the language, how the addition of only five words would solve the problem. As it was written, the President had to "report to Congress that . . ." (language that set standards). By dropping "that" and substituting "on the extent to which," the President need only make a report.

I do not know what happened next. But later that day, my friend Ed Long who worked for Senator Tom Harkin (a member of the subcommittee) showed me a copy of the final language. It read:

(N)one of the funds appropriated or otherwise made available by this Act may be made available to the Government of Mozambique unless the President reports to Congress on the extent to which . . .

It was total victory. In less than six months, the fortunes of aid to Mozambique had gone from total prohibition on funds from the SADCC account to the mildest of restrictions requiring only a report. Final language was agreed to on December 19. Congress passed the continuing resolution the following Tuesday. The following August, Mozambique and the United States signed an agreement under which the United States would provide $13 million in aid to Mozambique's railways.

But it is important to note how little power I had in this process. What I had was information, and access. Key players, each for his or her own reasons, allowed me to build support for the direct provision of aid to the government of Mozambique for the first time since 1985. Senator Kasten and his staff were always open about what they did and why they did it. That, too, made success possible. I was empowered by the State Department. Assistant Secretary of State Chet Crocker and his principal deputy on Mozambique, Roy Stacey, saw aid to Mozambique as critical. They believed that I could devise a successful congressional strategy, and find new people in Congress to support their efforts in Mozambique. Our contacts were mutually reinforcing. But every step I took in moving the issue forward was based on power or authority borrowed from others.

They were right to lend it, because Mozambique was and is one of the good guys. I had been an instrument—to weld together forces in Congress and the Administration in order to win. I also experienced a kind of internal redemption, since I was able to use contacts from my Contra days (days I now found morally ambiguous) for a cause that was without a doubt moral. There were good guys, the Mozambican government and its suffering people, and bad guys, RENAMO and its South African backers. This time the good guys won.

And finally Christmas came.

For me, it was my first adult Christmas. I bought a tree, a live one we could keep, to nourish the memory of our first Christmas together. I bought lights and ornaments. I went all out.

I bought her a tight pink skirt, so short that it stopped just an inch below her bottom. I bought her a pair of beautiful earrings, little pieces of colored stones set in smooth triangles.

But my piece de resistance was from a store called Slightly Laced, a green negligee with an ivory pattern that began at the neck and wandered down the front until it found the hem. When she opened it her eyes widened in amazement.

"At last a man who wants to see me in something beautiful."

"And out of it," I replied. We laughed.

We spent New Years Eve together, too. We had long planned to go dancing and there was a ball at the Kennedy-Warren building, one of Washington's most stately and prestigious. But then there were the lawyers. It would be too public. So we went to a local bar and cheered in the New Year, anonymously.

When Corinne stopped by two days later she was trembling. Allan had lost his temper and come close to hitting her. She didn't know what to do, but I did. I had found her a counselor, now I found her a lawyer.

When we spoke on Monday she was sick with the flu, so we spoke only briefly. Then there was a great snowstorm that shut Washington down. I couldn't call her; Allan was home. And she didn't call me. By Saturday I had convinced myself that he had killed her.

It was ten days before I heard her voice again. By then, silence would have been better. ■

CHAPTER SEVENTEEN

THE LAST CONTRA VOTE

January–February 1988

*T*he snow melted away and Corinne emerged with news. She had planned to move out of her house and into her mother's on January 23, but she now postponed until February 13. She said she was doing it for us. Allan was going on a long trip at that time, a chance to be together, alone, after she put Sam to bed at night.

I was stunned. How many times can a man be stunned and do nothing? As long as I remained attached to Corinne, the possibilities seemed infinite. I could leave or accept. So I was stunned. And I was getting good at it.

In the week before Allan left, relations warmed between them again. Life returned to something near normal—with the buying of groceries, the cooking of dinner, and long talks after Sam went to bed. Corinne felt comfortable, and would embrace him, a friendly act that upset him a lot. "What are you trying to do? You are sending me mixed signals."

Corinne was often home alone. So we, too, would have long talks.

We discussed an old theme in a new wrapper. Corinne felt like a failure. She put ten years into a marriage that hadn't worked. "You wouldn't understand, you were never in a real marriage," she said. That was true. I had been married barely a year, and I had been extremely ill for half of it.

"You wouldn't understand. I was in love with Allan. And I failed. Maybe there is something wrong with me. Maybe marriage is too hard." This went on and on for hours. I listened, and I sank deeper and deeper into despair.

Save for my speech, I had avoided the Nicaragua issue throughout the fall, content to read the papers, and keep up with Administration and congressional gossip. In the fall negotiations over Contra aid, I remained aloof.

House Speaker Jim Wright had agreed to extend the so-called humanitarian aid (contained in various short-term bills) to keep the Contras alive, but he would not increase their fighting capabilities with military aid. Nevertheless, the biggest (and most successful) Contra battles took place during that time. In a continuing resolution, the Administration and a Democratic Congress worked out a final compromise. If a cease-fire was not in place by January 15, the President would put forward a new aid proposal, and the House would vote (on February 3) and the Senate would vote (on February 4) on whether to approve it. In order for that aid package to go into effect, both House and Senate would have to approve. Another vote would then be held the following spring. If the package was defeated, there would be no guarantee of future votes. Given Democratic control of the House (and a Democratic leadership capable of blocking), this would be the last vote in which the congressional situation favored the Administration. Marlin Fitzwater, the President's spokesman, summed up their situation, "This is our last chance, and [the President] is not going to blow it."

In fact, there had been progress made in Nicaragua. *La Prensa* was publishing and opposition radio stations were operating. Opposition political rallies had been held. Perhaps most telling since the accord, Sandinista leaders had been preparing militants to engage in ideological struggle with the "class enemy." But there was no cease-fire, and Sandinistas were still insisting they would not negotiate with the Contras.[53]

The next debate would show whether Democratic leadership under Jim Wright could reassemble the liberal-moderate alliance liberals had caused to crumble in 1985. I had time, so I decided to take part.

The first part of that debate took place not in Washington but in Central America. In the second week of January the President's National Security Advisor Lt. General Colin Powell traveled to the region. In clear but diplomatic language, Powell explained to the leaders of the four democracies that they could not rely on Washington for "additional economic aid as a result of the difficulties caused by the Sandinistas being suddenly unrestrained by the Contras. If the Contras wither . . . there will not be a sudden surge of interest in things Central American or other kinds of aid."[54]

It was a threat. His words really meant, "Help us win this vote by criticizing the Sandinistas for non-compliance, or face losing your aid." Another official explained, "General Powell has told them he wasn't there to cry wolf; this was 'real wolf.'"[55] The *Washington Times* reported, "Most observers expect the presidents of Guatemala, Honduras, Costa Rica and El Salvador to denounce a lack of compliance on the part of Nicaragua's Sandinista government when they begin meeting later today."[56]

But Arias was not biting. He was actively working to save his agreement. On January 12 he ordered Contra leaders living in Costa Rica to resign or leave. The same day he sent a letter to Daniel Ortega criticizing him for failing to implement the treaty.[57] Arias challenged Ortega to act, and directly linked his compliance to the vote. If he advances toward democracy, if he lifts the state of emergency, if he builds a more pluralistic society, if he offers a general amnesty, and if he reaches an agreement with the Contras, then there is no more reason for aid to the Contras because there is no more reason for war.[58]

Arias was again rejecting the Contras while using them as an instrument to pressure Ortega.

At the presidents' meeting in San Jose the next day, Ortega agreed to open direct talks with the Contras and completely lift the state of emergency. It was lifted three days later, and the special tribunals to try suspected "counter-revolutionaries" were abolished.

Bob Leiken, Bernie Aronson, and Penn Kemble, the newly constituted Gang of Three, lobbied for the Administration's proposal while attempting to influence its content to make it most palatable to the House where the battle would be won or lost. I lobbied against the proposal, working closely with McCurdy's office. McCurdy no longer had an aide on Central America so his administrative assistant was assigned to cover the issue. While Steve Patterson possessed an uncanny, instinctive ability to capture Dave's thoughts and intentions on paper, he lacked Central American expertise. He called me for advice on a letter from Dave to President Reagan. That letter was subsequently signed by twenty swing voters. On January 21 it was sent to the President.

> We are convinced that Nicaraguan President Daniel Ortega is, for the first time in nine years, being forced to recognize and pay more observance to the democratic principles upon which his regime was empowered.
>
> The United States must exercise extreme care not to upset the delicate balance of [the negotiations between the Sandinistas and the Contras, and the Sandinistas and the four Central American democracies] by providing the Nicaraguan President with the very escape hatch he is seeking—newly approved U.S. aid to the Contras. . . .

It would be preferable to withhold any request, but if you believe you must absolutely come forward with a request for additional aid, we urge that all aid be non-lethal and be placed in escrow for this critical phase of the peace process. The United States must not be the obstacle to peace in Central America.

In the fall, the Administration had announced it would seek an additional $270 million for the Contras for the remainder of the President's term. In the early weeks of January, that sum was reduced, first to $150 million, then to $100 million, and finally to less than $50 million—because of congressional opposition.

On January 26 the President's Contra program was announced—$36.25 million for four months, including $3.6 million to buy weapons. Only the $3.6 million would be held in escrow until March 31. It would only be released if the President determined the Sandinistas were not complying with the Guatemala City Accord.

Closer examination of the bill (by Congress and the press) revealed it would actually provide $42 million, with a $20 million contingency fund that made spending rate per month higher than in any previous Contra aid bill.

This was important, but the key issue was military aid, the fact that Congress was being asked to approve it with no role in its release. Four members (all signers of Dave's letter) told me when I asked to speak to them, "Don't bother. The military aid issue sinks it."

Senator John McCain, a fervent Contra supporter but a realist, understood the situation and struggled to convince the Administration to back off. So did Bernie, Penn, and Bob. But this was an issue of fundamental principle for Elliott Abrams, and other administration hard-liners, who had succeeded in ousting Habib as negotiator, had argued in vain for a quick vote (after the impact of Ollie's testimony showed up in the polls), and trumpeted Contra military successes.

Elliott was sticking to his own timetable. This was no time for negotiations. That time would come (if ever) in two to four years. Now was the time to strengthen the Contras. He knew the President would go ahead with military aid on March 31. If they could just win this one vote, they could resume their preferred policy; the Iran-Contra scandal and the Arias plan would become mere footnotes in the successful prosecution of a war to destroy Sandinista military power. Elliott was joined by Colin Powell in his opposition to any surrender on military aid.

The Gang of Three and John McCain continued to support the President despite being rebuffed about military aid. McCurdy and his allies would not. But they were also not prepared to see the Contras completely abandoned. They needed an alternative—one that would justify (to voters) their opposition to Reagan while (equally important) maintaining pressure on the Sandinistas to comply with the peace plan. They met with Wright and presented their views. He agreed. The Democratic leadership would present its own plan for humanitarian aid later.

On the eve of the vote, the President tried to counter the Democratic leadership by offering an opportunity to vote on a Sense of Congress Resolution. He said he would abide by the resolution if both the House and Senate disapproved of military aid. A week earlier, the ploy might have worked. But swing voters now sensed it was an act of desperation and did not represent any real change in Administration position. By this time they distrusted any arrangement that was not codified in law. Swing voters still remembered the McCurdy letter of 1985 that I wrote, the President signed, and was sent to McCurdy in 1985.

I visited more congressional offices and had longer discussions with House members on this vote than on any I had ever worked on. And probably with less effect. Regarding the Contras, the key is framing the debate and writing the bill. Dave's letter and the McCurdy Group visit to Wright were crucial in defining an alternative acceptable to moderates. Powell's and Abrams's insistence on military aid insured most moderates would see the Administration bill as more of the same.

One member (who later voted in favor of military aid) acknowledged to me that the Administration had no plan, but he wanted to maintain military aid until a new Administration could take over and devise one.

Another member and I congratulated each other for our work in laying the groundwork for the Arias plan. We lamented becoming targets of both the left and right.

My most frustrating meeting was with Martin Lancaster, a new member from South Carolina. Every line of argument I stated, he finished. Every fact I had, he knew. Voting against the Administration troubled him, but he had worked hard to inform himself on the issue, and he would vote no.

Another told me, "I agree with everything you say, but I am voting with the Administration. I must stick with my commitments."

Steve Kinzer wrote a piece for the *New York Times* called "The Mood of Managua." It appeared on the morning of the vote:

> "There is definitely a new breeze blowing, at least for now," said one protest marcher. . . . "People are losing their fear."
>
> Political dissidents in Nicaragua have advantages today that they have not enjoyed for years. Not only can they scrawl provocative slogans on walls and doors, but they are also free to operate their own newspapers and radio programs. The state of emergency that had restricted civil and political rights since 1982 was lifted two weeks ago, and at the same time "people's tribunals" were abolished.
>
> In addition, the Sandinistas have opened direct cease-fire talks with the Contras, something they vowed for years they would never do. The first round of talks was held in Costa Rica last week.
>
> The changed climate is quite palpable, and no one who heard the aggressive anti-Sandinista chants that dominated the rally Sunday could doubt that activities are now tolerated that would have been immediately repressed six months ago.
>
> One dramatic change has been the reopening of the press. During years of censorship, only news that did not irritate the government could be disseminated. But today the Nicaraguan press is presenting news from a broader range of political perspectives than is available in El Salvador, Honduras, Guatemala and even Costa Rica, the countries characterized by the Reagan Administration as the Central American democracies. No other country in the region boasts a major daily newspaper that fundamentally questions the legitimacy and ideological foundation of the ruling group.
>
> "The motivation may be to improve their image abroad, but the Sandinistas are making concessions that benefit us here inside Nicaragua," said Ignacio Briones Torres, news director of the Roman Catholic radio station, which reopened in October after 21 months of forced silence. "It is hard for them because they are obsessed with controlling everything. But I think the Sandinistas, or at least Daniel Ortega and his people, are starting to value common sense over ideology."

They are engaged now in seeking a balance between the two programs, a formula through which they can permit enough democracy to please the outside world while not threatening their hold on power.

At dinner that night with two colleagues from the Foreign Operations Subcommittee, I predicted a twenty-vote margin for the Democratic leadership. I was wrong. The vote was agonizingly close, 219–212.

Sixteen of the twenty Democrats who had signed Dave's letter voted no. Dave spoke during the debate.

The Administration was right to challenge its Democratic opposition in the Congress in 1985 with having no alternative policy to the Contras. I agreed and voted with the President. Now in 1988, there are alternatives. The Arias plan is already in place and the Democratic leadership of this House has promised its every effort to bring forward a humanitarian assistance proposal later this month. These alternatives offered the best hope of forcing Sandinista compliance with the regional peace agreement.

I urged my colleagues not to "overplay our hand" by granting President Ortega an excuse to avoid compliance with the peace plan. The United States must not be the obstacle to peace in Central America.

This was not the last vote on Contra aid. It was not the time, when substantial progress is being made toward peace and democracy in Central America, to send—or even promise to send—more military aid to the Contras. Rather than offer Daniel Ortega a convenient escape clause, let's strengthen the United States' favorable position by challenging the Sandinistas to further concessions.

The modest amount of U.S. humanitarian aid to the Contras being contemplated by the leadership did not tilt the balance in the region or give Ortega an excuse to refuse to comply with the treaty. It would send a clear message to Nicaraguan leaders that tactics aimed at stalling the Central American peace process could be met by continued support to the Contras.

Adolfo Calero ironically explained in the *Washington Times* the next day why a majority of moderates had opposed the President's bill:

> Mr. Calero said an alternative aid package of food, clothing and medicine that leaders of both parties were said to be drawing up in place of the Administration package . . . "would only keep a healthy fighting force that wouldn't be able to fight. We want a healthy fighting force that fights."
>
> An Administration official predicted they would be back. "You have to remember we lost an [aid request in March of 1986] and won in June. We also came back in 1985 and won. There is a record of coming back."[59]

He was wrong. The moderate-liberal alliance had been reassembled and it endured. There would be other Contra aid debates, but this was the last one of significance. The Democratic alternative was later defeated. The loss came because the Administration rallied Republicans in opposition, and because a few too many liberals opposed aid in general. But these defections did not seriously affect the reborn moderate-liberal alliance. Many liberals, defying district voters and past statements about "fundamental principles," voted in favor of humanitarian aid to the Contras. They knew that without their votes moderates would be tempted to move back into alliance with the Administration. Some even came to share the view (of Wright and the moderates) that the Contras, supplied with modest economic aid, were an instrument to push continued Sandinista concessions. Unable to break the alliance, the Administration eventually worked out a package of humanitarian aid with the House Democratic leadership.

The day after the February 3 vote, Alfonso Robelo (bowing to the demands of Oscar Arias and to new political realities) resigned from the Contra leadership. ■

CHAPTER EIGHTEEN

ENDGAME

February–August 1988

*T*hat Saturday, for the first time, I went to Corinne's house. I was nervous, afraid I'd get lost in suburbia, afraid of Corinne. But it was pleasant, like old times at my place, with little fear of being caught. It was odd to feel this way in Allan's house.

I was depressed by long hours talking about how much she had loved Allan, about her failure in her marriage. I continued to doubt her, although I said nothing. While Corinne checked Sam, I looked at her books. I found some postcards and began to thumb through them. They were just cards she had sent Sam from Paris.

She was moving out the next week. That Sunday was Valentine's Day. We would finally go out to dance, ballroom.

On Wednesday, James LeMoyne came to town. It had been a year since I proposed to Corinne, and we were on the verge of being together. "You look terrible," James began. I explained. "Why don't you give up on it?" James asked.

"I don't like to give up. I didn't give up on Nicaragua until I had done all I could to set it right. And I won't give up now on Corinne, not now," I replied fiercely.

That Friday, I went back to Corinne's. It would be one of our best nights together. She answered the door wearing the micro-miniskirt I had bought her for Christmas, saying, "I am your . . . for the night." I let go for the first time in months; so did she.

That Sunday I bought her a dozen roses. And we went to the dance.

My experience with Corinne at the dance is best described by James Grady's Runner in the Street:

> And it was true,
> The absolute most wondrous night,
> A night of extreme enchantment.
> A night of living in my best dream.

> *And my worst nightmare.*
> *This was heaven: I held her in my arms . . .*
> *This was hell: I held her in my arms. . . .*
> *The circle of my grasp around her*
> *Marked the divine borders of the universe . . . ;*
> *I was everywhere at once*
> *And nowhere at all.*[60]

At the dance Corinne seemed distant. Over time, I gazed at other couples, jealously. The dance just wasn't fun.

When we returned to my place, I parked the car. She told me it was too late for her to come in. In front of my building we talked for another hour. She said everything had changed since Friday. She had not expected any rush of emotions when she moved out, but it came. "It will take time," she said. "How much?" I asked. "I don't know."

Events moved quickly, and inevitably, I suppose.

The next day she called and told me she felt better, that I should go ahead and give the party we had agreed to postpone. So, that Friday, we had the party. Only a few people there knew our story. Corinne, as usual, had to leave early. When she had gone, I asked Bob Kagan and his wife Toria what they thought. "Corinne was here?" Toria asked. "We couldn't tell." She had acted that night as if we were strangers. I brooded.

She called me the next morning. She felt much better, she said. "I can't wait to start looking at houses with you."

We met the following Tuesday in a carryout restaurant called McSenate. Corinne had withdrawn again. "You're putting too much pressure on me. I'm not ready for this. You've just got to give me time." Later she left a message on my machine: "I just called to say I'm sorry. I don't want to be this way, any more than you want to be the way you are, the way that you are feeling. Maybe we can meet tomorrow somewhere a little quieter. Call me tomorrow. That's fine. And I'm really sorry. Goodnight."

It was the first time she had ever left a message without saying, "I love you."

As she was leaving my apartment on Friday morning, I asked her, "Do you want to continue to go out? I mean, what's the point?" She grabbed me and said, "Don't you know that I have never loved anyone as much as you? That's why I'm here. I want to make this work. But time, Bruce. I need time."

I went to the doctor. Corinne and I had just had lunch. We seemed comfortable, our time together pleasant, but I didn't believe in it. I told the doctor I was out of control. I was drinking half a fifth of Scotch a night and smoking like an industrial pollutant. "I'm going crazy," I told him. "Have you told Corinne?" "No!" I said defiantly. "What kind of relationship is that?" he demanded. I was silent.

I don't remember what happened that evening. Accumulated emotional trauma caused me to withdraw, to become sullen and unresponsive. I didn't pressure; I asked nothing of her.

Again, she began to talk about our future. "I want to have a baby with you. No, don't answer," putting her fingers to my lips. "Just think about it."

By Friday I was feeling better, and she was gone again, uncertain of anything.

Every now and then I called my friend, John Miller, a congressional aide who had spent a year working with Ollie. John, too, had begun a relationship with a married woman. Their affair pre-dated mine. I would tell him Corinne was going to leave her husband soon. He would respond, "That's good news, get out."

"Corinne and I will be spending Valentine's night together," I would announce. "That's great," he responded. "Drop her. Don't you understand that nothing they say means anything? They are one bundle of contrary emotions being pulled in a million different directions. Leave her! Protect yourself."

To survive the madness, I drank and played racquetball. Sometimes I played with the most vicious hangover. It didn't seem to affect my excellent game.

In January a partner's personal crisis came to a head in the middle of a game. He looked up at the railing, saw a woman watching us, and said: "Do you play?" She nodded. "Take my place," he said, and walked off the court.

So Ellen played. And she quickly became my regular partner.

One night she invited me to join her for a drink. I had been planning to ask her but she beat me to it. "I was going to ask you."

"Why didn't you?"

"I couldn't afford another rejection today," I laughed.

We went to my usual bar on the night of the Contra vote. We drank, smoked, and I told her about Corinne. We laughed and I had a good time.

We went out again and she told me her story. She had been a Corinne, but her man had given up on her before she finally left her husband. "I wasn't thinking so when we were together, but I used him. He was the way out of my marriage."

Was that us?

I asked Ellen out to dinner, and took her for Chinese at the Great Wall. There was a parking place in front of her apartment in a very crowded neighborhood. It was fate.

I left after brunch the next morning. I arrived home to nap before Corinne arrived.

That night Corinne noticed the change. "I don't feel the pressure coming from you. This is better, much better. I really love you, you know."

The next week I went to Guatemala for a meeting with the President. Corinne's birthday was coming up. I bought her a new weaving and a red necklace. I bought Ellen a weaving, too.

I spent my first evening back with Ellen. The next night Corinne and I went to dinner at the elegant Mr. K's. Coming home I had to park east of 16th Street. Although I do this all the time, I am careful. There's more street crime there. That night I wasn't careful enough; on the corner of 16th and S, a mugger grabbed Corinne's purse. I instinctively grabbed his arm, he broke free, and I fell, scraping both hands and knees. Corinne found a cop who combed the neighborhood for the mugger and her purse. Amazingly, he found the latter.

My unsuccessful act of defending Corinne (the policeman said, "I admire your instincts, but not your common sense") ended my silence. I told Corinne I couldn't pretend anymore. I wanted everything or nothing. She said, "It's all right. It's all right. It'll be fine."

I broke up with Ellen the next night. We continued to play racquetball four times a week, but our relationship was over.

Corinne and I, on the other hand, were only a little better off. We didn't talk of the future, but there was tension. We were together Tuesday, Wednesday, and every other Saturday night, when Allan took care of Sam.

The night of Corinne's birthday, we went to Maison Blanche. I told her my parents were coming to Washington in late April, after I returned from a trip to Mozambique. She said we should have dinner with them. "Look, when you get back, the weekend you get back, we should spend the night together." We had not spent the night together even once since Guatemala. I didn't know what it was like to wake up with her without Allan's ring on her finger.

But there was no joy anymore. A darkness entered her. Before she took me to the airport for my departure to Mozambique, I made love with her desperately, but she was somewhere else. At the airport she left without seeing me board the plane. She explained lamely, "I have to get a toy for Sam."

I wrote her a letter from Mozambique . . .

> In the latest installment [of a novel I was writing], the love interest tells the hero that he is full of shit when he says he no longer believes. You can't escape, she insists. It is your generation. You are only waiting to find out what you believe in next.
>
> That is me, Corinne.
>
> For a long time, I believed in you and in us. You or your circumstances—I can't decide who, which, what—have made that belief dangerous to my survival. I mean after I have followed every twist, turn, double axle, inside out, upside down, triple flip in your/our/his saga.
>
> Let me say it: my one crystalline thought. You were a better lover and, perhaps more important, a better friend to me when you were Allan's wife than when you became something else.
>
> When I return to the United States, it is the truth and I must say it that I will at the very least try to believe in you again. I think it might be better to believe in Mozambique.

I returned on a Monday. We saw each other Tuesday night. I sat in my chair, she sat alone on the couch. I read to her what I had written. And then I said, "Corinne, in two and a half countries, I drink normally: Guatemala, Mozambique, and Miami—Miami's half a country. Here in the United States, here in Washington where we live, I am an alcoholic. I don't want to lie to you anymore. We can't live like this."

I sat there trembling. She came over, sat on my lap, and began to kiss me, without saying a thing. Then she led me to the bedroom. We made love passionately and gently. Rather she made love, and I responded.

Then I was sitting in the corner of my bedroom, sitting on a chair where there is no chair, listening to Corinne tell me, "Maybe we shouldn't see each other for three months. We've waited this long. Maybe that's what we should do."

There my memory shuts down. She left, nothing resolved. That night a toothache kept me up. I met her again the next evening, only to say goodnight.

Our plan, her plan (I just said okay) was to meet my parents, then spend the weekend together.

Thursday she canceled. She had forgotten a plan with her friend Mildred to go to Philadelphia. "Can't you postpone that? We've had our plan for months." "No, I can't." I didn't push.

Saturday she was cold and distant but brightened a little when she talked about Sunday.

Sunday came. Corinne called to tell me she was having problems with Sam. She told me to go ahead and meet my parents, she would come later. I said, "We'll wait." She called again to urge me to go. I changed the reservation. Finally she called to say that Sam was too upset for her to leave. I called my parents to cancel.

Monday she called to tell me that Allan had to work Tuesday night and could not care for Sam. She would spend the whole day with me on Wednesday.

What a terrible day. Corinne was working on an article friends of mine had commissioned. It was based on a draft I had written. She spent the day working on my computer. I spent the day talking on the phone and answering her questions. All day long she was distant. But there is one last part to the story:

She had also canceled our date for Friday. She would be too busy getting ready for her trip to Philadelphia, and she was still concerned about leaving Sam. From Matt McHugh's office I called for my messages. I found, "Hi. It is quarter of six and we are at my aunt's and we are going to eat here. And, okay, I'll talk to you later or tomorrow morning. And also I was thinking: let's do something Friday night. I think I was being too protective Sunday. Goodbye."

I screamed at my friend Gary Bombardier, "What is she trying to do to me? She's putting me down. Now she's taking me up again. What, after all this, does she want from me?"

It was the endgame.

But my parents were coming; I would not embarrass them. About an hour before they were due to arrive, I reached out to her. "No," she said, as I tried to lead her to the bedroom. "I can't," she said. Then, "Okay. I will help you, but I will not remove my clothes."

"No," I said. "No. It's over, isn't it?"

"Yes," she said.

"Okay, okay. Look I have to call my parents. Here's ten dollars. Go get me a bottle of Scotch. I'll call my parents."

"But you told me you're an . . . you have a . . . that you . . ."

"Yeah, I know. But if I can't tonight, I can't any night."

VISITING MOZAMBIQUE

In Mozambique, I met between fifteen and twenty members of the ruling party, FRELIMO, all of whom had major government positions either in the capital, Maputo, or in the second city of Mozambique, Beira. They were smart and dedicated, gentle and good. The arrogance I had seen in Sandinista or FMLN leaders was absent, as was the dogmatism. They were fierce only in their insistence on the reality of Mozambique and the right of Mozambicans to make decisions for their own country. They were prepared to experiment with a more open economy in which the more ambitious, hardworking—and lucky—could become rich, but they would not yield on the principle that the government had the right to pursue equity. Otherwise, every other question about governance, economics, and society was open to review.

The top leadership was my age (forty-four) or a few years older. So many of the others, filling responsible positions, seemed like youths. The governor of Sofala province, whose capital was Beira, was only thirty-one.

I spent two and one half hours with the president at his home. He told me two great stories. First, my fee was not paid by his government, except as a pass through. But such is solidarity among Africans that the money came directly from the president of the Ivory Coast, Humphrey Boigny, the conservative, free marketer to President Chissano, the nominal socialist and friend of Russia and China.

The second was even better. He spoke of an Eastern European president, he would not say who, who lamented that it was the Eastern Europeans who spoke of equality and prosperity but it was their Western European neighbors who were making such policies live.

This was my last message from Corinne:

My dear, I don't know what to say about your desire to understand why I changed, and why I decided you weren't a suitable life partner.

I didn't mean to lie when I said I misunderstood myself and my feelings. Yes, I loved you. Yes, I changed. What I misunderstood was that there are things that would lead me to reject you. . . . There were external factors I should have been aware of, internal feelings in my heart.

I loved you in a fairly straightforward way, without relation to the outside world. . . . We had a private affair, and I was happy in it.

The changes I started feeling weren't about Sam, but about you and me in relation to the outside world. They weren't about your being reliable and responsible—I know you are both. They were about your personal ways of relating to the outside world. And this is where it gets hard to explain, I feel I'm in murky waters . . .

I'll end now and call again when I have more peace and quiet.

■

Chapter Nineteen

Who Won Nicaragua?

February 1990

On February 25, 1990, the day after the Nicaraguan elections, I overslept. Newspaper deadlines were too early to include the election results, so I turned on *The Today Show*, then *Good Morning America* to see if they would recap the news at five of nine. They didn't, so I turned to other news of the day.

Just two minutes later, Bob Kagan called. "I have never been so delighted to lose a bet," he announced. I couldn't remember what he was talking about. (We had bet $25 on the elections.) Bob had insisted that, since I had argued for closing down the Contras in exchange for free elections, I had to bet the opposition would defeat the Sandinistas; that way my policy alternative would be proven correct. Reluctantly, I had agreed to the bet, though I would not agree that if the opposition lost, my position was wrong.

As a matter of fact, I had expected the opposition to lose. The polls, at least all the American polls, predicted the Sandinistas would win, by 10 to 20 percent. When the elections were first announced, my Nicaraguan friends convinced me that the opposition coalition UNO could win. Its candidate was Violeta Chamorro, the publisher of the opposition newspaper *La Prensa* and widow of Pedro Joaquín Chamorro. His January 1978 assassination, most likely the work of Somoza henchmen, had sparked the revolution that led to the coming to power of the Sandinistas. Violeta Chamorro had served in the first junta of 1979, and had left with Alfonso in 1980. But while she led *La Prensa* in its steady opposition to the Sandinistas, she stayed above the political fray, spurning alliance with any of the small opposition parties, or the exiled Contras. Her critics charged she was unsophisticated and, worse, that her Spanish was Nicaraguan argot. She would lose any debate; no journalist would take her seriously.

Ernesto Palazio (who had been the Contras's Washington representative from August 1986 until May 1989 when he was purged by Calero), Bermudez, and Mantomoros disagreed. "Her colloquial Spanish is her advantage. It is the same Spanish spoken by the Nicaraguan people. She alone can unite the opposition. Program is not important; let her lose the debates. What matters is her visits to the barrios of Managua and the villages of the countryside. She will be the symbol that will gather together their hatred of the Sandinistas. No one else can do it."

It made sense. I believed Palazio at the time. But the opposition parties failed to mount an effective campaign, while the Sandinista campaign was textbook—door-to-door canvassing, slick advertisements, a new image for Ortega, buttons, hats, banners, a presence throughout the country.

So that morning I demanded of Bob, "What are you talking about?"

"They won! They beat the Sandinistas. I owe you $25 and I'm glad to pay it."

I had not only expected a Sandinista victory, I was prepared to defend it, as another step in the easing of tensions between Nicaragua and its neighbors, between the Nicaraguan government and its people, and between Nicaragua and the United States. While there had been numerous violations by the Sandinistas in the electoral process, most observers agreed the election itself would be fair and its results should be respected. Democracy would have attained a real foothold in Nicaragua, and the opposition could use its strong presence in the Assembly to challenge the next six years of Sandinista rule.

Many observers believed the rigors of the campaign fundamentally changed the Sandinistas. Ortega put on colored shirts, campaigned with rock idols, reached out to the Church, took communion, and released political prisoners. Ernesto Palazio quipped to the *Washington Post* the day before the elections, "The Sandinistas are unrecognizable, they don't know what they are anymore." And I was convinced that Sandinista rule, reconfirmed, and tempered by a free and fair election, should be considered progress.

And then there was victory. Violeta Chamorro beat Daniel Ortega, 59 to 41 percent, a clean sweep. She won in every province except one, Rio San Juan (which has only 15,000 inhabitants). How did this happen?

A year before in El Salvador, Ortega had agreed in a meeting with the other Central American presidents, to move the elections then scheduled for November 1989 to February 1990. He committed his government to a timetable for voter registration and the campaign and, most important, to strict international supervision of the election.

That commitment came on the heels of pressure from other Latin leaders and Premier Felipe Gonzalez of Spain, who met with Ortega at the presidential inauguration in Venezuela. Their message was reinforced by congressional Democrats, who told Ortega that, with George Bush as the new president of the United States, he had an opportunity to end the Contra war and to normalize relations with the United States—but only if the Sandinistas held free elections.

The new Administration could have undermined this message by continuing the hostility of the Reagan Administration toward the Arias plan and its backers in Congress, or by sending a not-so-secret message to the Contras that their time would come again. But the new president and his top officials did neither. Instead they embraced the elections, and supported the Arias formula. They quickly reached an agreement with Congress on humanitarian aid to the Contras, limited to those Contras who remained peaceful in their bases.

The new Administration chose Bernie Aronson to administer the new policy. He was not the Administration's first choice, but that man was blackballed by conservatives for being insufficiently militant about Central America. Bernie was recommended by Senator John McCain and Representative Henry Hyde. They knew him to be militantly anti-Sandinista and pro-Contra. The new secretary of state, James Baker, saw in Bernie a man who had good relations with conservatives as well as close ties to moderate Democrats. George Bush and James Baker knew they had to pay attention to Central America because attention was demanded by their conservative supporters, but they did not want to think about it very much. Hopefully Bernie could manage it for them so it would not be too much trouble to them. He was right on the issues (from the conservative perspective), and he was a Democrat. His first job was to negotiate a deal on humanitarian aid, which he did.

By August, the Sandinistas and Nicaragua's internal opposition had reached an unprecedented agreement, which set forth rules for the February 1990 elections, and called for the disbanding of the Contras. Three days later, the Central American presidents agreed to a process whereby the Organization of American States and the United Nations would oversee the dismantling of the Contras.

The Sandinistas, making concessions to democracy, were ratcheting up the pressure and enlisting new allies in their effort to shut down the

Contras. Simultaneously, the Bush Administration was generating other types of pressure to ensure an honest election. In April, Ortega failed to convince Europeans to provide $250 million in aid. James Baker had asked his European counterparts to hold their pledges to $20 million, and condition them on free elections. The Administration also enlisted Soviet support. The Soviets informed Managua they would no longer support "inefficient revolutions," that only a real political opening and honest elections would attract western aid.[61]

In November the campaign began. Simultaneously cease-fire talks with the Contras commenced. When the talks collapsed, Ortega suspended the unilateral cease-fire in place since April of 1988. But remarkably, the campaign continued.

Chuck Lane of *Newsweek* described its progress in his final report before the elections:

> Ortega is the favorite. Recent opinion polls show his Sandinistas ahead; they are banking on public workers, land-reform beneficiaries, young people and soldiers. The Sandinista campaign is making ample use of government resources. Zipping from town to town in his motorcade, Ortega passes out thousands of Ortega T-shirts, caps, belt buckles, pens and notebooks to massive crowds brought in by state-owned trucks and buses. Meanwhile, internal disputes, the late arrival of $1.7 million from the U.S. National Endowment for Democracy, and even a broken knee Chamorro suffered in January have hobbled her campaign. Still, she has been gaining momentum recently, drawing on the many Nicaraguans who blame the Sandinistas for war, repression and poverty. . . . She arrives at rallies dressed in white, arms opened in a gesture of benediction, and her promises of economic improvement and an end to the military draft are drawing enthusiastic crowds.

Under the agreement made the year before, the Nicaraguan government permitted a massive international presence to monitor the elections. On election day, 1,400 international observers were able to visit 70 percent of the country's 4,394 voting stations. Both the UN and the OAS carried out quick counts as well as their own parallel full counts. Most important, the Nicaraguan people knew these agencies were watching the election.

People came to believe that once they had received their ballots from the polling stations and marked them, their votes would be truly secret. Nonetheless, the last poll taken by the *Washington Post* and ABC News showed Ortega winning 48 percent to 32 percent.

During the final week, both campaigns held major rallies in Managua. On the last Sunday of the campaign, UNO attracted an enthusiastic crowd of 50,000. The Sandinistas had tried to thwart it—curtailing bus and train links to Managua, and televising the movie *Batman* and the Mike Tyson–Buster Douglas fight on the morning of the rally.

Four days later up to 300,000 attended the Sandinistas' final rally. I talked to my Sandinista friend Monolo Cadero the next day; he was on cloud nine, convinced of victory the coming Sunday. His only concern was how quickly normalization of relations with the United States could occur. I shared his concern, and urged him to convince his superiors to be magnanimous and allow members of Congress who had supported the Contras to be election monitors. "If you deny them visas, they'll remember, and when the Administration comes to consult them on the pace of normalization, they'll say no, and it will be in large part your own fault for being petty and vindictive just as you're about to achieve your greatest victory." But as I reread the U.S. press during that time, I see stories forecasting a UNO victory.

Mark Uhlig of the *New York Times* wrote this on the day after the election:

> Across the country, beginning in the early morning, there was the almost surreal sensation of imminent change. Nicaraguans shared a widespread sense of awe at the power of their own votes, and disbelief that something so pervasive and apparently entrenched as the Sandinista Front had suddenly been swept aside. . . .
>
> [R]eporters and other outsiders who spent hours interviewing average citizens in working-class neighborhoods became convinced that the polls were misleading. Their view was that the electorate of about 1.7 million . . . was mouthing support for Mr. Ortega while secretly looking to oust the Sandinistas after a decade of civil war and economic ruin.

A week before the election, Uhlig had described a rally in Managua where he interviewed a woman who announced that she and the others would be voting for Ortega. Later she guided Uhlig from the crowd.

> "I am here because they know I live here," she confided, nodding toward some Sandinistas in red-and-black scarves. "But in this barrio we are voting for Violeta. Things can't go on like this. The people can't afford to eat."
>
> While the UNO is running on a vague and optimistic platform calling for a "social market economy," it is Ortega's party that is really on trial. A nearly toothless old woman, trucked to a Sandinista rally in Somoto, spoke for many last week, saying, "I'm inclined to vote for UNO."[62]
>
> "I say I'm going to vote for the front, but I'm going to cast my ballot for the UNO," said a 29-year-old waiter, using the colloquial expressions for the Government and the opposition. Like many other supporters of the 14-party opposition coalition, he talked about his views in a hushed voice and only after making sure that none of his coworkers were close enough to hear.[63]
>
> Maria de los Angeles Araica, a mother of three who works as a saleswoman in Managua's Eastern market, wears an Ortega T-shirt. But, she says, she'll vote for Chamorro.
>
> "We have to change things. We're sick and tired of poverty and hunger," she says. Then why the Ortega T-shirt? "It's free," she answers, laughing.
>
> Nearby, in a booth filled with Sandinista campaign flags and streamers, Bernardo Castro recalls the rallies for both sides he has attended as singer.
>
> "I was there just to sing and entertain," he says. Then, after some thought, he says in a low voice he wants UNO to win. "We all used to be Sandinistas, but then they changed their ways and became Marxist-Leninists. Ten years is enough."[64]

On the day before the election, Lee Hockstader and William Branigan of the *Post* wrote their final preelection story. In it, they took note of the discrepancy:

Most independent public opinion polls, including one by The Washington Post-ABC News, show Sandinista President Daniel Ortega comfortably ahead of his main rival, Violeta Chamorro. But the survey results seem at odds with reporters' random interviews on the streets, where discontent and resentment directed at the Sandinistas and their management of the economy are commonplace.

By Sunday, February 25, most reporters now believed their informal canvass was more reliable than polls. Polls are only good for exposing the surface-level response. At that level, many Nicaraguans were fearful, withholding from pollsters the truth. But when reporters took the time to penetrate layers of deception they found a people "seething with resentment." Many reporters had listened too attentively to the Sandinistas who, as Julia Preston of the *Washington Post* (perhaps in self-critique) noted on March 2, had "been fooling a good portion of international opinion and, not least of all, themselves."

A *Miami Herald* columnist who was never confused by the Sandinistas, or by the international opinion makers who listened to them, wrote on February 20:

> It is true . . . that Ortega's campaign has been better organized and has had more means than Chamorro's, and that it has had almost total control of the communications media. But it is highly unlikely that the most brilliant political rally that Sandinism could convoke, or that all the communion hosts consumed by Ortega before the television cameras, could outweigh the hunger, the insecurity, and the total lack of hope that the great majority of Nicaraguans suffer today.
>
> It seems clear to me: if the people turn out to vote, and if there is no electoral fraud, the opposition should win handily.

And it did. The reactions to this surprising event were, not so surprisingly, as varied as the people and political viewpoints that had been fighting over Nicaragua for the past thirteen years.

In a single day, Daniel Ortega managed to blame Washington for his defeat in one speech and claim victory in another:

We confronted a power in the political and electoral field, with the disadvantage of this power having a gun aimed at the entire people and nation. We had only our moral strength and a message of hope and faith for the suffering people.

They have a gun and a finger on the trigger and tell the people: If you vote for the FSLN, the war will continue, the embargo will continue, and the economic situation will continue to be disastrous. Conversely, if you vote for the other alternative, the war will end and the economic situation will improve.[65]

And:

... [I]f the Contras disappear, the United States lifts the embargo, and economic aid arrives, who would be the big winner of these elections other than the revolution and the Nicaraguan people? I repeat, when we planned the elections we said we would hold these elections, convinced that this would allow us to achieve peace faster and generate more economic resources for Nicaragua. Therefore, this victory for peace and this victory for an end to the economic and commercial blockade would constitute a victory of the people, the revolution, and the FSLN, a great victory for all of us.[66]

On the morning he lost, Ortega was conciliatory, accepting defeat graciously, pledging to work with the new government:

We leave victorious. Because we Sandinistas have sacrificed, have spilled blood and sweat, not to cling to government posts, but to bring to Nicaragua something denied it since 1821, when it became an independent nation.

Nicaragua was denied democracy, social and economic development, the right to speak out and organize ... the right of the poor to aspire to a better life. All this that was denied was achieved on July 19, 1979.

That same morning he went to visit the victor, Violeta Chamorro. But for many Sandinista militants, defeat was bitter:

"I felt as if the blood spilled out of my veins," (Christina) Zeledon said.

"I felt betrayed. When Daniel said, 'Free fatherland or death' at the end (of his concession speech), I felt something in my throat and I started to cry. Not because we lost but because I was angry. . . .

"Those who voted for UNO didn't feel the repression of Somoza. The humble people let themselves be bought with dollars. The UNO took advantage of their poverty," she said.[67]

The *New York Times* solicited opinions on the day of UNO victory.

Elliott Abrams: "When history is written, the Contras will be the folk heroes."

Jeane Kirkpatrick: "The Contras were far more successful than the press ever understood."

Larry Birns of the Council on Hemispheric Affairs (a left-wing organization): "I am filled with an inner rage that the corner bully won over the little guy. . . . The Sandinistas had the right to win, to rule a country that was not being visited by an extraordinary array of negative factors."

Two days later, the *Washington Post* ran an article about the reaction of foreign activists living in Nicaragua who had supported the Sandinistas:

A Brazilian filmmaker, Haroldo Avila, broke down weeping as he addressed Ortega (at a rally of militants). "The pain is so deep . . . to lose Nicaragua would be to lose life," he sobbed.

"I'm a little nervous here. I come from the United States. I'm not used to democracy," Paul Bohannon, a 32-year-old writer from Mendocino, California, told Ortega. He added passionately: "We love you people. We really need your leadership."

"They finally gave in to the suffering and the torture the Reagan and Bush Administration imposed on them," said Gen. Howe, a volunteer from Washington who coordinates 17 American solidarity groups in Nicaragua.

Referring to Nicaraguan voters, Monika Von Flowtow, 33, a

physical therapist from Santa Rosa, California, said: "I didn't ask myself what mistake I made. I thought to myself, they made the mistake."

On the other hand, a Soviet spokesman endorsed the elections and their outcome:

> "The two sides have concrete obligations and the Soviet Union is prepared to meet its obligations if Nicaragua follows suit. . . .
> "Regardless of who won, the Nicaraguans made their choice. They voted for peace, freedom, democracy, national reconciliation and . . . the country's economic revival and social progress."[68]

Some Sandinistas reflected on the mistakes that had led to their defeat. Dionisio Marenco, Ortega's campaign manager said, "In ten years, the front adopted the psychology of party in power. We were drunk with this idea that everything was OK. We lost our capacity to converse, to listen, to criticize ourselves, the capacity to measure, and the people punished us for that."

"Within Sandinismo, we militants became almost a sect. We didn't open up to outsiders," said Daniel Nunez, whose resume reflects the concentration of power. He heads the Sandinista farmers union and belongs to the lawmaking National Assembly and the [Sandinista] party's 102-member Sandinista Assembly.[69]

Perhaps the saddest and truest reaction came from Israel Galeano, better known as Commandante Franklin, the Contra military leader who had replaced Bermudez just a few days before the elections, in one final spurt of Contra reform. Speaking of the forces he now led he said: "We are a cancer nobody wants."

But my favorite one-line election analyses came from a peace activist in Binghamton, New York, and from Oscar Arias:

> Peace activist: "The people couldn't hold out for the government they really wanted."
> Arias: "Governments with 35,000 percent inflation do not win free elections."

As soon as the UNO coalition victory was clear, a new debate began in Washington: *Who won Nicaragua?* This was a debate we were not prepared for. Our earlier experiences had been: Who lost China? Who lost Vietnam? Winning wars in the third world was not something we were accustomed to.

The debate was a rehash of the same arguments that had been made for the last nine years. The right claimed that Contra military pressure had brought Ortega to the bargaining table, then to elections. Keeping Contra forces in their bases during the campaign simply ensured the elections would be honest. Liberals claimed the Contras were a pretext for the Sandinista hold on power, their repression of peaceful dissent. Only when the pressure was removed and replaced by diplomacy did the Sandinistas agree to free and fair elections.

When both arguments are reduced to their core assumptions, they become very simple. For conservatives, the key was aiding the Contras. For liberals, it was stopping that aid. There was also an ultraliberal argument, made by writers like Ry Ryan of the *Boston Globe* and Alexander Cockburn of *The Nation* who agreed with conservatives that the pressure was ultimately successful. Ryan wrote on February 28:

> "The steady message to the Nicaraguan government was: Drop dead or we'll kill you. And to the people: Dump your govern ment or watch your loved ones starve." This echoed the official Sandinista view.

But this was a sterile debate—yielding no winners, and no truths. All three major interpretations were fundamentally wrong. One must instead begin with a historical appreciation of the conflict between the Sandinistas and the Reagan Administration.

It was a conflict that could not be avoided. The Sandinistas swept to power in 1979 on the crest of a powerful and short-lived revolution that had united an entire people, then the whole world, against Somoza. They ascended at the end of a four-year string of American defeats in the third world, beginning with Vietnam. The Sandinistas had reason to believe they were the beginning of a revolutionary wave that would rid Central America of U.S.-backed military governments that ruled oppressively in El Salvador, Guatemala, and Honduras. From their first day in power, they plotted the extension of their revolution.

Ronald Reagan rode into Washington on January 20, 1981, on the crest of a very different revolution of ideological conservatives. These conservatives had witnessed that string of American defeats, as well as a steady Soviet arms buildup. They believed voters had given them a mandate—to restore military balance, and to take the fight to the Soviet Union and its allies, everywhere, in every theater, using every medium of combat.

And so, without further thought, each side did what brought on the Contra war. The Sandinistas threw tons of weaponry at an attempt by the Salvadoran guerrillas to seize power between Reagan's election and his inauguration. The new Administration responded by cutting aid. Even after the Sandinistas ceased to support the Salvadoran guerrillas, the Reagan Administration cut off wheat shipments. But the Sandinistas had always believed in the inevitability of confrontation; this only proved it. Later that year, when U.S. Assistant Secretary of State for Latin America Tom Enders proposed a deal whereby the United States would foreswear military action against the Sandinistas if they would agree not to subvert their neighbors, the Sandinistas did not even consider it for a minute.

At the same time the Administration began to assemble, train, and arm the men who would become the Contras, without ever defining an end-game, or presenting their project to Congress. That set the stage for the endless Contra wars waged in the United States Congress. Conservatives argued the importance of the Contras to vital U.S. security goals in the region, without showing how the pressure of the poorly trained and poorly led soldiers could possibly achieve them. Liberals promised that diplomacy would lead the Sandinistas to democracy and a regional peace treaty on security issues, once the Contras were disbanded.

In 1985 moderate Democrats led by Representative Dave McCurdy were becoming dubious about the liberal premise. In April when liberals attempted to end all aid, including aid for Nicaraguan refugees and funds to promote a regional treaty, these moderates made an alliance with the Administration.

The strategy of the moderates was not to escalate the war through military aid to the Contras. Rather, nonlethal economic aid would keep the Contras in place, and encourage a diplomatic settlement with the Sandinistas that would bring democracy to Nicaragua and a regional security pact based on the Contadora principles.

But the moderates' timing was terrible, for 1985 was the year of the hard-liners. Led by CIA Director Bill Casey and the new Assistant Secretary of State for Latin America Elliott Abrams, they consolidated their control over policy. That policy was military defeat of the Sandinistas.

By mid-1986, most McCurdy Democrats knew this, but not enough knew to prevent the Administration from winning an additional $100 million (including $70 million in military aid). During that year top administration officials nicknamed McCurdy "the Prince." The name was appropriate. His was a princely challenge, to force the Administration to change policy, not prevent day-to-day diplomacy. Besides, it would take royalty to challenge "King Reagan" and win.

A year after their June 1986 victory, Administration policy was seriously mauled by the Iran-Contra scandal and the Cruz resignation. But there was no alternative. Without one, it was only a matter of time before the Administration would reassemble the moderate Administration alliance.

Two other leaders emerged to take Reagan on: Oscar Arias and Jim Wright. Wright made an alliance with Reagan to present the Sandinistas with a united U.S. policy on negotiations. Arias used the one diplomatic alternative endorsed by the United States to convince the Sandinistas to concur with another less onerous treaty.

The Administration had hoped to trap the Democrats into supporting Contra aid when the Sandinistas rejected the Wright-Reagan plan. Instead it was the Administration that became trapped when the Sandinistas accepted the Arias plan, and when Wright, embracing that plan, reassembled the liberal-moderate alliance.

When the Administration opposed the new plan, Wright and Arias were left with the task of implementing it, and forcing it upon the parties in Nicaragua. Wright and Arias, who had opposed Contra aid on principle, now found they needed the Contras to win concessions from the Sandinistas. In fact, they needed both the conservatives' attachment to the Contras and the liberals' desire to be rid of them. If the conservatives had meekly accepted the Arias plan, Contras leverage would no longer have been credible. On the other hand, the liberals' intense opposition gave the Sandinistas hope that there would be an aid to the Contras.

And in every follow-up negotiation leading up to the election, *that* was the formula that worked. Liberals (whether Wright, Arias, David Bonoir of the House Democratic Leadership, or former President Jimmy Carter) wrestled concessions from the Sandinistas with the implicit or explicit promise that concessions would help eliminate the Contras and their conservative American support.

Wright and Arias's diplomacy was a substitute for the Reagan Administration posturing in its last seventeen months. Wright and Arias presented the new Bush Administration with a policy already in the initial stages of implementation. To its credit, the new Administration not only accepted the principles of Wright-Arias, but labored creatively to make them work.

Who won Nicaragua? In the complicated endgame that began with the agreement of the five presidents in Guatemala City, it would seem that everyone did. The liberal policy of working with the Central American presidents would not have succeeded without the conservative policy of threatening to unleash the Contras. But if credit must be given, it should go to the synthesizing abilities of House Speaker Jim Wright and the president of Costa Rica, Oscar Arias.

Why did the Sandinistas lose? That's simple: they failed to keep the peace and establish prosperity, then they allowed a free election. ■

CHAPTER TWENTY

FOURTH THOUGHTS

March 15, 1992

My fourth thoughts were provoked by the work of Bob Kagan, who was convinced that I should never have gone beyond second thoughts. In what I believe will become the definitive work on the United States and Nicaragua for the years 1977–1990,[70] Bob describes how the Sandinistas came to view their relationship with the Soviet Union as fundamental. He describes how their perception of changes in the Soviet Union more than any policy of the Bush Administration caused the Sandinistas to bend to the demands of the Arias plan.

If my book has a theme, it is a simple one. In the American debate on Nicaragua, there was a mindless right and a dishonest left, then there were those in the middle who were more thoughtful, wise, and (more important) right.

Our position was simple. The Sandinistas had chosen to embrace Soviet-style communism, and they were attempting to impose it on their own people and their neighbors. That belief put us in solidarity with the right. But the Contras, we argued, could not defeat the Sandinistas, and it would be politically impossible (and plain wrong) to deploy U.S. troops to do what the Nicaraguans could not or would not do themselves. That put us in solidarity with the left.

Split the difference, we argued. Don't abandon the cause of freedom in Nicaragua; use the Contras as leverage to win political concessions from the Sandinistas. It worked. We were right. Despite all of its problems today (and they are legion), Nicaragua is nonetheless a freer and a better place to live and bring up children. And in politics, that simple test signals success.

But free elections did not take place simply because the Sandinistas yielded to pressure from the Contra threat. The context had changed. Though often blind to their own domestic realities, the Sandinistas were never unsophisticated in analyzing their geopolitical context.

Daniel Ortega flew to Moscow in 1985 (to the outrage of Congress) not because he was unmindful of fallout in Washington, but because Washington was just not as important as Moscow. Ortega would visit Gorbachev, form a relationship with the new ruler of the Soviet Union, and demonstrate that he and no other in the Sandinista directorate was the indispensable link to the indispensable ally. Their relationship with the Soviet Union (above all else) was believed to be the key to Sandinista survival.

Soviet aid would continue at high levels until the day the Sandinistas were voted out of office. But the Soviet Union itself changed before that. In fact, Gorbachev brought continual change. What he sought was a new way of organizing society, a way that would unleash the creative and productive powers of the Russian people long crushed by stultifying bureaucracy and mind numbing and transparently mendacious ideology. The very social, political, and economic structures the Sandinistas hoped one day to emulate were being held up to public scrutiny in the Soviet Union, and were found sorely lacking.

Worse, from the Sandinista perspective, by 1987 the Brezhnev years of greatest Soviet assistance to third world liberation were being called "the years of stagnation." Worse still, some Soviet foreign policy specialists now saw that policy of supporting "liberation" as the cause for the breakdown in U.S.-Soviet relations, now deemed vital to economic and social change.

> It is our conviction that the crisis was caused chiefly by the miscalculations and incompetent approach of the Brezhnev leadership toward the resolution of foreign policy tasks.
>
> Though we were politically, militarily (via weapons supplies and advisors), and diplomatically involved in regional conflicts, we disregarded their influence on the relaxation of tension between the USSR and the West and on their entire system of relationships. There were no clear ideas of the Soviet Union's true national state interests. These interests lay by no means in chasing petty and essentially formal gains associated with leadership coups in certain developing countries. The genuine interest lay in ensuring a favorable international situation for profound transformations in the Soviet Union's economy and socio-political system. However, at that time it was believed that no transformations were needed.[71]

Do I think the Sandinistas read those words and made adjustments accordingly? I have no idea. But it doesn't really matter. The Sandinista leaders were Soviet specialists, just as the Somozas before them had been American specialists. The Sandinistas lived and breathed the changes and movements arising in their one indispensable ally. At some point they must have concluded that they could no longer count on a government in economic collapse, profound ideological transformation, and global retreat.

The Sandinistas came to realize that they would ultimately have to make a deal in the region where they lived with the one superpower that overshadowed all others. However, they also understood that within that superpower is a Congress that can restrain its Administration, at least at times. They also knew there were several presidents and political forces in the region who, for their own reasons, would oppose that superpower continuing aid to the Contras.

Sometime between 1987 and 1989, the Sandinistas came to believe that their survival depended on the regional balance of forces in the Americas. They concluded that they must win enough friends in the region (not the distant Soviet bloc) to shield them against the imperial force to the north.

The question became what price would the U.S. Congress, their Central American neighbors, and other regional actors (like Venezuela) demand to shut down the Contra program and renew economic aid. That price was political relaxation, and eventual free and fair elections.

Grudgingly, but after clear political calculation, the Sandinistas did take these steps, beginning in the fall of 1987 and culminating in the elections of 1990. Ironically, it was the Soviets' task in Nicaragua, after eighteen months of negotiations with the new U.S. Administration, to convince the Sandinistas that President Bush would indeed accept the results of a free election, even if the Sandinistas won. The Sandinistas made their final estimate, calculated they could win, and agreed to elections on February 22, 1990.

The final game played out as we predicted, but we had never factored fundamental change in the Soviet Union into our analysis. The calculations we made as moderates in 1985 and 1986 always assumed Soviet involvement in the region to be constant.

In sum, our predictions were correct—but only because of developments we never envisioned. Indeed, one must fairly say that the facts and assumptions that brought us to our preferred policy of 1985 and 1986 were just plain wrong. Without change in the Soviet Union, a policy of half-hearted support for the Contras to create pressure for internal change in Nicaragua would never have worked. Without it, there would have been endless, low-level conflict, and annual Contra war in the U.S. Congress until one side or the other just gave up.

In 1982, two major forces in American foreign policy (informed by their separate analyses of Vietnam as well as political events of the '70s) were poised to fight major legislative battles over how to deal with a new revolutionary regime in Nicaragua. From 1985 until 1987, a few moderates (fewer than twenty members of the House and even fewer reporters and so-called policy intellectuals) successfully muddied that debate, and eventually insisted on their own policy. In retrospect, I think that perhaps the powerful right and the equally powerful left should have been allowed to fight it out, with clear winners and losers. The results of such debate might have yielded principles to better guide U.S. foreign policy makers on decisions regarding new third world conflicts in the post-Cold War period.

But we happy few did not let that happen.

Or maybe, without knowing it, we happy few moderates were the ones already in touch with a new Zeitgeist, a sense of rightness regarding our policy alternative despite our ignorance of its major enabling factor—the collapse of the Soviet Union. ■

Epilogue

2006

There was no neat ending to my story with Corinne. Shortly after her last message we started to see each other again. That stopped after three meetings and took up again two months later.

Each time we reunited she was more distant and less willing to explore the magic we had between us. Even the sexual ardor subsided. I had served my purpose.

For me, the whole experience was about my need to realize the great dream—the fusion of one human being with another, the unity of two bodies and two souls, a way to reach beyond ordinary human experience. For her, our love was an explosive device placed under the chassis of a bad marriage. When she told me "I feel like I belong to you" and "it is all yours," she was simply lighting the fuse.

At that point she was still attached to me, but as her husband, step by step, relinquished his hold on her, her passion for me slowly died. What Corrine alluded to in her final message, my "personal ways of relating to the outside world," is now obvious. It was my health.

Neither she nor I knew at the time, but two years after our last rendezvous the horrible muscle pain I had suffered for fourteen years was finally given a name—Fibromyalgia. More than any other person, Corinne appreciated the limitations chronic disease imposed on me, how much it disrupted my life, how it made me feel hopeless. If my health had been normal I would already have been married, a big-time lobbyist with a house in the suburbs and 2.3 children. It was illness that made me available to play a starring role in her end-of-marriage drama. It was also because of my illness that she could so easily let me go, with so little explanation, so little comfort given to a man who had steadfastly stood by her. That was my purpose—to be steadfast, and to threaten her husband's self-respect until it demanded he let her go.

By the time she finally left for good, I believe Corinne allowed almost no room for memory of the passion we had shared. Perhaps at times she allowed herself to remember it, but only as something slightly disturbing and out of character from her past, and it surely faded as she grew accustomed to her new life of freedom and quiet purpose. Within a year of our parting, Corinne was engaged. Within eighteen months she was married, and on her way to a new career in India.

Her leaving left me worse than distraught, it left me completely empty. For me, our passion was not just a tactic in a game, but something grand. I wanted the transcendence of ever-closer physical and emotional bonds.

It was a year after Corinne was married that I learned the name of my illness. Fibromyalgia is a disease of muscles that doesn't originate in the muscles but in the brain. It causes mild to severe pain, occasionally to constantly. It isn't hard to guess what combination of these characteristics I have. There is no cure.

Surprisingly my business weathered my illness and depression induced by Corinne's leaving. The new Nicaraguan government of President Chamorro selected me as its lobbyist. And after a number of close calls that might have been calamitous to its aid, in 1996 the government of Mozambique embraced wholesale economic reform, along with greater aid.

In 1999 the people of East Timor voted their choice between autonomy within Indonesia and independence, and won their independence by an overwhelming margin. But that successful act of self-determination unleashed a paroxysm of Indonesian and Indonesian-backed militia violence. As it had for many months leading up to East Timor's referendum, the U.S. Congress pressed the Administration to help end Indonesia's occupation. President Bill Clinton announced a suspension of all U.S. aid to Indonesia until its withdrawal. Congress also supported a coalition force led by Australia that pushed out the marauders. Today East Timor is struggling mightily to forge a democracy and a viable economy. Timorese citizens are still waiting for decent medical care, jobs and education, but they are free.

When it became clear that both Mozambique and East Timor had achieved positive outcomes, I quietly resigned, in 1999. My pain had become fierce, and constant. I had surgery for Chron's disease, but in recovery I noticed an increase in fatigue. In 2001 even walking became difficult. In the fall of 2002 I was diagnosed with and treated for Parkinson's. By the end of that year the Parkinson's was causing sleep disorders—both sleepwalking and a tendency to fall asleep against my will and without my knowing. I began to have very troubling problems with my balance.

But five years after I retired, I envisioned a magical combination; it required one person from the Nicaraguan embassy, one from the Guatemalan embassy, and myself. We would reveal how debilitating corruption is to a developing country, how the previous governments of both countries robbed them blind, and how U.S. assistance was needed to aid their recovery. We were a hit. Both countries received increased U.S. funds, and both received additional funds for their anticorruption units.

Then, for some obscure reason, I was denied a meeting with Vice President Eduardo Steyn of Guatemala. I phoned a colleague from the embassy and announced that I could no longer work for Guatemala gratis.

Within twenty-four hours I received a formal invitation to visit Guatemala, all expenses paid.

MIRACLE IN GUATEMALA

But I am not still writing to tell you about what's happening in Guatemala. I am writing to tell you about the woman who finally eclipsed Corinne. When I arrived in Guatemala she was waiting for me there.

Nely is a young mother of three from El Salvador struggling to finish her college degree. A mutual friend had asked me to help her do that. She had written me twice, we had spoken on the phone once, and she had invited me to visit her.

Amusingly, our first date was horrible, a nightmare date from hell. But we went out again anyway the next night, on the spur of the moment, and things turned first pleasant, then lightly amorous. I asked her to join me for a ride in one of the foreign ministry's chauffeur-driven Mercedes. We drove for hours, traveling through the small towns that surround Guatemala City, and in each town we found more common ground, more attraction. We met the next night, and the next, and by my last night in Guatemala we were engaged.

Have I rediscovered the grand passion I had with Corinne, where transcendence only comes through greater and greater acts of domination? Surely not.

If anyone dominates now it is Nely, the beautiful Salvadoran tigress. Nely and I also share warmth, mutual support, and a love that is gentle and hopeful, not aggressive and desperate. When in odd moments during

Figure 19: The miracle in Guatemala. Author photo.

turbulent thunderstorms that reach into my open-air patio in my home in El Salvador, producing many little lakes that are flat and unmoving in the aftermath, I remember and wonder.

Almost Final Note on Nicaragua: January 1, 2006

This would certainly be a neat place to end. But it would be unfair not to speak also of changes in the general contours of Nicaraguan history since I began my story. The war in the '70s was a war of nearly an entire country against one strongman, his family, and their personal army, the Guardia Nacional. Thankfully, the people won. That was the first civil war, against the very corrupt Somocistas.

But the people were immediately betrayed when the Sandinista forces, the men with the guns, decided to seek an alliance with and emulate the Soviet Union. The second civil war pitted the Sandinistas, with a very strong social base among the poor, against another group, the Contras. Though they could never generate the level of military force the Sandinistas had, the Contras were sufficiently powerful to force the Sandinistas to accept a democratic compromise in the wake of the collapse of their main benefactor, the Soviet Union.

And the Sandinistas lost that election. What was sadly most notable during the presidency of the victorious Violeta Chamorro was that the Somocistas were able to rebuild their party in the context of a coalition to retake the presidency the next time around. Whereupon President Arnoldo Aleman repeated the now-familiar looting of Nicaragua's treasury begun during the earlier Somocista governments.

But Aleman miscalculated in choosing his successor, Enrique Bolaños, who attacked corruption in Nicaragua with a vengeance (even without a party of his own or strong allies). In so doing, Bolaños upset not only the Somocistas, but the Sandinistas. It is only a slight exaggeration to say that an alliance of Sandinistas and Somocistas rules the country from the National Assembly even with Aleman under house arrest. ■

AFTERWORD

*For the Second Time Daniel Ortega Surprises the World, This Time by Winning**

Various illnesses and other delays have pushed the publication of this book right up to the eve of the 2006 election in Nicaragua. We decided we could not release this book until I prepared an afterword on the election.

Trying to make sense of this election is one of the hardest pieces of analysis I have ever attempted. Every actor played his role predictably except for the United States and President Enrique Bolaños, and the United States only acted unpredictably because of the legacy of Acting Assistant Secretary of State for Latin America, Otto Reich.

But before we examine these two men who assumed power in 2001, we must look at party development in the 1990s. A fourteen-party coalition vaulted Violeta Chamorro to a 59-to-41 percent victory in 1990. During the reign of Violeta, only the Constitutional Liberal Party, a dissident movement to the traditional liberal party of Somoza, worked hard at party building. Running initially alone, Arnoldo Aleman lost his bid for mayor of Managua. The second time he received the UNO endorsement and won. And always he continued party building. The uniting principle was always loyalty to him.

When Aleman ran for president in 1996, he ran as part of the Liberal Alliance and the National Liberal Party (NLP), Somoza's old party. But after the election, he ignored both the Liberal Alliance and the NLP and organized his administration around the Constitutional Liberal Party. People from other parties received positions in his administration, but as individuals.

---

*This trip was made possible by the contribution of some very veteran comrades: Bruce Nussbaum (Vietnam and *the current conjuncture*) and Jim Peck (China and *the principal contradiction*) and some more recent: Bill Clarke (El Salvador and *the general context*) and George Biddle (Central America *and everywhere else*).

Figure 20: Picture of the author with two former dictators, Wojciech Jaruzelki of Poland and Daniel Ortega of Nicaragua. Author photo.

In 2001 he was so strong he ran his designated successor, Enrique Bolaños, exclusively on the PLC ticket.[72]

After he lost the election to President Chamorro in 1990, Daniel Ortega faced successive attacks on his leadership, and after each attempt that he defeated, power and control were more centralized in his own person.

Toward the end of his term, Aleman began to hear that he could face and be convicted of charges of corruption; after all, he and his closest cronies had stolen upwards of $100 million. And Ortega rightly feared charges of abuse of his stepdaughter as well as responsibility for human rights crimes during the war. So Aleman and Ortega joined forces to put a stranglehold on three institutions that could come after them or interfere with their plans for domination: the Supreme Court, the auditor's office, and the Supreme Electoral Council. They also passed laws in the Assembly that automatically gave to the former president and the candidate coming in second seats in the Assembly, as well as immunity to all members of the Assembly.

All of this was built on a corrupt system of patronage and graft.

Aleman was replaced by his vice president, Enrique Bolaños. Although Bolaños had campaigned against corruption and knew all the rumors about Aleman, it was only the finding of evidence of rather minor corruption that caused President Bolaños to launch a major investigation into the previous government's record.

Bolaños was inaugurated on January 10, 2002. Sometime thereafter, Aleman made himself President of the National Assembly. What sealed his fate was when Otto Reich became Assistant Secretary of State for Latin America on March 11, 2002. Otto was famous—some would say infamous—for his performance at the public diplomacy office where he and his staff would gather information, some would say disinformation, on the internal conflicts in Central American countries, especially Nicaragua.

He only had a recess appointment in 2002 which allowed him to stay in office for a year unless Senator Dodd would allow a hearing and a floor vote—which he would not. Well, this was Otto's brief chance to make and implement policy. He embraced the issue like he did free Cuba or the contras in Nicaragua, but more so.

> Corruption is an issue that people are often reluctant to talk about openly, but it is probably the single largest obstacle to development. Those who steal from the public purse are doing as much harm to their country as a foreign invader would. The fact is that corruption not only cuts economic growth, but it also puts a strain on democracy by eroding public trust and a sense of public responsibility.[73]

One of Otto's ideas was to deny visas to corrupt officials so they could not enjoy their ill-gotten gains in the United States, especially Miami which was a second home to so many of them. Here he faced the almost united opposition of all other assistant secretaries from other regions. And this was at a time when the bar to pass over was much higher, having to find absolute, concrete information about money laundering or drug trafficking because corruption itself was not a legal reason. A year and a half after he left, the President signed orders that made corruption an issue by which one's visa could be lifted at a slightly lower level of proof.

Sometime in 2002, Otto told Bolaños that the United States would be completely behind his efforts to root out corruption. It would not have been that easy to do because Aleman had been close to the activist community in south Florida in favor of more aggressive action toward Cuba. Aleman had been their friend and recipient of their largess.[74]

But Otto was, as the left-liberal press kept hammering, a right-wing ideologue. What right-wingers, at least American ones, have is an aggressive belief in the rule of law and stopping corruption. Otto reaffirmed US policy to continue opposing the Sandinistas in their bid for office, but also extended it to oppose the PLC. In the formulation of policy, the specific issue was the single factor of the pact. The larger issue was corruption. Two years after Otto left office, Bolaños was reported to have said, "When I came into the presidency I wanted to tackle corruption, so we could reduce poverty, which is the main shame of such a rich, wealthy country."[75]

Perhaps most galling to Nicaraguans is that prosecutors have turned up $1.8 million worth of lavish personal expenses on Aleman's government-paid American Express cards. That amount is almost unfathomable here in the Western Hemisphere's second poorest country (after Haiti). After many decades of U.S. tutelage mixed with bouts of invasion and occupation, 80 percent of Nicaragua's five million people live in poverty and half earn less than $1 a day, a condition that supporters of globalization consider essential to lining their coffers.[76]

It is one thing to dig up so much dirtiness; it is another to use it. The obvious first choice was the PLC because that is who brought Bolaños to power, especially the forty-three PLC members of the Assembly who could in multiple alliances with small parties form a majority to strip Aleman of his immunity. But the PLC remained a caudillo party and only eight members broke with Aleman to support Bolaños.

The richest man in Nicaragua, at least the richest Nicaraguan, famously said in referring to the upcoming election in November 2002, "Just do the math." He was referring to what should have happened if the right split on the first round and the Sandinistas received their customary 36 to 40 percent. Under the rules adopted by the National Assembly at the goading of Aleman to please Daniel, a minority candidate could win and avoid a second round if he received at least 35 percent and no other candidate was within 5 percent of that number.

At that time, this was a self-serving question to justify his contribution to the PLC, the Sandinistas, and the new party of Eduardo Montealegre, the U.S. government's candidate. Because at that time, there was a strong fourth candidate, an ex-Sandinista mayor of Managua whose total votes drawing from the Sandinistas most certainly would have put the election into a second round. But he died and the math changed. His replacement at best could have won half of what Herty Lewites could draw.

But when Bolaños did the math after finding out how weak he was among PLC delegates, he realized there was only one alternative. They had beaten him, they had jailed him, and they had confiscated his property and almost killed him. He had devoted his life to oppose them. But now he found that there was something more important and alliance with the Sandinistas was essential in his efforts to oppose corruption.

In his first year, he put together a coalition in the assembly of forty-seven deputies of whom thirty-eight were Sandinistas, which stripped Aleman of his immunity. In September the government charged Aleman with money laundering, embezzlement, and other crimes during his time in office. In December a Sandinista court, run by a Sandinista judge, found him guilty and sentenced him to twenty years. The government investigations were led by the deputy assistant attorney general who had been the former ambassador for the Sandinistas to Washington, who before his defection had sold the Embassy's residence and given half the proceeds to Pastora.

That September and then again in December, Bolaños and Ortega worked out an agreement to run the Assembly together and the Sandinistas accepted a non-Sandinista as president. The next year was probably the politically most congenial and productive of the Bolaños years. Here was the laying of a foundation for steady economic progress, and steady progress was also made in developing corruption cases and sending them to court.

The Bolaños administration with Sandinista assistance was very successful in changing Nicaragua's macroeconomic environment. It stabilized the nation's finances, gutted during Aleman's final year, and successfully negotiated support from the IMF for a new three-year Poverty Reduction and Growth Facility. Over the course of 2003, it put in place the remaining preconditions for a massive pardon of Nicaragua's $6.4 billion foreign debt.

But the Sandinistas were not sitting on their laurels. In 2002 the FSLN surprisingly voted for the re-election of Roberto Rivas as president of the Supreme Electoral Council. This was another step in consolidating their hold on the Cardinal. They also secured their hold on the Supreme Court. The FSLN was able to increase the number of Supreme Court members to parity with the PLC after the election of one of their own as Court president.

Ortega's success in enlarging his power produced a predictable reaction. Since 2003 U.S. diplomatic representatives have worked both openly and surreptitiously to thwart the possibility that a split in Liberal ranks could provide Ortega with his comeback chance. In November 2003 Secretary of State Colin Powell went so far as to declare that Ortega (along with Arnoldo Aleman) was a figure of the past. The United States combined public statements by the secretary and other high officials with pressures to keep the liberals politically united.[77]

I am clear on what happened next, but not why Bolaños switched partners. On his own or under extreme U.S. pressure, I do not know.

In December 2004, the United States Embassy offered to mediate among the different parties to help them find the right combination to establish an effective and stable leadership. The U.S. ambassador, Barbara Moore, talked with everybody except the Sandinistas. The bad blood between the parties was very strong due to the terrible things Bolaños had said about their leader, Aleman. And yet Ambassador Moore was able to unify the PLC and the president's party based on five agreements, and upon these create a new legislative leadership.

In short order, the PLC reneged on all the agreements. They had one and only one goal: the release of their leader, Aleman. They could not return to their old role as the party of governance. Only the leader mattered.

For Bolaños, no scenario with the FSLN or the PLC made sense. The American obsession with the Sandinistas ruled them out; the PLC's obsession with Aleman made them impossible partners as he quickly found out in 2004. Since January 2004, he ruled in essence with the international community—the World Bank and various nations. They were his protection against a creeping constitutional coup and his partners in maintaining macroeconomic programs that by 2004 were producing. After he ended his partnership with the Sandinistas in the Assembly, Bolaños essentially did only the routine with the Assembly and made his initiatives through the international community. In fact, the first two years following the pact parties taking over the Assembly were nothing but misery. That is, until Ortega made a pact with Bolaños giving the latter anti-coup insurance. It guaranteed he could serve out his term.

Following their losing leadership posts in the Assembly, the Sandinistas did the math and it was time to reinvigorate the pact. With the pact together they could on a much greater scale transfer powers from the executive to the legislative. Daniel Ortega had already increased his power within the judicial branch and was becoming the dominant force. And the activities of his partner, Aleman, would always be restricted by the courts, for was not Ortega the courts? In December 2004, pact parties won control of the Assembly and a Sandinista was made and continues to be President of the Assembly.

In any possible scenario Ortega could envision, he would remain the dominant power. The only exception was an outright victory by Montealegre for president and an outright majority for his party in the Assembly, but that was not possible. Montealegre's campaign manager was a disaster, and he himself was too arrogant to heed almost unanimous opinions of his other political advisors.

Daniel Ortega could see that he would not lose his informal power, but he wanted more. At the very least he wanted the trappings of power, but perhaps also the formal power to do something positive. The question now is, Whose positive? Hugo Chavez's or Tony Blair's? But how could Daniel Ortega make the math worth? With Herty Lewites's presence on the ballot, Ortega would have a hard time making 35 percent.

Then Herty died. Now reality caught up with the richest man in Nicaragua and it became urgent for the parties on the right to seriously consider their options. I learned they tried mediation in May of 2006 with former President of El Salvador Calderon Sol. The PLC and ALN, the party of Eduardo Montealegre, met and tried mediation. PLC candidate Rizzo was prepared to accept anything that would keep him in the race and unite the ALN and the PLC. The trouble was, Aleman was disposed not to accept anything. Eduardo demanded a signed resignation statement that he would keep and only release if Rizzo broke any of their agreements. Eduardo's demand for a letter was the pretext Aleman needed to say no.

By the time I arrived in Managua the day before the November 2006 election, the only thing unsettled was second place. Everybody except the

American ambassador believed that Daniel would take first place and have the requisite 5 percent over 35 percent lead to avoid a second ballot. The ambassador spoke of polls by the private sector that had Eduardo first.

U.S. policies had been to support the anticorruption drive and oppose the pact and corruption, while finding a way to reunite the right. That was impossible. If you opposed corruption, you had to oppose Aleman and his party because it could not be anything but his party.

In the past, it had been possible for the U.S. government to oppose a major corrupter or human rights violator, hoping the people of that country would somehow sideline him. But if they didn't, we would find some way of reversing policy and secretly supporting him because he was our friend in the fight against communism. Otto's legacy was to negate that practice and summon a new one. Corruption in one state in Latin America affects all others, so finding an excuse to make an exception in Nicaragua means making an exception for all.

And the price was dear but worth it: Daniel Ortega is back in power, but I am optimistic. Although Ortega pulled many nasty tricks on his way, they are not the same Sandinistas and this is no cold war. The president of Venezuela is no Yuri Andropov, the former KGB's spy chief and later president of the Soviet Union, an empire with armaments almost equal to ours, who if his kidneys were healthy, would have modernized the Soviet Union without allowing it to fragment.

This story of Sergio Ramirez retold by Stephen Kinzer, though old, is illustrative of the Sandinistas' ability to be different over time.

Kinzer: When I asked him if the Contra War could have been avoided, he recalled the moment in 1981 when he received Assistant Secretary of State Thomas Enders who came to Managua with an offer.

Ramirez: You have to put yourself back in that moment to understand the emotions on both sides. Enders came with a message. He told me: Reagan thinks he can live with the Sandinistas as long as you confine your revolution within your own border, promise not to help guerrillas in El Salvador or anywhere else, and cut your own ties to the Soviets. If you ask me, now sitting in this room, what I think of the offer, I say I think it sounds like a pretty good deal but at the time we refused even to discuss it. We saw it as a trap. The gringos would cut us from our friends, isolate and then attack and destroy us. As for El Salvador, we considered support of that cause to be both a revolutionary duty and a strategic necessity We thought that was inevitable and that we had to prepare for it. We had no confidence in the United States. There was a lack of maturity on both sides.[78]

Make an educated judgment. Is there a way the Sandinistas will share power with an Aleman-controlled PLC? The pact, yes, but no formal coalition with Aleman.

So was it worth it, putting corruption above beating Daniel Ortega?

Absolutely. And this is a victory for the audacious Otto Reich, the stubborn Enrique Bolaños, and the United States. But mainly it is a victory for Otto Reich. He may not like being a hero because of the victory of the Sandinistas, and he isn't. It is in the why of their victory that he has his. The United States took a principled stand on corruption and stood by it.

Is that all there is? Not quite.

Finally, in the era of Hugo Chavez and not Yuri Andropov and the Sandinistas described by Sergio Ramirez, do I have doubts about the Sandinistas?

Indeed. But I have more hope. ■

NOTES

1. Augusto Sandino, a Nicaraguan guerrilla leader of the '20s and '30s, raised an army to fight an occupation by U.S. Marines. Shortly after their withdrawal and a reasonably fair election, Sandino retired from battle, only to be assassinated by the first Somoza. The latter had been installed by the United States as the first commander of the National Guard, which was to have been a professional army in the service of the new, freely elected government. After ridding himself of Sandino, the first Somoza subsequently deposed the president and installed himself. Source: Shirley Christian, *Nicaragua: Revolution in the Family* (New York: Vintage Books, 1986), pp. 9–25.

2. Robert Leiken, *Soviet Strategy in Latin America* (Washington, DC: Praeger, 1982), p. 72.

3. Negotiations promoted by Columbia, Mexico, Panama, and Venezuela, the Contadora negotiations, named after an island off Panama, were intended to resolve the security issues of Central America.

4. The use of this term was clearly ironic, a reference to the four leftist leaders in China, led by Chairman Mao's wife, who were purged in 1978.

5. This turned out to be Walter Cronkite's last hard-news story.

6. Common Cause is a good-government, reformist lobby in Washington, and the organization recently had decided to work to stop Contra aid.

7. Bob Kagan, untitled manuscript, 1985, p. 92.

8. *Report of the Congressional Committees Investigating the Iran-Contra Affair* (Washington, DC: 1987), p. 39.

9. Ibid., pp. 60–62.

10. Ibid., pp. 61–62.

11. Ibid., p. 62.

12. Ibid., p. 68.

13. Ibid., pp. 64–65.

14. His body was found a week before I left Guatemala.

15. From *The Godfather*.

16. *Report of the Congressional Committees Investigating the Iran-Contra Affair*, op. cit., pp. 64, 65.

17. There is much controversy about Ollie's famous story regarding the use of proceeds from the Iran sales to support the Nicaraguan Contras. I find these criticisms compelling but I like Ollie's story better.

18. *Report of the Congressional Committees Investigating the Iran-Contra Affair*, p. 221.

19. Ibid., p. 225.

20. Ibid., pp. 66–67.

21. Ibid, p. 70.

22. Theodore Draper, *A Very Thin Line: The Iran-Contra Affairs* (New York: Hill and Wang, 1991), pp. 346–51.

23. The preferred goal was a complete defeat of the Sandinista political and military machine. Second best would be a coalition government. Third best would be a free and fair election with stringent international controls and oversight. Fourth would be a new election with weak international oversight.

24. Arturo's son did, as did Bob Leiken, his close advisor. Both had just written articles supporting a long political and military struggle. That day, the *Miami Herald* had speculated that Cruz did, too. That article had disturbed Arturo greatly.

25. *San Diego Union*, March 29, 1987.

26. *Hartford Courant*, February 6, 1987.

27. Branigan attained significant credibility with moderates when he became the first newspaperman to describe the systematic underreporting of Sandinista human rights violations as reported by America's Watch.

28. John Barry, *The Ambition and the Power* (New York: Viking, 1989), p. 310.

29. What I know about those next eighteen days I have gleaned from the press, alks with key people after the fact, and from two books, John Barry's and a second, Roy Gutman's *Banana Diplomacy* (New York: Simon and Schuster, 1988).

30. *The Ambition and the Power*, op. cit., p. 311. 1989.

31. Ibid., p. 312.

32. Ibid., p. 320.

33. Ibid., pp. 327–28.

34. Ibid., p. 328.

35. Ibid., pp. 330–31.

36. Ibid., p. 332.

37. Ibid., p. 335.

38. Ibid., p. 344.

39. *Banana Diplomacy*, op. cit., p. 347.

40. Ibid., p. 348.

41. *Washington Post*, August 10 and 11. 1987.

42. The first arrow was Arturo Cruz's resignation, the second arrow was the scandal, and the third arrow was the Arias plan now endorsed by all five countries in Central America.

43. From Goethe.

44. During a private presidential visit, a motorcade can drive through red lights only if part of it is already in the intersection when the light turns red.

45. *Tikkun*, January/February 1988.

46. *The Village Voice*, October 1987.

47. As recorded in the *Congressional Record*.

48. He was especially outraged that Mozambique opposed U.S. positions at the United Nations more than 90 percent of the time.

49. Based on whether they voted yes or no on military aid in 1985.

50. I have spoken with other lobbyists, including those who always look so supremely confident, as though they own the halls of Congress, and they, too, admit that sometimes they freeze and have to wait for another opportunity. I know this but I am still furious with myself every time it happens to me.

51. Members can change their votes at any time until the chair announces the time for voting is over. If a member does change his vote, that change is noted in the *Congressional Record*.

52. It should be noted that by 1991 more than 200 pieces of church property had been returned, that the new constitution of 1990 guaranteed private property, and that almost all Soviet-bloc advisors had left Mozambique. The State Department had been right about the eventual trend, but it was wrong with its numbers.

53. In El Salvador, on the other hand, the Duarte government had begun negotiations with the FMLN, albeit with little progress.

54. *New York Times*, January 13, 1988.

55. *New York Times*, January 14, 1988.

56. *Washington Times*, January 15, 1988.

57. *New York Times*, January 14, 1988.

58. *Washington Times*, January 16, 1988

59. *Washington Times*, February 4, 1988.

60. James Grady, *Runner in the Street* (New York: Simon and Schuster, 1984), p. 237.

61. *Newsweek*, March 12, 1990.

62. *U.S. News and World Report*, February 26, 1990.

63. *The New York Times*, February 22, 1990.

64. *USA TODAY*, February 22, 1990.

65. Foreign Broadcast Information Service (FBIS), March 1990, p. 21.

66. Ibid., p. 26.

67. *Los Angeles Times*, February 28, 1990.

68. *Washington Post*, February 28, 1990.

69. *Los Angeles Times*, March 4, 1990.

70. Robert Kagan, *Twilight Struggle* (New York: Free Press, 1996).

71. Kurt Campbell and S. Neil MacFarlane, eds., *Gorbachev's Third World Dilemmas* (London: Routledge, 1989), p. 41.

72. Mark Kaster, "The Return of Somocismo," NACLA Report on the Americas, September/October 1996.

73. Otto Reich "A New Vision for Development and Prosperity in our Hemisphere," Embassy of the United States, Caracas, Venezuela.

74. Bill Berkowitz, "Working for Change," September 20, 2005.

75. Anna Gawel, "New Year, New Hopes for Nicaragua," Washington Diplomat, Diplomatic Pouch, December 2005.

76. (Really, this is the source) Craven Sellout "Say It Isn't So, Arnoldo," The Assassinated Press, September 11, 2002.

77. David Dye, "Democracy Adrift: Caudillo Politics in Nicaragua," *Hemispheric Initiatives*, 2004, pp. 30–45. This book is far and away the best book on this period, but especially on how the pact worked.

78. Stephen Kinzer, "A Country Without Heroes," *New York Review of Books*, July 19, 2001.

INDEX